Designing Networks and Services for the Cloud

Huseni Saboowala

Muhammad Abid

Sudhir Modali

Cisco Press

800 East 96th Street

Indianapolis, IN 46240

Designing Networks and Services for the Cloud

Delivering business-grade cloud applications and services

Huseni Saboowala

Muhammad Abid

Sudhir Modali

Copyright © 2013 Cisco Systems, Inc.

Published by:
Cisco Press
800 East 96th Street
Indianapolis, IN 46240 USA

Printed in the United States of America

First Printing April 2013

Library of Congress Control Number: 2013938238

ISBN-13: 978-1-58714-294-9

ISBN-10: 1-58714-294-5

Warning and Disclaimer

This book is designed to provide information about designing networks and network services for the cloud. Every effort has been made to make this book as complete and as accurate as possible, but no warranty or fitness is implied.

The information is provided on an "as is" basis. The author, Cisco Press, and Cisco Systems, Inc., shall have neither liability nor responsibility to any person or entity with respect to any loss or damages arising from the information contained in this book or from the use of the discs or programs that may accompany it.

The opinions expressed in this book belong to the author and are not necessarily those of Cisco Systems, Inc.

Trademark Acknowledgments

All terms mentioned in this book that are known to be trademarks or service marks have been appropriately capitalized. Cisco Press or Cisco Systems, Inc. cannot attest to the accuracy of this information. Use of a term in this book should not be regarded as affecting the validity of any trademark or service mark.

Corporate and Government Sales

The publisher offers excellent discounts on this book when ordered in quantity for bulk purchases or special sales, which may include electronic versions and/or custom covers and content particular to your business, training goals, marketing focus, and branding interests. For more information, please contact: **U.S. Corporate and Government Sales** 1-800-382-3419 corpsales@pearsontechgroup.com

For sales outside of the U.S. please contact: **International Sales** international@pearsoned.com

Feedback Information

At Cisco Press, our goal is to create in-depth technical books of the highest quality and value. Each book is crafted with care and precision, undergoing rigorous development that involves the unique expertise of members from the professional technical community.

Readers' feedback is a natural continuation of this process. If you have any comments regarding how we could improve the quality of this book, or otherwise alter it to better suit your needs, you can contact us through e-mail at feedback@ciscopress.com. Please make sure to include the book title and ISBN in your message.

We greatly appreciate your assistance.

Publisher: Paul Boger

Associate Publisher: Dave Dusthimer

Executive Editor: Brett Bartow

Managing Editor: Sandra Schroeder

Senior Project Editor: Tonya Simpson

Editorial Assistant: Vanessa Evans

Cover Designer: Mark Shirar

Composition: Bumpy Design

Business Operation Manager, Cisco Press: Jan Cornelssen

Manager Global Certification: Erik Ullanderson

Senior Development Editor: Christopher Cleveland

Copy Editor: Keith Cline

Technical Editors: Sunil Cherukuri, Dave Lively, Ravi Varanasi

Indexer: Tim Wright

Proofreader: Debbie Williams

CISCO.

Americas Headquarters
Cisco Systems, Inc.
San Jose, CA

Asia Pacific Headquarters
Cisco Systems (USA) Pte. Ltd.
Singapore

Europe Headquarters
Cisco Systems International BV
Amsterdam, The Netherlands

Cisco has more than 200 offices worldwide. Addresses, phone numbers, and fax numbers are listed on the Cisco Website at **www.cisco.com/go/offices.**

CCDE, CCENT, Cisco Eos, Cisco HealthPresence, the Cisco logo, Cisco Lumin, Cisco Nexus, Cisco StadiumVision, Cisco TelePresence, Cisco WebEx, DCE, and Welcome to the Human Network are trademarks; Changing the Way We Work, Live, Play, and Learn and Cisco Store are service marks; and Access Registrar, Aironet, AsyncOS, Bringing the Meeting To You, Catalyst, CCDA, CCDP, CCIE, CCIP, CCNA, CCNP, CCSP, CCVP, Cisco, the Cisco Certified Internetwork Expert logo, Cisco IOS, Cisco Press, Cisco Systems, Cisco Systems Capital, the Cisco Systems logo, Cisco Unity, Collaboration Without Limitation, EtherFast, EtherSwitch, Event Center, Fast Step, Follow Me Browsing, FormShare, GigaDrive, HomeLink, Internet Quotient, IOS, iPhone, iQuick Study, IronPort, the IronPort logo, LightStream, Linksys, MediaTone, MeetingPlace, MeetingPlace Chime Sound, MGX, Networkers, Networking Academy, Network Registrar, PCNow, PIX, PowerPanels, ProConnect, ScriptShare, SenderBase, SMARTnet, Spectrum Expert, StackWise, The Fastest Way to Increase Your Internet Quotient, TransPath, WebEx, and the WebEx logo are registered trademarks of Cisco Systems, Inc. and/or its affiliates in the United States and certain other countries.

All other trademarks mentioned in this document or website are the property of their respective owners. The use of the word partner does not imply a partnership relationship between Cisco and any other company. (0812R)

About the Authors

Huseni Saboowala is engaged at Cisco as a senior technical leader in the areas of Software Defined Networking, Cloud, and Unified Communications. He currently focuses on evangelizing the role of the network and network services in accelerating the adoption of cloud services by enterprises. His proposals have won Cisco-wide recognition and awards, and he continues to cultivate business-driven innovations that further enrich application-network interactions. Within Cisco SRG, he leads the architecture and deployment of a custom private cloud, driving his concept to reality across several groups. He has filed patents and spoken on Cloud and UC to large audiences on several occasions. Before joining Cisco, Huseni held several positions, including at Nortel, TTI (acquired by Sonus Networks), and dynamicsoft (acquired by Cisco). Over the past 18 years, his activities have ranged from solution architecture, design, validation, and deployment to leadership of global teams, innovation coaching, and developing technology strategies. He holds a Bachelor's degree in Electronics Engineering from the University of Bombay, and a Master's degree in Software Engineering from Kansas State University.

Muhammad Abid is an innovator who is currently working as a senior product manager in the Services and Routing Group at Cisco. He is engaged in developing the next generation of platforms and innovative technologies that will support data center interconnect and software defined network (SDN) frameworks and play a key role in enabling cloud-based services and applications. Prior to this, he was focused on architecting solutions and driving technology roadmaps across multiple business units for unified communications, collaboration, and threat defense. Before joining Cisco, Muhammad held several positions, including at T-Systems, Padcom, Telcordia, and Latham & Watkins. Over the past 18 years, he has been involved in building innovative products and designing and architecting networks for service providers and enterprises. He has also validated mobility solutions for enterprises and performed technical audits on service provider equipment and networks. He holds a Bachelor's degree in Electrical Engineering from the City University of New York and an Executive Master in Technology Management degree from the Stevens Institute of Technology in New Jersey.

Sudhir Modali is a thinker and innovator currently putting his creative mind to work as a product manager at Cisco, working on products that fuel data center and cloud architectures. He currently focuses on the evolving application requirements and the corresponding network architectures that enable some of the biggest cloud services in the world. His expertise comes from multiple positions he has held at Cisco over the past 13 years, including customer support (TAC); QA lead; technical marketing in areas such as service provider, enterprise, and data center networks; and technologies such as data, voice, and video. He has developed and is a major contributor to several certification courses for data center and cloud fields within Cisco. He holds a Bachelor's degree in Industrial Electronics from Shivaji University (Solapur, India).

About the Technical Reviewers

Dave Lively is currently a director in the Cloud Architectures/Sales team at Cisco. His team focuses on driving the architectures for early/emerging opportunities to leverage cloud computing in various markets/verticals in the service provider space. He has also worked extensively on the engineering side, focusing on system architecture, strategy, and validation for the cloud computing and data center markets. His teams have developed the end-to-end system architecture for the data center and *Next Generation Network* (NGN), including both network and compute infrastructure and management/ orchestration. Before working in cloud computing, Dave led the systems efforts for Cisco's multiscreen IP video strategy, enabling service providers to deliver video to the television, the PC, and the mobile phone. In addition, he has served in multiple companies in various product management, marketing, and engineering capacities, working across various technologies, including optical networking, WAN optimization, content networking, VoIP, VoATM, and broadband. He also worked in software and hardware engineering and holds a Bachelor's degree in Computer Engineering from Virginia Tech.

Sunil Cherukuri is a senior technical lead at the Cisco Systems Development Unit (SDU), focusing on Cloud solutions since 2009. He has more than 14 years of experience with design, validation, and deployment of end-to-end networking solutions spanning VoIP, cable, MPLS, security, and cloud architectures. He holds a Master's degree in computer engineering from North Carolina State University. He has presented to both internal and external audiences at various conferences and has represented Cisco in a number of customer events.

Sunil currently works on designing and validating the Cisco Architectures and Orchestration systems for Cloud Computing solutions, for end-to-end functionality, scalability, resiliency, automation, and service delivery, and for delivering the CVDs for the VMDC cloud architectures and related cloud orchestration and cloud assurance systems. He also assists service providers and major enterprises in the design and deployment of such services. He previously worked on designing and validating scalability and performance of large-scale network-based security services, including IPsec and SSL VPN, firewall, IPS, and DDoS.

Dedications

Huseni Saboowala:

I dedicate this book to my wife, Insiya, our daughter, Alisha, and my parents, Ruby and Hakim. They are my inspiration in everything I do. Writing this book wouldn't have been possible without their patience, encouragement, and unyielding support. I love you all!

Muhammad Abid:

This book is dedicated first to my family, my wife, Nadia, and my two awesome children, Zayd and Khadeeja. Without their love, encouragement, support, and patience, I would not have been able to achieve my dream of writing this book. Second, to my mom, Safia, and dad, Gulzar, who instilled in me a strong work ethic, persistence, and a will to never give up. Lastly, to my brothers, sisters, and in-laws, who have always been there full of encouragement. I know they will be very delighted by what follows.

Sudhir Modali:

I dedicate this book to my family, to my wife, Subha, and our son, Ananth, my source of inspiration and drive to work on this book; my mom and dad, who have shaped my thinking and are a guide at all times; my sister and brother, who are a source of encouragement in all my endeavors. I know they are proud of my achievements and are close to me in this moment of elation.

Acknowledgments

Dave Lively, director SP Cloud Architecture Technical Sales at Cisco, for his outstanding contributions to this book. Along with deep technical and strategic inputs, his review comments included valuable pointers on enhancing the flow and readability of the book.

Kiran Rane, senior director Cisco SRG Engineering, for his unwavering support throughout this journey and his encouragement during some of the challenging times.

Ravi Chandra, VP/GM, SRG Operations, for sharing his deep insights on the cloud market and needs of Cisco SRG's enterprise and service provider customers.

Pravin Akkiraju, chief executive officer VCE, for spending time and inspiring us with his vision and strategy for the role of networks in solving some of the biggest challenges facing enterprise cloud adopters.

Kelly Ahuja, SVP/GM, SP Mobility Group, for sharing deep insights about how the service providers are looking to evolve their networks to monetize cloud-generated opportunities.

Suresh Thirunavukkarasu, director, product management, Rony Gotesdyner, senior product line manager, Mani Ramasamy, principal engineer, and Chandrodaya Prasad, manager product management at Cisco SRG, for their solid feedback and suggestions on Cisco Cloud Connectors.

Monique Morrow, distinguished consulting engineer at Cisco, for sharing her insights on the future of cloud and networks.

Mike Sullenberger, distinguished engineer and Nic Doyle, principal engineer at Cisco, for their valuable contributions to the NGN section of the book, with a focus on cloud security.

Mostafa Mansour, technical marketing engineer at Cisco SRG, for sharing his expertise on NGN infrastructure and data center interconnect technologies.

The technical reviewers, Ravi Varanasi, engineering director for Cloud Security, and Sunil Cherukuri, senior technical leader at Cisco, who provided excellent technical coverage and kept this book accurate and easy to navigate. Despite their busy travel schedule and ongoing engagements, both Ravi and Sunil stepped up and delivered high-quality input, which enabled the book to benefit from their expertise.

We also want to extend our sincerest gratitude to the following managers and colleagues for their support in this project: Mark Lohmeyer, Vinod Peris, Deependra Vaidya, Jason Rolleston, Marcelo Magno, Afaq Khan, Padmini Sridhar, Ashok Ganesan, Charles Yager, Jeff Raymond, Lakshmi Sharma, Ritch Dusome, Matthias Falkner, and Scott Yow.

Finally, the Cisco Press team: Brett Bartow, the executive editor, for seeing the value and vision provided in the original proposal and believing enough to provide us the opportunity to build this book. In addition, Christopher Cleveland, senior development editor, for his relentless push to develop our rough manuscript into a fine piece of technical literature and pushing the entire team to meet our deadlines. Lastly, Tonya Simpson and everyone else in the Cisco Press team who spent countless hours normalizing the manuscript and its technical drawings and content; their effort can be seen throughout the book pertaining to our ideas, words, and pictures, presented in ways that we ourselves could never have imagined.

Contents at a Glance

Contents

Introduction

The cloud and the services it has to offer have garnered significant interest worldwide. The cloud offers an elastic model that allows infrastructure capacity to be increased and decreased on demand. The cloud's usage-based model helps governments, educational institutions, and enterprises to increase business agility and reduce costs by seamlessly moving applications and consuming infrastructure resources from the cloud. The cloud's role as an enabler of newer economics for IT is now widely understood.

Despite all the benefits, enterprises have been cautious to adopt the cloud because of concerns around *availability*, *security*, and *application performance*. Lack of visibility and control combined with the need to maintain compliance with regulatory requirements are cited as other reasons that have thus far inhibited the adoption of the cloud.

Business-grade cloud services aim to address these concerns and enable these organizations to adopt the cloud with confidence. These advanced cloud services require that the cloud data centers, networks, applications, and services be tightly integrated. The network is the only entity that interacts with all the elements of a cloud service and is ideally positioned to address the barriers to cloud adoption.

Evolved networks and network services enable the provider to offer cloud services with security, performance and availability *service level agreements* (SLA). These advanced networks provide appropriate levels of visibility and insight that can help businesses with performance and compliance verification. In addition to boosting cloud adoption, such capabilities fuel premium cloud service offerings and enable competitive differentiation.

These cloud-aware networks have additional intelligence—service, location, and cost awareness—that facilitate the seamless extension of IT resources, delivered as an optimized cloud service that can scale rapidly and cost-effectively. The rich set of *application programming interfaces* (APIs) available for automated provisioning of these networks and network services facilitate simplified management and zero-touch operations, which help in driving down costs further.

Networks inherently carry tons of information, including user location, device capabilities, topology, and end-to-end performance characteristics. When exposed appropriately through well-defined APIs, such information can be consumed by cloud applications to fine-tune and customize their efficient delivery. The future holds the promise of increasingly rich application-network interactions.

Cisco, with an industry-leading portfolio of cloud-ready networking products and services, is in a unique position to provide end-to-end architectures for differentiated cloud services. Cisco's innovative platforms extend from the *customer premise equipment* (CPE) at the enterprise branch, to the service provider IP NGN, to the service-rich network fabric in the data centers. Large sets of documentation from various business units are available on these cloud products and solutions from Cisco. In addition, select cloud solutions in the form of CVDs (*Cisco Validated Designs*) are available, as well.

These product documentations and CVDs are implementation heavy, and usually do not address the design choices, application needs, end-to-end cloud service delivery, or business aspects of cloud services. For those seeking to understand the design and architecture of networks and network services pertaining to the delivery of business-grade cloud services, there is no single source of reference available today.

This book provides a concise and easy-to-understand view of how evolved networks and network services can be designed to enable a secure, resilient, and SLA-driven cloud experience. In addition, the book explains how intelligent networks can help providers simplify the complexity of managing cloud services and reduce costs through efficient scaling and improved capacity utilization. The end-to-end service delivery concepts are reinforced with illustrative examples. The goal is to boil down and simplify the design and architectural details and present them in one reference, augmenting the existing installation and configuration guides of the various cloud-related products and solutions already available from Cisco.

The book does not attempt to be prescriptive about how these network services can be put together into a particular cloud solution and dive into the detailed configurations/ CLIs needed to implement the cloud services, because these are tied to the specific requirements of that deployment. The book provides the architectural knowledge that will help you understand the role and capabilities of these advanced networks and network services, along with the design factors to consider for their insertion into a cloud service. For the next steps, CVDs are recommended for obtaining detailed design information on specific cloud solutions that have been qualified by Cisco, and consultative engagements with Cisco Advanced Services are recommended for customized cloud solutions.

Objectives of This Book

The book can help you understand the role of networks—encompassing data center networks, service provider IP NGNs, and the customer premise equipment—in the delivery of business-grade cloud services. The architecture of networks and network services is discussed in context with the underlying trends shaping the technical and business landscape of these cloud services and applications. A major focus is the evolution of today's networks and network services—new technologies and platforms—and how they can be designed to ensure the accelerated adoption of the cloud by addressing the primary inhibitors: availability, security, visibility, and application performance.

The book is organized into four parts: Part I discusses the basics of virtualization and the cloud and the role of networks in clouds. Part II focuses on virtualization-aware data center networks that enable flexible virtual network services for the cloud. Part III covers the evolution of IP NGNs and services for the cloud. Finally, Part IV explores the critical role of the CPE as a control point in accessing cloud services, and then delves into end-to-end cloud SLAs that enable guarantees in the delivery of premium cloud services.

Who Should Read This Book?

The book is intended primarily for a technical audience involved in designing, architecting, deploying, and delivering cloud services. Cloud and network visionaries, architects, and engineers at cloud service providers, network service providers, managed service providers, or even enterprises looking to build their own cloud, stand to benefit from the wide range of topics covered by the book.

The book would also prove valuable to cloud consumers, both businesses and individuals, who want to better understand the technical and business landscape surrounding premium cloud services. It can help them make informed choices and enable them to have an engaging discussion with their provider on how they can achieve their security and performance goals while reaping the benefits of the cloud.

How This Book Is Organized

This book is organized into 13 chapters distributed across 4 parts, and although it can be read cover to cover, it does allow for readers to move between chapters and parts, covering only the content that interests them. The four parts of the book are described as follows.

Part I introduces virtualization concepts across compute, network, and storage domains and how virtualization proved to be the cloud harbinger. Part I then covers basics of cloud (the characteristics, the deployment and service models, and the benefits and cloud service management) before diving into the critical role of the network in enabling business-grade cloud services.

Part II covers the all-important data center networks, underlining the importance of a virtualization-aware network fabric and the flexibility provided by virtual network services. It also discusses the concept of network containers and how security and optimization can be designed in this dynamic multitenant environment.

Part III examines the role of the service provider IP NGN in enabling the flexible and highly available extension of resource pools across geographically dispersed data centers. How can network intelligence be leveraged to optimize the placement of cloud services? This section then delves into designing secure access to the cloud and protecting the cloud edge from various attacks. Aspects of application performance are also examined to ensure that the cloud services and applications deliver an enhanced user experience that is expected from business-grade cloud services.

Part IV discusses the critical role of the CPE as a control point in accessing hybrid cloud services. It builds on the material covered earlier and breaks down the complexity of end-to-end SLA guarantees. This part then rounds off the book, with a peek into the future of cloud and networks.

An overview on each of the 13 chapters follows.

- **Chapter 1, "Virtualization":** Provides a brief history of virtualization, before discussing the core concepts for virtualizing the three pillars of the data center: server, network, and storage. Zooming into the server space, the chapter explores compute, memory, and I/O virtualization. Network virtualization concepts are examined with illustrative examples, and the chapter wraps up with a discussion on storage virtualization and the synergies from combining compute, network, and storage virtualization.

- **Chapter 2, "Arrival of the Cloud":** Describes how virtualization enables the transition to the cloud, followed by its definition and key attributes. It then delves into the underlying trends driving the adoption of cloud and also examines the key inhibitors. Finally, the chapter explores the game-changing benefits and impact of the cloud.

- **Chapter 3, "Cloud Taxonomy and Service Management":** Covers the classification of cloud services into the *software/platform/infrastructure* (as a service) SPI model and examines various cloud deployment models, including the evolution toward the intercloud. The chapter then explores a cloud ecosystem before concluding with an overview of cloud service management.

- **Chapter 4, "Networks and Services in the Cloud":** This key chapter explains how networks can help overcome the barriers that inhibit the CIOs from wholeheartedly adopting the cloud. How can these network services be monetized? And how are these networks and network services poised to play an increasingly critical role in the next stage of the cloud journey? The chapter ends with a discussion on the evolution of today's networks to meet the challenges of the cloud.

- **Chapter 5, "Role of the Network Infrastructure in a Virtualized Environment":** Discusses the factors influencing evolution of the network fabric due to virtualization and defines the critical components required of the network infrastructure in the virtual environment.

- **Chapter 6, "Securing and Optimizing Cloud Services":** Security is one of the most important services that is part of any data center architecture. An understanding of business and application workflow is key in designing a security framework. In a cloud-enabled data center, predefined instances can be used to provision security compliant (PCI-DSS, HIPAA, GLBA, SOX, and so on) frameworks. Virtualizing the services enables multitenant-capable security deployment models while retaining the characteristics of a virtual machine such as mobility, elasticity, and manageability.

- **Chapter 7, "Application Performance Optimization":** This chapter focuses on delivering a seamless and persistent cloud experience irrespective of the location and mode of connectivity.

- **Chapter 8, "IP NGN Infrastructure That Supports Cloud Services":** Delving deeper and showing how the IP NGNs are evolving to accommodate the transition to the cloud, this chapter describes various data center interconnect technologies, which enable the flexible, high-availability extension of resource pools across geographically separated data centers. The chapter also focuses on various route optimization techniques

- **Chapter 9, "Securing Cloud Transport and Edge Using NGN Technologies":** Focuses on protecting the cloud edge from various attacks and providing secure access to the cloud to place and consume cloud services and applications.

- **Chapter 10, "Optimizing and Accelerating Cloud Services":** Explains how the network infrastructure needs to become more intelligent; that is, it has to become service, location, and cost aware and enable optimal placement and accelerated delivery of cloud services and applications.

- **Chapter 11, "Connecting Enterprises to the Cloud":** Focuses on the need for enterprises to connect to multiple cloud providers, along with their own data centers. Various cloud connect examples illustrate how these organizations are able to leverage the CPE as a control point toward achieving secure, optimized, and cost-effective access to cloud services.

- **Chapter 12, "End-to-End Cloud SLAs":** This chapter deals with the complexity of cloud SLAs and elaborates on the models that you can use to simplify the delivery of these SLAs. The chapter then delves into end-to-end SLAs and how they can be enabled through a service overlay approach.

- **Chapter 13, "Peeking into the Future":** The final chapter explores two major phenomenon poised to change the future of cloud (the intercloud and the Internet of Things) and the critical role of the network in enabling their success. The chapter then delves into emerging network trends and innovations around application-network interactions and *software-defined networking* (SDN).

Chapter 1

Virtualization

In this chapter, you learn about the following:

- General concepts and a brief history of virtualization
- Virtualization of the server and its components
- Network virtualization and virtualization-aware networks
- Storage virtualization

The journey toward the cloud begins with virtualization. Virtualization has emerged as the key *disruptive* technology that has catalyzed and enabled data centers to deliver cloud services. Compute, networks, and storage form the three infrastructure pillars of today's data center. This chapter explores the abstraction of these vital resources, with a deep dive into server, network, and storage virtualization. The fluidity of the infrastructure brought about by the virtualization of these key data center resources is fundamental to the enablement of the cloud.

The idea of virtualization is not new; it has been around since the days of the mainframe. But more recently, the term *virtualization* has gained a broader, more inclusive connotation beyond server virtualization. We begin this chapter by seeking a generic definition of virtualization, while examining the basic concepts and history associated with it.

Virtualization Basics

Virtualization can be defined as the abstraction of physical resources into logical units, such that a single physical resource can appear as many logical units and multiple physical resources can appear as a single logical unit. The primary motivation behind virtualization is to hide the physical characteristics and irrelevant details of these resources from their end users. Thus, each user gets the illusion of being the lone user of that physical resource (one-to-many virtualization). Or multiple physical resources appear as a single virtual resource to the user (many-to-one virtualization).

One to Many

Consider the familiar example of virtualizing an x86 server, where software, called *virtual machine monitor* (VMM) or *hypervisor*, allows multiple *virtual machines* (VM) to run on the same physical server, as illustrated in Figure 1-1. Each VM emulates a physical computer by creating a separate operating system environment. The ability to run multiple VMs means that we can now simultaneously host multiple operating systems on the same underlying physical machine. Each operating system gets the illusion that it is the only one running on that host server. One physical machine has effectively been divided into many logical ones.

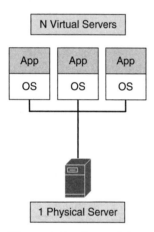

Figure 1-1   *One-to-Many Virtualization*

Virtual LANs (VLAN) are another example of one-to-many virtualization, where a single physical network is partitioned into many logical ones. Instead of setting up separate physical networks for each user group, a single physical network infrastructure can suffice, with each user group assigned to a separate logical network (VLAN).

Many to One

The classic example for many-to-one virtualization is that of a load balancer, which front-ends a group of web servers. As shown is Figure 1-2, the load balancer hides the details about the multiple physical web servers and simply exposes a single *virtual IP* (VIP). The web clients that connect to the VIP to obtain the web service have the illusion that there is a single web server. Many physical web servers have been abstracted into one logical web server.

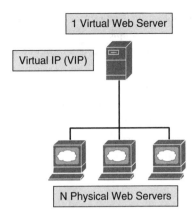

Figure 1-2   *Many-to-One Virtualization*

Virtualization: A Brief History

The concept of virtualization has been around since the 1960s, when IBM implemented it to logically partition mainframe computers into separate VMs. This partitioning enabled mainframes to run multiple applications and processes at the same time, which improved their utilization. Such multitasking allowed better leveraging of those expensive investments.

Over the next two to three decades, the need for virtualization declined as inexpensive PCs and servers became available. In addition, client/server applications became prevalent, and the trend shifted toward distributed computing. Furthermore, the universal adoption of Windows and Linux led to the emergence of x86 servers as the dominant compute platforms. Unlike mainframes, however, these servers have not been designed for virtualization. To enable the virtualization of x86 servers, specialized software called *hypervisor* was developed by companies such as VMware, Citrix, Microsoft, and others.

The term *virtualization* has evolved beyond server virtualization into a significantly broader context. Today, it represents any type of process obfuscation where a process is removed from its physical operating environment. Therefore, virtualization can be applied to other areas of IT, such as storage, network, applications, services, desktops, and many more. This chapter focuses on *server virtualization*, *network virtualization*, and *storage virtualization*, which together form the foundation of today's virtualized data center. The sections that follow explore these diverse forms of virtualization, starting with the most familiar one: server virtualization.

Server Virtualization

Server or compute virtualization is the most popular and visible form of virtualization today. We briefly touched on this form of virtualization as an example of one-to-many virtualization and saw how low-level software (hypervisor or VMM) allows multiple operating systems to run concurrently on a single host computer. As Figure 1-1 illustrated, each operating system, along with its applications, runs in complete isolation as a VM on top of the hypervisor, under the illusion that it is the sole operating system running on that physical machine.

To successfully virtualize the system and enable multiple VMs to run concurrently on the same host, hypervisors dynamically partition and share the available physical resources, such as CPU, memory, and I/O devices. The functionality of the hypervisor varies greatly based on the architecture and implementation.

Drivers for Server Virtualization

Before we move ahead to examine the approaches to server virtualization and the various components involved, the list that follows looks at the trends that have been responsible for driving the unprecedented growth of this phenomenon:

- **Underutilized servers:** Each year, enterprises procure large numbers of servers for hosting applications and services in their data centers. Each server would typically be dedicated to a particular task or application, and so there would be a server for *supply chain management* (SCM), another for *customer relationship management* (CRM), and so on. Thanks to Moore's law, the capabilities of these servers have been increasing exponentially, roughly doubling every 18 months. The software running on these servers often needs no more than 10 percent to 20 percent of the processing power of the server. This low average server utilization leads to a huge amount of wasted computing resources.

  Virtualization allows multiple independent environments to coexist on the same physical server, which significantly drives up the utilization of servers, making more efficient use of the company's investment in servers. The increased utilization means that fewer physical servers are now needed in the data center.

- **Shift toward greener IT:** With increased energy costs and environmental regulations, there is increasing pressure on IT to lower the energy consumption from power and cooling in their data centers. As described earlier, virtualization addresses the server underutilization issue and reduces the number of physical boxes needed, which in turn reduces the space requirements of the data center.

  This reduction in the number of servers has a dramatic impact on power-consumption and cooling requirements. An idle or near-idle server consumes a significant amount of base power. So, a single server with 50 percent utilization consumes much less power (by extension produces much less heat) than five servers running at 10 percent utilization. The reduced space and power requirements result in lowered electricity and cooling costs and a greener data center.

Approaches to Server Virtualization

In general, there are two approaches to x86 virtualization: hosted and bare metal.

In hosted virtualization, the hypervisor runs as an application on the *host* operating system. Then multiple *guest* operating systems could run as VMs on top of this hypervisor. This type of hypervisor is also referred to as a *Type 2 hypervisor*. Microsoft Virtual Server and VMware Server, and numerous endpoint-based virtualization platforms such as VMware Workstation, Microsoft Virtual PC, and Parallels Workstation, are hosted hypervisors.

In contrast, in bare-metal virtualization, the hypervisor runs directly on the host's hardware. Multiple guest operating systems could then run on top of this hypervisor, which falls into the *Type 1 hypervisor* category. The popular Type 1 hypervisors available in the market today include Citrix XenServer, VMware ESXi, Linux KVM, and Microsoft Hyper-V. The Linux KVM hypervisor has been increasing in popularity recently, but its classification as a Type 1 or Type 2 hypervisor remains mired in some debate. Many consider it a Type 2 hypervisor because KVM is essentially a Linux kernel module and is loaded by the Linux host operating system. Others make the case that Linux with KVM module is the hypervisor running on bare metal, thus making it a Type 1 hypervisor.

Type 1 hypervisors are typically more efficient because they have direct access to the underlying hardware and can deliver superior performance as compared to their Type 2 counterparts. Figure 1-3 illustrates both hypervisor types side by side and helps visualize the performance difference. For Type 1 hypervisors, any system call made by the guest operating system has to go through fewer software layers. However, Type 2 hypervisors support a wider range of platforms and I/O devices, because they run on top of a standard operating system such as Microsoft Windows or Red Hat Linux. Therefore, Type 2 hypervisors have been popular in clients such as PC/laptops/tablets, where support for a wide variety of I/O devices is an important factor.

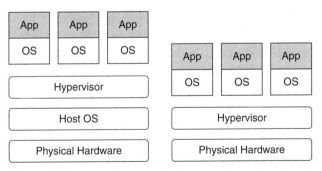

Figure 1-3 *Hosted Virtualization (Left) and Bare-Metal Virtualization (Right)*

In servers used in data centers to host applications, Type 1 hypervisors are typically deployed. In this book, unless mentioned otherwise, consider the term *hypervisor* to mean a Type 1 or bare-metal hypervisor.

Components of Server Virtualization

CPU, memory, and I/O are typically considered the three vital resources of a server. Correspondingly, the three key components of server virtualization are *CPU virtualization*, *memory virtualization*, and *I/O virtualization*. The sections that follow take a look at all three components, starting with the virtualization of the x86 CPU.

CPU Virtualization

x86 operating systems are designed to run directly on the bare-metal hardware, so they naturally assume they fully "own" the computer hardware. In fact, in the four privilege levels (or rings) offered by the x86 architecture (Ring 0, 1, 2, and 3) to manage access to the hardware resources, operating systems expect to run at Ring 0 (most privileged), whereas user applications typically run at Ring 3 (least privileged). Virtualizing the x86 architecture requires placing a virtualization layer under the operating system to create and manage the virtual machines that deliver shared resources.

Full Virtualization, Paravirtualization, and Hardware-Assisted Virtualization

Unfortunately, though, certain x86 instructions cannot effectively be virtualized, and the difficulty in trapping and translating these sensitive and privileged instruction requests at runtime was a significant challenge for x86 architecture virtualization. Two techniques that have been used to resolve this challenge are full-virtualization (using binary translation) and paravirtualization.

Full virtualization involves binary translation, replacing nonvirtualizable instructions with equivalent sequences of instructions. Paravirtualization involves modifying the operating system kernel itself to replace nonvirtualizable instructions with hypercalls that communicate directly with the virtualization layer hypervisor. Although paravirtualization provides lower virtualization overhead and thus accelerated performance, its obvious downside remains the need to modify the guest operating system. This is not an option for operating systems such as Windows where the source code is not available for modification. The open source Xen hypervisor is the most visible user of the paravirtualization technique.

Both of these techniques achieve the goal of operating system independence from the underlying hardware but present trade-offs in performance and compatibility. An alternative approach is hardware-assisted virtualization, which enables efficient full virtualization using help from hardware capabilities, primarily from the host processors. Here an unmodified guest operating system executes in complete isolation. With hardware-assisted virtualization, the hypervisor can efficiently virtualize the entire x86 instruction set by handling those sensitive and difficult-to-virtualize instructions using a classic trap-and-emulate model in hardware, as opposed to software. Intel VT-x and AMD-V are examples of hardware-assisted x86 virtualization technologies.

Memory Virtualization

Beyond CPU virtualization, the other critical part of server virtualization is memory virtualization. This involves sharing the host physical memory (machine memory) and dynamically allocating it to VMs, as illustrated in Figure 1-4. VM memory virtualization is similar to the virtual memory support provided by modern operating systems. Applications see a contiguous address space that is not necessarily tied to the underlying physical memory in the system. The operating system keeps mappings of virtual page numbers to physical page numbers stored in page tables. All modern x86 CPUs include a *memory management unit* (MMU) and a *translation look-aside buffer* (TLB) to optimize virtual memory performance.

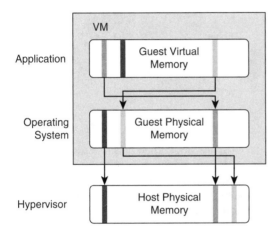

Figure 1-4   *Three-Layer VM Memory Access*

Shadow Page Tables

In the server virtualization scenario, with several VMs running on a single host system, another level of memory virtualization is required. As shown in Figure 1-5, the guest operating system continues to control the mapping of virtual addresses to the guest memory physical addresses; however, the guest operating system cannot have direct access to the actual host physical memory. Hence, another translation is added, in which the hypervisor steps in and assumes responsibility for mapping guest physical memory to the host physical memory.

To avoid the performance hit due to the double translation for every memory access, shadow page tables can be employed to accelerate the mappings. Here, the hypervisor maps the guest virtual memory directly to the host physical memory, as illustrated in Figure 1-6. How is this direct lookup made possible? Quite simply, it takes some good old-fashioned bookkeeping work by the hypervisor to make this possible. Whenever the guest operating system changes the virtual memory to physical memory mapping, the hypervisor updates the shadow page tables accordingly, thus enabling a direct lookup.

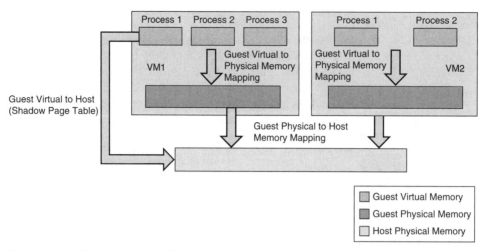

Figure 1-5   *Shadow Page Tables*

Hardware Approach

Second-generation hardware virtualization technologies, such as Nested Page Tables from AMD or Extended Page Tables from Intel, avoid the bookkeeping overhead of the shadow page table method, partly by brute hardware force. They employ a "super-TLB" that stores both virtual to guest physical translation and guest physical to host physical translation and enables significant performance gains.

I/O Virtualization

Having covered VMs (CPUs) and then virtual memory, this discussion now turns to the final component of the server virtualization story: *I/O virtualization* (IOV). As the name suggests, IOV involves virtualizing the I/O path from the server to the peripheral device, enabling multiple VMs to share an I/O device. As shown earlier in the case of CPU and memory virtualization, even in IOV we have a software approach and a hardware approach.

Software IOV

In the software-based IOV approach, the hypervisor virtualizes the physical hardware and presents each VM with a standardized set of virtual devices. These virtual devices effectively emulate well-known hardware and translate the VM requests to the system hardware. For instance, in network I/O, most virtual server systems currently use a software virtual switch, such as the Cisco Nexus 1000v, inside the hypervisor to share access to the *network interface card* (NIC) among the VMs. Virtual NICs and virtual switches create virtual networks between VMs without the network traffic consuming bandwidth on the physical network.

Although software-based methods for IOV typically provide richer functionality and better manageability, they exhibit higher CPU utilization and lower throughput. Every time an I/O operation occurs, the hypervisor is involved; this CPU overhead quickly adds up in the case of network interfaces, which perform gigabytes of I/O every second.

Hardware IOV

This CPU overhead issue leads to the hardware approach to IOV, introduced by Intel with VT-d and AMD with AMD-Vi technologies. With these hardware extensions, the hypervisor can safely assign physical hardware directly to VMs, ending the need for them to funnel all their I/O through the host, thus reducing CPU overhead and achieving native-level I/O performance for VMs.

To be practically feasible, this approach needs the I/O device to be shared among multiple VMs. *Virtual interface cards* (VIC) on Cisco *Unified Computing Systems* (UCS) address this challenge through self-virtualization, whereby a single VIC can present up to 256 virtual interfaces to the VMs running on the host. As illustrated in Figure 1-6, each of these virtual interfaces can be configured as either a virtual NIC for LAN access or a *virtual* Fibre Channel *host bus adapter* (vHBA) for storage access and then assigned exclusively to a particular VM.

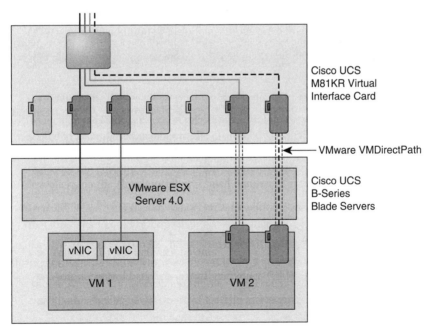

Figure 1-6   *Hardware IOV with Cisco UCS Virtual Interface Card (Source: Cisco)*

In addition, hypervisor bypass technologies on the UCS enable the VM to directly communicate with the physical port, without going through the hypervisor layer. Such optimization, illustrated in Figure 1-6, leverages hypervisor technologies such as VMware VMDirectPath and helps to reduce the CPU overhead created by software switching within the hypervisor, and can lead to greater than 30 percent improvement in virtual I/O performance.[1]

To standardize hardware virtualization and promote greater interoperability, the *PCI Special Interest Group* (PCI-SIG) developed the *Single Root I/O Virtualization* (SR-IOV) standard, which virtualizes a single physical PCIe device to appear as multiple PCIe devices. SR-IOV is being implemented within a growing number of devices, including the Cisco VIC illustrated earlier in Figure 1-6.

Taking the Single-Root IOV concept a step further, Multi-Root IOV moves the adapters out of the server and into a switching box. This allows the adapters to be shared across many physical servers, which drives up adapter utilization. Fewer adapters mean less power and cooling. Also, adapters take up a lot of space in servers, and moving them out of the server could potentially shrink a 2U server to a 1U server.

Figure 1-7 shows an example where multiple servers such as web, CRM, and SAP each use a single high-bandwidth IOV adapter to connect to the external I/O switching box, which in turn provides connectivity to all kinds of network and storage devices over diverse I/O protocols such as 1G/10G Ethernet, Fibre Channel, iSCSI, *Fibre Channel over Ethernet* (FCoE), and so on. The servers are isolated from changes to the network technologies that happen only at the switching box (for instance, moving from 4-Gb Fibre Channel to 8-Gb Fibre Channel).

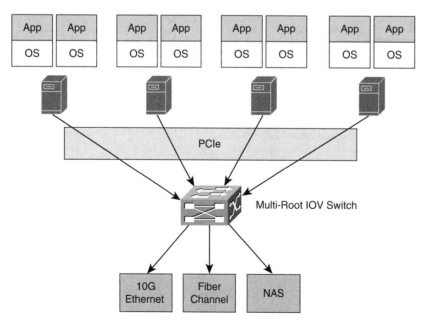

Figure 1-7   *Sharing I/O Adapters Across Servers with Multi-Root IOV*

Benefits and Risks of Server Virtualization

Virtualizing the servers in a data center can bring several direct and indirect gains, as outlined in the list that follows:

- **Server consolidation:** Applications running on servers typically use less than 20 percent of the available capacity. Server virtualization allows multiple VMs to run on the same physical server, thus increasing the utilization of the servers. This results in fewer physical servers in the data center, with correspondingly lower maintenance costs.

- **Reduced carbon footprint:** With server virtualization reducing the number of physical boxes needed, a data center with a smaller space can suffice. This results in reduced electricity and cooling costs and a greener data center.

- **Automation and agility:** Server virtualization enables the creation, modification and de-allocation of a variety of operating system environments, rapidly and with ease. This allows IT to respond with agility to the needs of the business. Adding new capacity is as simple as starting up a few VMs, which can take minutes instead of hours and days. Other IT tasks such as workload balancing and failure recovery become relatively easier to automate as well.

- **Business continuity:** In post-disaster scenarios, the task of restoring systems and migrating applications to the new environment is expedited by server virtualization. This enables the business to rapidly return back to normalcy.

- **Multi-operating system testing:** Server virtualization speeds up engineering processes, including development and test, because it makes it easier to create different operating system environments. Virtualization allows developers to test and to compare application feature and application performance across different operating environments.

As highlighted in the preceding list, server virtualization brings several near-term and long-term benefits. But does that mean that all should close their eyes and jump on to this bandwagon? Is it appropriate for everyone? What are the issues to be aware of before, during, and after the transition from physical to virtual? Here are a few items to watch out for:

- **Software licensing:** One of the most significant virtualization-related issues to be aware of is software licensing. Virtualization makes it easy to create new servers, but each VM requires its own separate software license. Organizations using expensive licensed applications could end up paying large amounts in license fees if they do not control their server sprawl.

- **IT training:** IT staff used to dealing with physical systems will need a certain amount of training in virtualization. Such training is essential to enable the staff to debug and troubleshoot issues in the virtual environment, to secure and manage VMs, and to effectively plan for capacity.

- **Hardware investment:** Server virtualization is most effective when powerful physical machines are used to host several VMs. This means that organizations that have existing not-so-powerful hardware might still need to make upfront investments in acquiring new physical servers to harvest the benefits of virtualization.

As seen from the rapid adoption of server virtualization in data centers around the globe, clearly the belief is that the upside to server virtualization outweighs the risks involved. But virtualizing the servers alone, without the virtualization of the network connecting these servers, would leave an unsecure and inefficient data center that does not scale too well. The section that follows examines the drivers for virtualizing the network, how virtualization concepts can be applied to the network, and the resulting gains.

Network Virtualization

Today, networks are everywhere, ranging from small *local-area networks* (LAN) all the way to the biggest network of all: the Internet. *Network virtualization* can be defined as the application of virtualization concepts to these networks. As discussed earlier in this chapter, virtualization can be exhibited in several different forms: one to many and many to one. Both forms apply to the virtualization of networks. On one hand, network virtualization includes logically segmenting a physical network into multiple virtual networks; on the other hand, it also includes consolidating multiple physical networks into one virtual network!

In either form of virtualization, network resources can be deployed and managed as logical services rather than as physical resources. Because we have abstracted out the physical characteristics of these network resources, we would be dealing only with virtual network services and can therefore expect virtualization related benefits such as increased agility and flexibility, improved network resource utilization, and reduced capital and operating costs.

Drivers for Network Virtualization

Several trends are driving the move toward virtualization of the network:

- **Privacy and regulatory compliance:** Privacy concerns are increasing, as is the need for enterprises to adhere to regulatory compliance. Both of these trends mean that even within the company, there is a need to isolate traffic between different user groups, such as engineering, marketing, legal, HR, or finance. And the need is even higher to separate partners, vendors, and guest traffic.

  In some instances, user groups are created to meet regulatory compliance requirements, such as separating bankers and traders in a financial company. Mobile devices such as tablets and smartphones might need to have their traffic separated, depending on whether they are IT approved, the applications they support, or the data bandwidth they generate.

Before network virtualization, such requirements would typically have meant having separate physical networks for each of these groups. In addition, network service nodes such as firewalls or load balancers would have to be separately deployed for each such physical network. This inefficient use of network resources would expectedly lead to not only a huge increase in network *capital expenditure* (CapEx) but also a significant increase in *operating expenditure* (OpEx) because of the maintenance requirements of separate physical networks.

- **Underutilized networks and network services:** As in the case of server virtualization, even networks face the trend of ever-powerful network boxes, which are underutilized. In the previrtualization era, multiple physical networks would be present in the same enterprise, and in such cases if the enterprise desired to acquire a new firewall appliance, it had to purchase a separate appliance for each physical network. This was cost-prohibitive and led to underutilized network devices.

  Enter network virtualization, and a single physical network would be segmented into multiple virtual networks. The firewall appliance with multiple virtual contexts could be shared among the various virtual networks, with a dedicated virtual firewall context per virtual network. This could dramatically improve the utilization of the firewall device and lower the overall cost to the enterprise.

- **Network management complexity:** Networks are getting larger and more complex. A growing number of network devices are present in today's data centers, ranging from access, aggregation, and core switches to load balancers, firewalls, session border controllers, WAN accelerators, deep packet inspection devices, and more. Managing all these devices separately, and coordinating the configuration across each of them to achieve the desired end-to-end network behavior, has become a significant challenge.

  Virtualization can help reduce this complexity in a couple of ways. First, because virtualization abstracts away the physical details of the network device, the network administrator has to deal only with managing the network at a logical level. This should help simplify the management of the network. Second, with the capability to combine multiple physical network devices into a single network device, virtualization can help reduce the number of network points that have to be managed.

- **Security:** Network security continues to stay in the limelight as hacker attacks on several high-profile targets on the Internet continue. A significant number of security exposures result from configuration errors on the various network security devices. As described earlier, when the network contains a large number of such security devices, overall network security requires the perfect coordination of their configuration.

  Virtualization reduces the number of configuration points in the network, which in turn lowers the complexity and the probability of misconfiguration, ultimately leading to successful enforcement of the desired security policy.

Logical Segmentation: One to Many

With one-to-many network virtualization, a single physical network is logically segmented into multiple virtual networks. As illustrated in Figure 1-8, each virtual network could correspond to a user group, providing the necessary traffic isolation and access restrictions for that group. At the same time, network services from a common physical service node are shareable across virtual networks. The sections that follow delve a little deeper into how virtual networks provide such path isolation, access authorization, and service sharing.

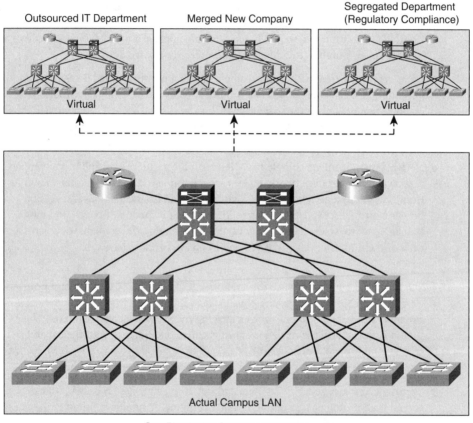

Figure 1-8 *Logical Separation of One Physical to Multiple Virtual Networks (Source: Cisco)*

Path Isolation

End-to-end path isolation requires virtualization of the network devices and their interconnecting links. VLANs have been one of the most visible examples of network virtualization, having existed in some form or the other since long before x86 server virtualization existed. Typically, all hosts from a user group are mapped to a single VLAN, and because network switches restrict traffic from flowing between VLANs, traffic isolation can be achieved between user groups. To extend this path isolation across switches, VLAN tagging (802.1Q) can be used to carry VLAN information between switches.

VLANs would suffice for segmenting Layer 2-only networks, but today's hierarchical networks likely involve a mix of Layer 2 switched networks (at the access) and Layer 3 routed networks (in the core). In this case, you need to extend the Layer 2 isolation of VLANs over the Layer 3 routed core, to provide end-to-end path isolation for each virtual network. To achieve this, you need to virtualize the Layer 3 network devices and their interconnecting links.

You can virtualize the Layer 3 network device (router) by using technology called *virtual routing and forwarding* (VRF). VRF technology allows multiple virtual routers to be created within a single physical router. A virtual router corresponds to a user group and includes its own IP routing table, forwarding table, network interfaces and routing protocols. Thus, separation is achieved at both the control plane and the data plane level, and users in one VRF cannot communicate with users in other VRFs unless such connectivity is explicitly configured. Figure 1-9 shows a single router abstracted into multiple virtual routers.

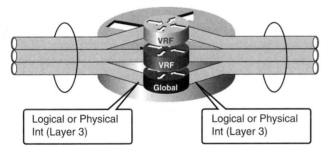

Figure 1-9   *Virtual Routing and Forwarding (Source: Cisco)*

Virtualization of the interconnecting links depends on how the virtual routers are connected to each other. If the virtual routers are directly connected to each other, you can use VRF-lite, a hop-by-hop virtualization technology. Each of these directly connected network devices and their physical interconnections are virtualized. On the data plane, you can use labeling techniques such as 802.1Q to virtualize the connecting link, as shown in Figure 1-10.

When the virtual routers are connected over multiple hops through an IP cloud, tunneling techniques are needed to virtualize the path between the virtual routers, as illustrated in Figure 1-11. *Generic routing encapsulation* (GRE) and *Multiprotocol Label Switching* (MPLS) *virtual private networks* (VPN) are examples of technologies used to create such tunnels. GRE tunnels provide a simple way to separate traffic by encapsulating packets within tunnel-identifying headers. This way, the tunnels can traverse multiple hops.

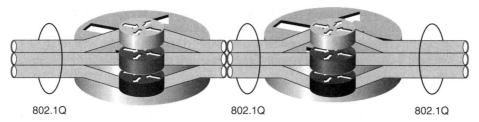

Figure 1-10   *Layer 2 Labels: Virtualizing the Direct Link Between Virtual Routers (Source: Cisco)*

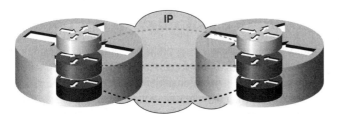

Figure 1-11   *Tunnels: Virtualizing Multihop Connection Between Virtual Routers (Source: Cisco)*

At the endpoints of the tunnel, mapping is done between the VRF for the user group and the GRE tunnel, as shown on the right side of Figure 1-12. On the left side of the same diagram, you see the mapping between the access network segmentation technology (VLAN) and the corresponding VRF for the user group. Thus, the path isolation for the user group could effectively be extended from the VLAN in the Layer 2 access network, all the way across the Layer 3 network using VRF separation on the network devices and GRE tunnels over the interconnecting links. In the case of directly connected devices, the same path isolation is achieved with VRF-lite, and 802.1Q VLAN labels replace GRE tunnels.

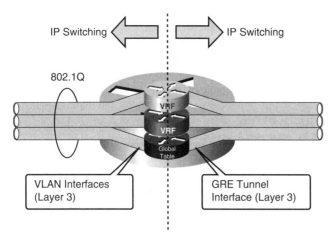

Figure 1-12   *Mapping VLAN > VRF > GRE (Source: Cisco)*

GRE tunnels are well suited to one-to-many connectivity, but MPLS VPN (another tunneling technique) is better suited for any-to-any connectivity within a user group. Unlike GRE tunnels, MPLS VPNs do not have to manage multiple point-to-point tunnels to provide a full mesh of connectivity within the virtual network (or user group). Traffic separation is achieved through the use of labels attached to packets. Beyond isolating the network traffic for each group, virtual networks need to provide access control and enable sharing of network services across groups.

Access Control

Users accessing the network need to be authenticated first. Standards-based technologies such as 802.1X can be leveraged to achieve identity-based authentication. Once authenticated, the user is then authorized to enter an assigned network partition (for example, VLAN) and access the network resources and services belonging to its group. In this way, a user is associated with a virtual network. Furthermore, users can be subjected to different policies attached to each user's virtual network (for example, a *quality of service* [QoS] policy attached to VLAN).

Sharing Network Services

Network services such as firewalls, traffic accelerators, intrusion detectors, and load balancers can be shared across authorized user groups by virtualizing them. For example, a physical firewall could be virtualized into multiple virtual firewalls, with each virtual firewall providing services to one user group. Each user group can then enforce its own policies on individual virtual firewalls, while the enterprise owns and maintains a single physical firewall appliance. Such network services virtualization provides efficient use of network resources while reducing the overall number of network devices.

Figure 1-13 illustrates virtualization of firewall and load-balancing services on a Cisco *Data Center Services Node* (DSN). The DSN consists of a Cisco Catalyst 6500 Series switch loaded with firewall (*Adaptive Security Appliance* [ASA]) and load-balancer (*Application Control Engine* [ACE]) modules. You can logically separate these network service modules into multiple virtual devices that allow dedicated instances of network services to be allocated to each virtual network. Figure 1-13 illustrates how a virtual firewall (vASA) and a virtual load-balancer (vACE) service are made available for each VLAN.

The preceding examples focused on the segmentation of the enterprise data center or campus networks into several virtual networks, but you can extend the logical separation concept to other networks. Service provider networks built as virtual networks on top of the physical resources of the network infrastructure provider are another such example.

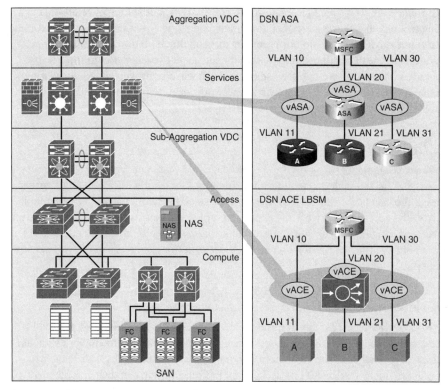

Figure 1-13 *Cisco DSN: Network Services Virtualization (Source: Cisco)*

Network Consolidation: Many to One

Many-to-one virtualization is exhibited when multiple physical networks (or network devices) are combined together into a single logical network (or network device). An example, illustrated in Figure 1-14, is Cisco's *Virtual Switching System* (VSS), allowing two network switches to be managed and monitored as a single logical switch. Such consolidation facilitates a single point of management and a simplified network, resulting in improved operational efficiency.

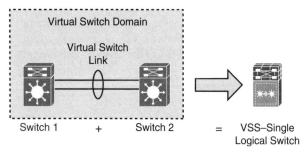

Figure 1-14 *Consolidation of Multiple Physical Network Devices into one Logical Device (Source: Cisco)*

VSS also enables significant improvement in network-capacity utilization by eliminating the active-passive model required by redundancy protocols such as *Spanning Tree Protocol* (STP) that allows one path to carry traffic while the other path sits idle and stays unused until a failure occurs. Using VSS in combination with the *Multichassis EtherChannel* (MEC) link aggregation technology allows all links to be active and passing traffic, resulting in significant CapEx savings.

Software Defined Networking

Taking this consolidation concept one step further is the Software Defined Networking (SDN) architecture, which aims to essentially abstract the entire network into a single virtual switch. One of SDN's great promises is simpler management, separating logical connections from the underlying physical infrastructure.

In a classical router or switch, the fast packet forwarding (data path) and the high-level routing decisions (control path) occur on the same device. In the SDN architecture, leveraging key protocols such as OpenFlow, the data and control functions are decoupled. The data path portion still resides on the switch, while high-level routing decisions are moved to a separate controller, typically a standard server. As shown in Figure 1-15, the OpenFlow switch and controller communicate via the OpenFlow protocol, which defines messages, such as packet-received, send-packet-out, modify-forwarding-table, and get-stats.

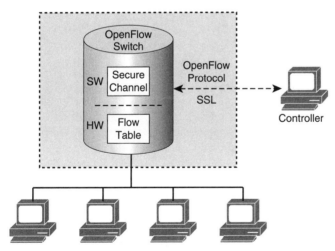

Figure 1-15 *OpenFlow Controller and Switches (Source: Openflow.org)*

The data path of an OpenFlow switch presents a clean flow table abstraction; each flow table entry contains a set of packet fields to match and an action (such as send-out-port, modify-field, or drop). When an OpenFlow switch receives a packet it has never seen before, and for which it has no matching flow entries, it sends this packet to the controller. The controller then decides how to handle this packet. It can drop the packet or it can add a flow entry directing the switch on how to forward similar packets in the future.

A single controller could potentially manage all the OpenFlow-enabled switches in the network. Instead of separately configuring multiple network devices, network administrators need to configure only a single controller that can automatically govern the behavior of switches and routers. In effect, the administrator's task is simplified to managing a single huge virtual switch, without having to bother about the details representing the physical topology of the underlying networks—a compelling example of many-to-one virtualization.

Virtualization-Aware Networks

The advent of server virtualization brings an increasing number of VMs running in the data center today; however, classical network switches are not aware of VMs. To them, a particular physical port with its various security and QoS policies corresponds to a NIC on a server. The reality, though, is that multiple VMs are running on that server sharing a NIC, each potentially with distinct security and QoS requirements. To enable network administrators to configure separate security and QoS policies per VM, the network needs to virtualize the physical port and allow configuration of policies per virtual port, with each virtual port corresponding to a *virtual NIC* (VNIC), as illustrated by Figure 1-16.

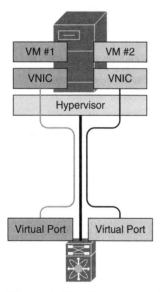

Figure 1-16   *Server Virtualization-Aware Network Switch (Source: Cisco)*

Solutions are available from networking vendors such as Cisco, with its *Virtual Machine Fabric Extender* (VM-FEX) technology, and Blade Networks (acquired by IBM), with VMReady functionality; these essentially allow the network to become virtualization aware and work at VM-level granularity. The VM-FEX technology leverages the *virtual interface card* (VIC) discussed earlier in the "Server Virtualization" section to present each VM with virtual ports on the physical access switch. VM traffic tagged with VM identifying information (VNTag) is sent directly to the upstream physical switch, bypassing the vSwitch in the hypervisor. Based on the information in the tag, the virtualization-aware external switch applies appropriate QoS and security policies while switching the VM traffic. Standardization activities are ongoing in the IEEE to address the challenges of networking in a virtualized environment, and the resulting standards tracks include IEEE 802.1 BR Bridge Port Extension and IEEE 802.1Qbg *Ethernet Virtual Bridging* (EVB).

Benefits and Risks of Network Virtualization

The following list summarizes the primary benefits of network virtualization, discussed in the preceding sections:

- **Improved utilization** of network resources, with multiple users and groups sharing the same physical network.

- **Increased flexibility** by allowing the network to more rapidly respond to changing business needs. Separate virtual networks can be rapidly added for regulatory compliance with new laws or integration of an acquired company

- **Reduced cost of ownership**, by allowing network services to be centralized and shared across multiple closed user groups.

- **Ease of management**, brought about by a single point for managing multiple networks and by abstracting away the details of the physical nodes and topology.

- **Better security** gained from centralizing the security services and from simplified management of security policies

Network virtualization's benefits should be weighed against the risks that it introduces:

- Just as with virtualization in general, network virtualization brings additional *debugging complexity*. This results from the need to map problems noticed on a virtual network to the responsible physical network, or to map problems noticed in the physical network to the affected virtual networks. Both cases could lead to an increase in time needed to identify and resolve network outages or brownouts.

- Another expected downside of network virtualization is the *loss of physical separation*, which may be important for customers with stringent policies or ultraconfidential data.

Widespread deployment of network virtualization over decades of use is testimony to its success and the significant benefits it brings. The maturing of some of these network virtualization technologies has provided a solid foundation to leverage and build on. In addition, the emergence of virtualization-aware networks and software-defined networking is providing exciting opportunities for future innovations.

Having looked at server virtualization and then network virtualization, the discussion now turns to the third pillar of data center virtualization: storage.

Storage Virtualization

Because virtualization is defined as the abstraction of physical details, it could be argued that at some level everything in storage is virtualized; for example, technologies such as RAID hide the details of the underlying storage hardware from the operating system and applications. In today's world, however, the term *storage virtualization* usually means the process of combining multiple physical storage devices into logical storage devices.

In the modern sense, there are really two major kinds of storage virtualization: one at the block level and one at the file level. Block storage virtualization refers to the abstraction of physical storage such that it may be accessed without regard to the physical location or structure of the storage, thus providing flexibility in the management of storage. Block storage virtualization is often simply referred to as storage virtualization, and is used by databases that need block-level access to data. The data disks for block virtualization will typically reside on *storage-area networks* (SAN). File storage virtualization, in contrast, provides abstraction for data accessed at the file level from the physical location where the files are stored. This type of storage virtualization is targeted for applications that access data as files rather than as blocks. The files are typically stored on *network attached storage* (NAS) file systems. This coverage focuses on block virtualization.

Drivers for Storage Virtualization

Storage using disk arrays suffered from a few issues. Various storage management functions were limited to the disks in the array and could not be expanded beyond the array. In addition, arrays belonging to different vendors had different architecture and management interfaces. This meant that multiple arrays could not be managed from the same console or that replication between the arrays was difficult. What was needed was a way to pull these storage management functionalities out of the internal controllers of the storage array and into a virtualization layer located above the various heterogeneous storage arrays. Storage virtualization solutions from several vendors today provide such functionality.

How Storage Virtualization Works

Quite simply, storage virtualization works through mapping. The storage virtualization layer creates a mapping from the logical storage address space (used by the hosts) to the physical address of the storage device. Such mapping information, also referred to as *metadata*, is stored in huge mapping tables. When a host requests I/O, the virtualization layer looks at the logical address in that I/O request and using the mapping table translates the logical address into the address of a physical storage device. The virtualization layer then performs I/O with the underlying storage device using the physical address, and when it receives the data back from the physical device, it returns that data to the application as if it had come from the logical address. The application is unaware of this mapping that happens beneath the covers. Figure 1-17 illustrates this virtual storage layer that sits between the applications and the physical storage devices.

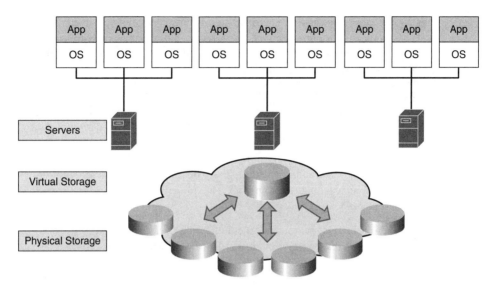

Figure 1-17 *Storage Virtualization Mapping Heterogeneous Physical Storage to Virtual Storage*

Common Implementations of Storage Virtualization

The sections that follow examine some of the familiar approaches to deploying storage virtualization.

Array-Based Storage Virtualization

In an array-based approach, the virtualization layer resides inside a storage array controller, and multiple other storage devices, from the same vendor or from a different vendor, can be added behind it. That controller, called the *primary storage array controller*, is responsible for providing the mapping functionality. The primary storage array controller also provides replication, migration, and other storage management services across the storage devices that it is virtualizing.

Network-Based Storage Virtualization

A network-based implementation is the most commonly deployed approach for storage virtualization. The virtualization layer resides on a networked device sitting in the SAN, such as an appliance or a network switch. This approach provides true virtualization, abstracting a variety of storage devices, which can be managed from a single management interface. Network-based virtualization can be done with one of the following approaches:

■ **Symmetric or in-band:** With an in-band approach, the virtualization device is sitting in the path of the I/O data flow. Hosts send I/O requests to the virtualization device, which perform I/O with the actual storage device on behalf of the host. Caching for improving performance and other storage management features such as replication and migration can be supported. One possible caveat is that the virtualization device risks being the performance bottleneck because all I/O passes through it (perhaps resulting in network bottlenecks and application latency).

- **Asymmetric or out-of-band:** The virtualization device in this approach sits outside the data path between the host and storage device. What this means is that special software is needed on the host, which knows to first request the location of data from the virtualization device and then use that mapped physical address to perform the I/O. Although this approach has the obvious advantage of avoiding a performance bottleneck, it has additional complexity because of the changes required on the host side. Also, caching is not an option anymore because I/O does not pass through the mapping device.

- **Hybrid split-path:** This method uses a combination of in-band and out-of-band approaches, taking advantage of intelligent SAN switches to perform I/O redirection and other virtualization tasks at wire speed. Specialized software running on a dedicated highly available appliance interacts with the intelligent switch ports to manage I/O traffic and map logical-to-physical storage resources at wire speed. Whereas in typical in-band solutions the CPU is susceptible to being overwhelmed by I/O traffic, in the split-path approach the I/O-intensive work is offloaded to dedicated port-level ASICs on the SAN switch. These *application-specific integrated circuits* (ASIC) can look inside Fibre Channel frames and perform I/O mapping and reroute the frames without introducing any significant amount of latency.

Benefits and Risks of Storage Virtualization

The list that follows recaps the major benefits associated with storage virtualization:

- **Ease of storage management:** Single pane of glass for managing all storage, thus simplifying storage administration and reducing operational expenses.

- **Increased efficiency through greater utilization of storage:** This is achieved through resource pooling, migration, and thin provisioning. When all available storage capacity is pooled together, the admin can easily allocate new logical disks from the pool, allowing all available storage to potentially be used. In addition, thin provisioning allows storage space to be easily allocated to servers, on a just-enough and just-in-time basis, reducing unused overallocations of storage.

- **Support for heterogeneous storage arrays:** Helps avoid vendor limitations. Also, because storage disks from multiple vendors can be interchangeably used, capital expenses are reduced.

- **Higher availability of storage:** No downtime is required, and concurrent I/O access can be maintained while migrating data, resizing disks, or taking snapshots.

Risks worth considering include the following:

- Performance can be a concern, especially for in-band deployments, where the virtualization controller or appliance can become a bandwidth bottleneck.

- Interoperability among vendor products is still evolving.

- Failure of the virtualization device, leading to loss of the mapping table.

The benefits of storage virtualization certainly outweigh its limited risks, especially if you carefully consider the risks applicable to the particular situation in advance. You can avoid single points of failure by smarter design, and you can avoid interoperability-related surprises with due diligence. With the significant gains that it brings to the table, storage virtualization is here to stay and will change the way storage is managed.

Summary

Virtualization is the abstraction of a physical resource into one or more logical resources. Either a single physical resource can provide the illusion of multiple logical ones or multiple physical resources can appear as a single logical resource. In this chapter, you learned how the virtualization concept applies to IT resources such as compute, network, and storage, which are the three building blocks of today's virtualized data center.

The success of server virtualization has been hailed as a transformational event in IT. Without network and storage virtualization, though, the data center would continue to run inefficiently. In fact, when these virtualization technologies come together, there are synergies to be leveraged. For instance, network virtualization when combined with server virtualization can result in virtual network ports and network policies that stick to VMs. Even as a VM migrates to another server for workload balancing or other reasons, the network policies move with it, resulting in unchanged accessibility and security for the VM. Another example is where server and storage virtualization can combine to efficiently and cost-effectively extend business continuity/disaster recovery capabilities to remote sites.

Together, these three virtualization technologies help build a dynamic, flexible, and efficient infrastructure that allows IT to be responsive to business needs, dramatically improve utilization of resources, and lower capital and operating costs. Ultimately, they enable today's data centers to be ready for the cloud.

Review Questions

You can find answers to these questions in Appendix A, "Answers to Review Questions."

1. CPU, memory, and I/O virtualization are components of which of the following?
    a. Network virtualization
    b. Server virtualization
    c. Storage virtualization
    d. Desktop virtualization

2. VLANs are a widely used virtualization technology for providing isolation at which layer?

   a. Layer 1
   b. Layer 2
   c. Layer 3
   d. Layer 4

3. Which full-mesh technology is used for network path isolation over multiple IP hops?

   a. VLAN
   b. MPLS VPN
   c. GRE tunnels
   d. 802.1Q

4. Which of the following are benefits of storage virtualization?

   a. Ease of management
   b. Thin provisioning
   c. Support for multivendor storage
   d. All of the above

References

1. Cisco Virtual Interface Card (VIC) Throughput Improvement: http://www.cisco.com/en/US/solutions/collateral/ns340/ns517/ns224/ns944/white_paper_c11-593280.html

- VMware History of Virtualization: http://www.vmware.com/virtualization/history.html

- VMware white paper: "Understanding Full Virtualization, Paravirtualization, and Hardware Assist" (http://www.vmware.com/files/pdf/VMwarevirtualization.pdf)

- Memory Virtualization – Shadow PT, Nested PT, Extended PT: http://www.anandtech.com/show/2480/10

- Server Virtualization: http://www.itmanagement.com/faq/server-virtualization/

- Cisco Network Virtualization Solutions: http://www.cisco.com/en/US/netsol/ns658/index.html

- Cisco Network Virtualization solutions for the Campus: http://www.cisco.com/en/US/solutions/collateral/ns340/ns517/ns431/ns658/net_brochure0900aecd804a17db.html

- Cisco Data Center Virtual Machine Fabric Extender (VM-FEX): http://www.cisco.com/en/US/netsol/ns1124/index.html

- OpenFlow: https://www.opennetworking.org/standards/intro-to-openflow
- Virtualization: The Foundation of Data Center Transformation: http://www.infostor.com/storage-management/virtualization/2010/virtualization-the-foundation-for-data-center-transformation.html

Chapter 2

Arrival of the Cloud

In this chapter, you learn about the following:

- Phases of virtualization and how virtualization enables the cloud

- Essential characteristics of the cloud

- History of the cloud

- Trends driving the adoption of the cloud

- Benefits and major impact of the cloud, and the challenges impeding its rapid adoption

Phases of Virtualization

As discussed in Chapter 1, "Virtualization," the rapid adoption of server virtualization has been driven initially by the significant *capital expenditure* (CapEx) and *operating expenditure* (OpEx) savings realized by consolidation. Apart from the reduction in server spend, the decreased number of physical servers in the data center results in additional savings in the form of lower power consumption and reduced space and cooling requirements. Cost can be a powerful motivator and has pushed a lot of enterprises to embark on their virtualization journey.

Along with cost reductions, virtualization in this early phase also enabled IT to rapidly provision new servers, dramatically improving deployment speed. Before virtualization, fulfilling a new server request entailed several cumbersome steps, including the initial procurement and mounting of the physical server, the wiring of the network connections, and then the subsequent operating system installation, network configuration, and installation and test of supported applications. With virtualization, the same fulfillment process simplifies to first selecting the appropriate *virtual machine* (VM) template file and then firing up the VM on an appropriate physical server. As shown in Figure 2-1, the workflow shortens from days/weeks to minutes/hours, enabling IT to respond rapidly to service requests.

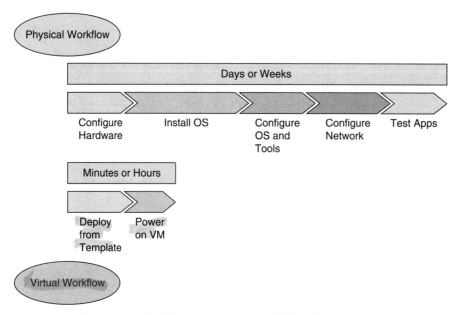

Figure 2-1 *Virtualization Phase 1 Benefit: Rapid Provisioning*

As enterprise IT started leveraging virtualization to reduce costs and increase deployment speed, they became familiar and comfortable with the concept of virtualization. The next natural step in the virtualization journey was to go beyond looking at a single resource at a time (simple virtualization) to distributed virtualization, as illustrated in Figure 2-2. In this second phase of virtualization, abstracted IT resources such as servers, storage, and networks are treated as pools of resources that can be managed in aggregate rather than as isolated silos. Thinking about IT resources as an entire system allows IT to move resources on demand to efficiently balance computing loads and use capacity more efficiently. This mobility of virtualized resources can unleash powerful capabilities.

For example, when a spike in demand occurs for an application, a physical server hosting multiple VMs running that application could get overloaded with respect to CPU, memory, or I/O resources. To preserve the performance of the application, some of those VMs could be migrated to less-loaded or more-powerful servers. Or if a physical server needs to undergo maintenance, all the VMs running on it could be migrated off before the maintenance and then returned back to it once the maintenance is completed, leading to a significant improvement in service availability.

Equally important, the capabilities just described lend themselves to automation, with scripts that can be triggered by events such as CPU utilization crossing a predefined threshold or the arrival of a scheduled maintenance window.

This advanced phase of virtualization adoption brings improved service availability, automation, and a tremendous amount of flexibility to IT operations. Essentially, IT becomes more nimble and can respond more quickly and efficiently to changing business needs.

Virtualization Enables the Cloud

We discussed how virtualization benefits evolved from increased resource utilization, cost reduction, and deployment speed to increased responsiveness and application uptime, leading to greater flexibility in responding to rapidly changing business requirements. The next logical step forward in this journey, illustrated in Figure 2-2, is delivering these resources (not just servers, but storage, networks, applications, services, or any other IT resource) as a service to the consumer. These consumers request resources through a self-service portal, and IT can deliver the requested resources in an automated manner, by allocating those resources on demand, where and when needed. This model of IT-as-a-service could also be described as an example of cloud computing.

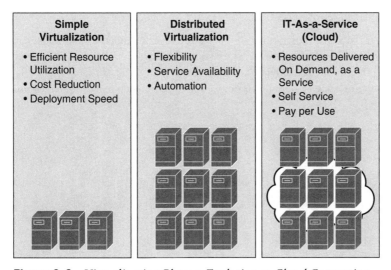

Figure 2-2   *Virtualization Phases: Evolution to Cloud Computing*

Before we go ahead and define cloud computing, let's review the four fundamental capabilities that virtualization helps to enable, which ultimately pave the path to cloud computing:

■ **Hardware abstraction:** Virtualization enables IT resources to be abstracted from the underlying hardware, allowing them to move around freely, from one server to another, across clusters or even across data centers.

■ **Resource pooling:** Resources across the data center, when virtualized, can be readily put together into a giant resource pool. From this pool, resources are allocated on demand. The resource pool is shared across services and enables optimization of resource utilization.

- **Automation and elasticity:** Virtualized resources can be managed in an automated fashion, which allows IT to respond quickly to scale out and scale in requests. If manual involvement were required for responding to these service requests, IT would be unable to respond rapidly enough or to sustain the economies of scale advantage.

- **Isolation and multitenancy:** Virtualization enables logical partitioning of a physical resource, such that the physical resource can be securely shared between multiple users. Hypervisors allow multiple VMs on the same server to run in isolation of one another. Network virtualization segments the network into multiple virtual networks, and the traffic on each of these virtual networks is isolated from the others.

What Exactly Is Cloud Computing?

More than a new technology, cloud computing is really an *operations model* for delivering IT services. Cloud computing can be defined as a model where IT resources are abstracted from the underlying infrastructure and provided *as a service*, *on demand*, and *at scale* in a multitenant environment.

Although not as facile as the illustration in Figure 2-3, a recommended way to understand cloud computing is to examine its key characteristics. There is a lot of confusing marketing messaging from vendors and providers around cloud, with some of them simply relabeling their existing offerings as cloud offerings. (The term for such marketing innovation is *cloud-washing*.)

Figure 2-3   *Cloud Computing Explained (Courtesy: Geekandpoke.com)*

The following essential properties, illustrated in Figure 2-4 and defined initially by the United States *National Institute of Standards Technology* (NIST), can be used as a litmus test to confirm whether the latest offering you are looking at is really cloud computing:

- **Self-service:** Cloud consumers can request for the cloud service on their own, typically through a web-based portal or through *application programming interfaces* (API), without the need for interaction with the service provider's staff over the phone or via other means such as email or chat. Such a portal allows the consumer to select and then customize the desired services. Consumers today are increasingly accustomed to helping themselves; an analogy can be found in the banking sector, with the popularity of the self-service provided by ATMs.

- **Ubiquitous access:** Cloud consumers can access cloud services over the network in a standard manner without needing any special proprietary technology. The access can be done using a web browser or from an application installed on a laptop, tablet, or smartphone. An example is accessing the Gmail cloud service from an iPad tablet connected to the Internet via a WiFi hotspot, while enjoying a café latte at Starbucks. And no, the café latte is not included as a defining characteristic for ubiquitously accessing cloud services.

- **Resource pooling/multitenancy:** IT resources are pooled together, with the pool being shared across consumers in a multitenant fashion. Resources from the pool are dynamically assigned and reassigned to consumers, when and where needed. The consumer is typically unaware of the specific physical location of the resource allocated from the resource pool.

  For example, a cloud provider may pool a particular type of network resource in its data center, such as VLANs, into a resource pool. When a consumer requests network segmentation services, one of the VLANs from the pool is allocated to that consumer.

  As described in the previous section, virtualization provides the hardware abstraction and facilitates this pooling of resources. Virtualized resources in the pool can be shared across services and across consumers, achieving high levels of resource utilization. The isolation of logical resources is another key capability brought about by virtualization that enables the secured sharing of resources across tenants.

- **Rapidly scale on demand:** Based on the demand of the cloud consumer, the cloud service can rapidly scale capacity up or down. To the consumer, the cloud appears to offer a limitless amount of resources that they can request, expand, or contract their usage of as needed, and release when done. The cloud can respond to these changes in demand at the speed of automation.

  Consider the example of an online dating company using the cloud to host its web service. The company gets mentioned on Oprah and becomes wildly popular overnight. To keep up with the huge upsurge in compute, storage, and network requirements, the company needs tens of new servers, hundreds of gigabytes of additional storage, and several gigabits per second of networking bandwidth, which typically would takes days or weeks to set up. A cloud provider, however, can rapidly provision and make these additional capabilities available to the consumer within minutes or seconds.

The automation and elasticity capabilities brought about by virtualization, and discussed in the previous section, help enable this essential cloud characteristic. Virtualized resources can be provisioned and deprovisioned in a completely automated manner, with zero human touch, allowing the cloud to rapidly respond to changing demand from the cloud consumer.

■ **Measured service/usage based billing:** The resources required for the service are metered in a fashion similar to utilities. Such metering allows the consumer to be billed for only the resources used and for the period they were used (usage-based billing). This is one of the principal attractions of the cloud for a lot of consumers, especially small and medium-sized businesses: not having to make upfront investments, but rather paying for the service based on its usage.

Consider the example of a payroll-processing company, which leverages the cloud to obtain the extra processing power during the last two to three days of the month. Instead of procuring the servers needed for that month-end spike in processing demand, and keeping those servers idle the rest of the month, the company has opted for the cloud. The cloud provider bills them only for the two to three days that they use the cloud, and this makes great economic sense for the company.

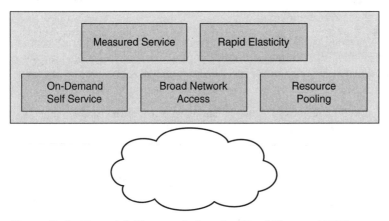

Figure 2-4   *Essential Characteristics of a Cloud (Source: NIST)*

A Little History

Although cloud computing is considered the latest mega-trend in IT today, the idea has been around since the 1960s, when J. C. R. Licklider described his concept of an intergalactic network where everyone would be able to access programs and data at any site, from anywhere. In addition, John McCarthy, a computer scientist at Stanford, espoused the concept of computing power being made available as a utility, akin to water and electricity, in the early 1960s. But the software, hardware, and infrastructure technology available at that time could not support converting those visionary concepts into reality.

Those ideas had to wait all the way until the late 1990s, when Salesforce.com pioneered the concept of software-as-a-service, delivering *customer relationship management* (CRM) and other enterprise applications via a simple website. And in 2006, Amazon introduced its S3 storage and EC2 compute services as part of its *Amazon Web Services* (AWS) offering. The idea was to sell unused capacity in the huge data centers running Amazon.com's retail business. S3 and EC2 were the first true infrastructure cloud computing services, making storage and compute available as a service, with pay-per-use pricing models.

In 2008, the launch of Google App Engine marked the entry of the Internet search leader into the cloud computing market, offering services that enable application developers to rapidly develop and then deploy their applications on an automatically scalable web application platform. And finally, in 2010, Microsoft launched the Windows Azure cloud, marking a major shift from the software giant's traditional focus on the desktop. In addition to these leaders, the recent emergence of major telco carriers such as AT&T, Qwest, and Verizon (with its acquisition of Terremark in 2011) as cloud providers has helped propel cloud services into the mainstream of IT.

Cloud computing today delivers an increasingly wide range of IT services, including application software, development platforms, servers, networks, and storage. Typically, these services are delivered from huge data centers equipped with an enormous amount of computing, network, and storage resources. However, computing infrastructures have not always been centralized like this.

In fact, computing infrastructures began in a centralized fashion with the mainframe in the 1960s, which gave way to minicomputers; both were aggregated models of data center computing and provided little control and flexibility to their users. This was followed by the decentralized infrastructure phase, where computing power was available right at the user's desktop. This model allowed users to manage their own compute and data, essentially becoming their own system administrators, which, as you can imagine, ended up being very inefficient. Over the past few years, several trends have been driving the rise of cloud computing services delivered from huge data centers, swinging the pendulum back toward centralized computing infrastructures. We examine those trends in the next section.

Trends Driving the Growth of Cloud Computing

Today, cloud computing services are experiencing rapid growth in various market segments, including consumer, small-to-medium business (SMB), education, government, and even enterprise. But, as discussed previously, cloud is not new, and concepts such as computing as a utility have been around for decades. So, why is it now that the cloud model is gaining traction? Let's examine the trends that are driving the rise and the subsequent adoption of cloud computing:

■ **Maturity and widespread adoption of virtualization:** Virtualization has been considered by many as the principal catalyst in enabling the rise of cloud computing.

Even though it may not be listed as an essential characteristic of the cloud, the reality is that virtualization is an indispensable ingredient to almost all clouds. As described in the "Phases of Virtualization" section, earlier in this chapter, as virtualization technologies matured and saw widespread adoption, delivering IT resources-as-a-service (that is, cloud) was a natural next step. Virtualization makes the cloud technically feasible and economically attractive for the provider by enabling capabilities such as hardware abstraction, resource pooling, automated elasticity, and multitenant isolation, which were discussed earlier in the chapter.

Providers can significantly improve profitability by offering what seems to be a dedicated service to the customer, only doing so on a shared infrastructure. The increased infrastructure utilization brought about by virtualization leads to reduced CapEx and lowered power and cooling costs for the service provider. In addition, the automated, zero-touch operations enabled by virtualization help drive down administration costs and significantly lower the provider's OpEx. These factors have contributed to the emergence of a wave of cloud providers.

■ **IT as a competitive advantage for the business:** With the economic turbulence witnessed over the past several years, enterprise IT groups are being asked to do more with less (reduce IT overhead without impact to business revenues). At the same time, IT is expected to be able to rapidly roll out services to support new business initiatives and decommission obsolete services on demand. When the business grows, IT is expected to be able to scale out rapidly to support that growth. Similarly, during a downturn, there is a need to scale in.

The adoption of cloud services allows IT to dynamically scale out and scale in on demand, only paying for the actual services consumed, enabling IT to operate with increased agility and reduced costs and providing a competitive advantage for the business. Consider the example of a social gaming company whose latest game goes viral, shooting up in popularity almost overnight. IT will need to procure and spin up a bunch of new servers/storage/networking resources to keep up with the increasing load. If these resources are not added quickly enough, a lot of users trying the game might leave dissatisfied with the gaming experience. An agile and faster-responding IT could prove to be a huge differentiator for the business.

■ **Rapid growth in the number of high-speed Internet users:** The past decade has seen a tremendous increase in bandwidth available to businesses and consumers alike. Next-generation mobile Internet technologies such as *Long Term Evolution* (LTE) allow high-speed access to the cloud even when outside the office or home. This has vastly expanded the target market for cloud offerings, allowing a large number of cloud services, including ones with rich media, to be accessed by cloud consumers.

Apple's iCloud music-sharing service is an example of a cloud storage service that would not have made sense a few years ago. But with the large number of Internet-connected devices from which users like to access their music today, storing them in the cloud seems simply logical.

- **Increased collaboration within and between organizations:** Rapid globalization over the past few years has resulted in virtual teams spread across multiple continents, spanning partner, vendor, or customer organizations, together working toward a common goal. This has led to an increased need for collaboration within and across organizations, on a global scale. The ideal location for hosting such collaboration is not inside the firewalls of any one of the organizations involved, but instead out in the cloud.

  Consider the case of an organization looking to enable high-definition video conferencing among its headquarters, the globally distributed branches, and its partners and vendors. Leveraging a collaboration cloud service such as Cisco TelePresence Exchange enables such a capability, allowing users from anywhere to share video, documents, and so on during the real-time collaboration session. No one organization has to bear the burden of hosting the conferencing exchange and providing the necessary service scale with a global footprint.

- **Killer apps from industry leaders:** The success and popularity of several cloud offerings by leading players in the technology industry has led to consumers becoming increasingly comfortable with the concept of using services from the cloud. While the initial adoption was driven by individuals for their personal use, enterprises also started by leveraging cloud services in non-mission-critical, noncore areas such as email and document sharing. The success they achieved with cloud services in these areas has increased their trust in the cloud.

Despite some negative press about outages and the lack of meaningful *service level agreements* (SLA) (covered in detail in subsequent chapters in this book), on the whole the cloud market has been filled with a lot of positive customer experiences. Several small and medium-sized businesses, and even some larger ones, have successfully switched over to Google's cloud-based email service Gmail, shedding their long serving in-house shrink-wrapped email solutions such as Exchange or Lotus Notes. Apart from the cost savings from the subscription pricing, and the ability to automatically receive free updates and patches, Gmail has enabled their work force to be more productive, with instant access to their email from anywhere, anytime, and from any device. Such positive experiences have prepared customers to increasingly move their core functions into the cloud.

Impact of the Cloud

Beyond providing benefits to both consumers and providers, which are evidently visible and driving the rapid growth of cloud computing today, the cloud has the potential to create far-reaching impact, which can rival the scale of the previous major disruption— the Internet. As the cloud becomes more widespread, it will unleash game-changing benefits, with a global scope. The sections that follow examine two such impacts.

Spur Innovation and Entrepreneurship Globally

One of the biggest barriers for innovators to try out new ideas, or for entrepreneurs to start a new company, is the upfront investment needed in IT resources. Cloud computing makes a large amount of computing, storage, network, development platform, or software resources accessible with near zero initial investment and a low ongoing expense. Individuals and start-ups anywhere on the planet (as long as they have access to a quality Internet connection) can reap these benefits, allowing the cloud to make a truly worldwide impact. This global democratization of access to IT resources has the potential of ushering in a new wave of business and technical innovations, which has only just started. Let's consider two examples:

■ A couple of young technology innovators have a brilliant idea for developing a web-based productivity application that can improve the efficiency of its users. Without much funding to support their efforts, and a significant IT setup being needed for developing and testing their application, the innovators may have given up on transforming their idea to reality. Instead, they turn to the cloud and work on developing their application on IT infrastructure resources from cloud providers such as Amazon AWS or Rackspace, thus obtaining their IT infrastructure with almost no upfront investment and a flexible pay-as-you-go billing scheme.

Later, when their application is developed and ready for launch, they could make their web application available on the same cloud infrastructure provider, starting off with only a few servers to handle the initial load. As the application grows in popularity, they are quickly able to provision more servers from the cloud provider to run with their application, to adequately handle the increasing load. If the application did not become popular, and the venture had to be abandoned, they simply deprovision their cloud resources, and the billing stops right away. A few months later, learning from the failure of their previous venture, the duo is ready to try out another idea. The cloud not only lowers the barrier to innovation, but equally significantly, it encourages risk taking by reducing the cost of failure. Unsuccessful innovation attempts can fail fast and fail often.

■ An entrepreneur planning to start her own small financial services business is looking to minimize the initial setup and ongoing expense of running the business. Some of these include setting up email and file servers, storage systems, and servers for shrink-wrapped software for CRM, accounting, and collaboration. The upfront costs for procuring the hardware and software needed for the aforementioned list, in addition to the facilities costs, can add up to a significant amount, and could easily make starting the business beyond her reach. Even if she manages to secure funding for the initial setup, the ongoing expenses associated with the maintenance and staffing requirements for the same could make the business unsustainable.

With a cloud-based approach, the entrepreneur could avoid those high infrastructure costs by adopting cloud email services from Google's Gmail for Business or by using cloud file-sharing and storage services from Dropbox, Box.net, or Microsoft

SkyDrive or CRM software from Salesforce.com. Such services help her avoid setup costs and are usually relatively inexpensive, with a monthly or annual subscription fee. The pricing tiers are usually based on the usage or number of subscribers, which allows the expenses to grow in line with the business. An additional advantage with this approach is that she can access these services anytime, anywhere, and from any device (PCs, tablets, or smartphones) with an Internet connection and collaborate with her employees and business partners. As with the previous technology innovation example, clouds can help lower the barrier for entrepreneurs around the globe trying to launch their small business in any field.

Collect and Analyze Big Data

Over the past several years, the amount of data available in our digital universe has increased exponentially. The IDC 2011 study "Extracting Value from Chaos" predicts that the world's information is more than doubling every two years, with close to 8 zettabytes (that is, 8 trillion GB) expected to be created in the year 2015, as illustrated in Figure 2-5. Entertainment media, video surveillance, healthcare and other sensor networks, along with data from social media sites such as Facebook and Twitter, are fueling this growth.

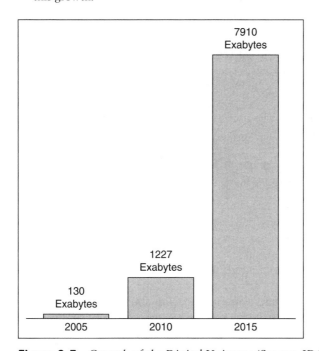

Figure 2-5   *Growth of the Digital Universe (Source: IDC)*

Clouds obviously can play a major role in collecting and storing this huge pile of information. Storing data in the cloud makes the data more accessible to a wider set of individuals and organizations, irrespective of their location. But more important, clouds can provide the huge amount of processing capacity needed to analyze and make sense of this stored data. Such compute power can be either in the form of real-time processing or large-scale batch processing. Several smaller companies simply cannot afford the upfront costs for the computation infrastructure needed to analyze such vast amounts of data. The cloud allows them the opportunity to perform this processing on a large number of servers, paying only for the time used.

This ability to analyze large sets of data, rapidly and economically, is valuable in a number of domains, most notably the following:

- In medical research, big data techniques can be used to analyze large numbers of patient and medical records to learn more about a disease. Pharmaceutical and biotechnology companies can run huge batch jobs for analyzing disease causing proteins, such as the recent research by ETH Zurich University to identify drugs for resistant bacterial strands. The job of analyzing such massive amounts of data with their own computational infrastructure would usually take several months. With access to vast amounts of readily available and affordable compute, network, and storage resources in the cloud, however, the task was accomplished in less than two weeks.

- Big data analytics is being increasingly leveraged for fraud prevention. A good example is BillGuard, which detects anomalies in a consumer's credit card billing by comparing with several data sources, including crowdsource information from millions of other consumers. This helps quickly identify hidden charges, billing errors, misleading subscriptions, or even fraud. The ability to collect and store huge streams of data from multiple sources and then run powerful data mining algorithms over such data stores to yield actionable information in an economic fashion is a job cut out for the cloud. Massive amounts of cloud-based IT resources can be rapidly employed to match the volume and velocity of incoming data.

- Analytics, when applied to the huge amount of data available to a business, can help identify actionable insights, which a business can use to remain agile and enhance its competitiveness. Social media information related to the business, its products, and competitors could also be integrated into such analysis on a real-time basis. Several resource-constrained organizations, despite being technically savvy, are unable to justify the investment for setting up the huge data farms needed for big data analytics. Cloud-based big data platforms make it practical for these organizations to access massive amounts of compute/network/storage resources for short and semipredictable amounts of time and extract valuable business intelligence from the overwhelming amount of data available to them.

These are only a few examples; the possibilities are nearly endless. Software technologies such as Apache Hadoop, which is an open source manifestation of the MapReduce idea, are available to process huge amounts of data in parallel on large compute clusters. Amazon integrated this with their cloud, when they offered Amazon Elastic MapReduce, enabling users to crunch huge amounts of data with ease and at a relatively inexpensive usage-based price.

Cloud computing is opening this field to players of all sizes who have a smart idea about the application of big data analytics. Such a confluence is poised to usher in an era of research breakthroughs and bring us closer to answering some of the most complex questions facing mankind.

Cloud Challenges

In many ways, we are currently in the first phase of cloud adoption, with a lot of enterprises leveraging the cloud to lower costs and increase agility. These users are currently moving what Geoffrey Moore describes as *context* applications (applications such as email and backup, which are not the core competency or differentiator for that business) to the cloud, while the *core* applications still remain on-premise. What challenges currently impede the rapid and widespread migration of these core workloads to the cloud? Let's examine some of the critical ones: security, compliance, SLA, and interoperability.

Security

For a lot of enterprises looking to move their core business applications and data into the cloud, security is the single most important factor holding them back. When considering a cloud provider, these are some of the questions regarding security that are top of mind for these enterprises:

- Can we trust our cloud provider to protect the confidentiality and privacy of our business and personnel data?

- And can we trust them to keep our cloud assets and network traffic isolated from other cloud tenants?

- What about securing the access to our cloud assets with multiple levels of authorization?

- Do we have control over where and how our data and application gets deployed?

- What kind of protection do we have against malicious attacks bringing down our cloud service?

The relevant threats that these enterprises are looking to protect against include data leakage, data modification, data disclosure, identity theft, intrusions and takeover, and service disruptions. They are looking for cloud providers that can ensure such protection, before they decide to migrate into the cloud completely.

ince

prises in different vertical markets must comply with legal requirements and with the regulations applicable to that industry. When an enterprise in such markets is considering a cloud provider, it needs answers to these questions:

- Can our provider ensure that their cloud facilities, IT infrastructure, and other components comply with a certain regulation?

- Can we restrict the storage location and transit path for our data based on geographic or jurisdiction boundaries?

- Does the provider maintain a record of who accessed our cloud infrastructure and data and when?

- Does the provider enable the collection of detailed audit records, which include measurements and logs related to these questions?

Some of the regulations that enterprises need to contend with today include *Payment Card Industry Data Security Standard* (PCI-DSS), *Sarbanes-Oxley* (SOX), *Health Insurance Portability and Accountability Act* (HIPAA), and state-specific laws such as Massachusetts Privacy Law 201 CMR 17 or Nevada SB-227. When they move to the cloud, enterprises need a cloud provider that is both able and willing to help them meet compliance requirements.

SLA: Reliability and Performance

A *service level agreement* (SLA) is a contractual agreement between a cloud provider and the cloud consumer and covers the definitions of the service and the metrics to objectively measure the condition of the service. Chapter 12, "End-to-End Cloud SLAs," covers the topic of cloud SLAs in detail. In the meantime, let's look at two key facets of an SLA: reliability and performance. Cloud reliability is typically associated with the availability of the cloud system, and putting a mission-critical application in the cloud without appropriate levels of reliability can prove costly. The questions for the cloud provider about reliability include the following:

- How do you define an outage?

- How many 9s availability do you guarantee? (For example, five 9s means a downtime of around 5 minutes a year.)

- How much in fines or damages will you repay if your lowered availability results in revenue loss?

- Does your service depend on other cloud providers? If so, what is their availability and the availability of the network between the two clouds?

- What is the combined availability of the complete system?

Performance of applications in the cloud is a major concern as organizations contemplate migrating *quality of experience* (QoE)-sensitive applications to the cloud. There are multiple facets to application performance, and questions that cloud providers need to answer about such include the following:

■ Will there be enough bandwidth for the application in the cloud?

■ Will the latency be low enough to avoid perceptible deterioration in the user experience?

■ With there be enough compute and storage resources available to the application on the shared cloud infrastructure?

■ And here's the big question: How reliable will the performance of our application be to its end users?

Reliability and performance of the cloud have been put in the spotlight with some high-profile outages and service deteriorations at leading cloud providers. Enterprises are understandably cautious about moving their core applications to the cloud without adequate guarantees.

Interoperability

Provider lock-in is another big concern for enterprises planning to adopt cloud services. Currently, standards in the cloud world are still evolving, and so moving from one cloud provider to another is not a trivial task. The possibility of such lock-in creates anxiety on the part of the consumer, who fears being stuck with a provider that does not deliver the performance, reliability, or features that the consumer needs. Interoperability between clouds can span several layers, including cloud management interoperability and virtual machine image interoperability. Enterprises need answers to the following questions about interoperability:

■ Which virtualization technologies do you support?

■ Which platforms (for example, Java or .NET) do you support?

■ What kind of storage access mechanisms (for example, Cloud Data Management Interface [CDMI]) do you support?

■ Which cloud management *application programming interface* (API) (for example, VMware vCloud, Amazon EC2) do you support?

■ Are my workloads and associated SLAs transferable?

Interoperability in the cloud world is still evolving, and standards will emerge gradually. In the meantime, enterprises may have to look for cloud providers with the most flexible options or for those that have common technologies/APIs supported by at least one other cloud provider.

Summary

The cloud has finally arrived. The adoption of virtualization, the penetration of broadband Internet, and other trends have contributed to making the cloud concept, introduced as far back as the 1960s, a reality. Today, cloud services are thriving and are being used by individuals, businesses, educational institutions, and the government to solve real-world challenges, both business and technical.

The adoption of the cloud is fueled by the benefits that it brings. Cloud consumers are looking to the cost benefits and increased agility offered by the cloud. Providers can offer innovative cloud services while lowering their CapEx and OpEx, leading to increased profitability. Beyond those visible advantages, however, the real impact of the cloud is only beginning to be felt. The effect on innovation, entrepreneurship, collaboration, and big data analytics will be profound and far-reaching. We are just beginning to fully understand the real capabilities unleashed by the cloud and its applications in other domains.

Even with all these benefits, the cloud does face several significant challenges to widespread adoption. Concerns about data privacy and security, compliance with regulations, workload portability between cloud providers, and reliability and performance SLAs are holding back enterprises from moving their core applications into the cloud. Figure 2-6 illustrates these inhibitors weighing against the accelerators driving the adoption of the cloud. Throughout the rest of the book, you learn how cloud providers can effectively address these challenges and thus enable their customers to migrate to the cloud with confidence.

The next chapter covers cloud services, their classification, and their deployment models. We also look at the cloud ecosystem, which depicts the various entities involved in a cloud solution, and their interactions.

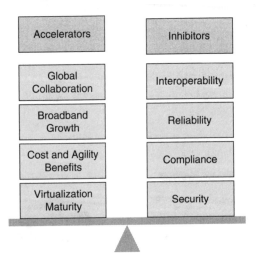

Figure 2-6   *Cloud Computing Adoption: Balancing Forces*

Review Questions

You can find answers to these questions in Appendix A, "Answers to Review Questions."

1. Which of these is one of the biggest obstacles to cloud adoption?

   a. Security

   b. SLA

   c. Interoperability

   d. All of the above

2. According to NIST, which of the following is an essential characteristic of the cloud?

   a. Security code

   b. Commodity hardware

   c. Self-service

   d. Collaboration

3. Which of the following cloud offering was the earliest to market?

   a. Amazon AWS

   b. Salesforce.com

   c. Microsoft Azure

   d. Google App Engine

References

- Journey to the Cloud via Virtualization: http://www.forbes.com/2010/06/21/virtualization-cloud-computing-technology-vmware.html

- Brief history of Cloud Computing: http://www.undertheradarblog.com/blog/a-brief-history-of-cloud-computing/

- Big Data predictions: http://tdwi.org/Articles/2011/03/16/Big-Data-Analytics-Predictions.aspx?Page=1

- Big Data Medical Research Example with ETH Zurich University: http://www.prnewswire.com/news-releases/ibm-and-eth-zurich-use-cloud-computing-to-combat-increasingly-resistant-bacteria-125203869.html

- Cloud Computing Killer Apps, James Urquhart: http://news.cnet.com/8301-19413_3-20030948-240.html?tag=mncol;title

- IDC/EMC Research on Explosion of Data in Digital Universe: http://www.emc.com/leadership/programs/digital-universe.htm

- Cisco Cloud Computing: Data Center Strategy, Architecture and Solutions: www.cisco.com/web/strategy/docs/gov/CiscoCloudComputing_WP.pdf

- Understanding Cloud Compliance Issues: http://searchcloudcomputing.techtarget.com/tip/Understanding-cloud-compliance-issues

- Review and Summary of Cloud Service Level Agreements: http://www.ibm.com/developerworks/cloud/library/cl-rev2sla.html?ca=drs-

- Cloud Interoperability: Problems and Best Practices: http://www.computerworld.com/s/article/9217158/Cloud_interoperability_Problems_and_best_practices?taxonomyId=158&pageNumber=1

Chapter 3

Cloud Taxonomy and Service Management

In this chapter, you learn about the following:

- Classification of cloud services
- Cloud deployment models
- Actors in the cloud ecosystem
- Cloud services management

Cloud Service Models

Cloud computing is fundamentally changing the way information technology resources are offered and consumed. Chapter 2, "Arrival of the Cloud," defined *cloud computing* as the delivery of abstracted IT resources *as a service*, characterized by on-demand scaling, self-service, and pay per use. Today, various clouds offer a wide range of services, such as compute, storage, network, development platforms, databases, messaging systems, and application software. In fact, the term *XaaS*, or *anything-as-a-service*, has been used to describe the increasing variety of services available from the cloud.

For the most part, these cloud services have been commonly classified into three categories:

- **Software-as-a-service (SaaS):** In this category, applications are delivered on demand as a service to the cloud consumer, typically on a subscription basis. This is the most visible form of cloud computing, and examples include Google's Gmail, Salesforce. com's CRM, Microsoft's Office365, and Cisco's WebEx offering.

- **Platform-as-a-service (PaaS):** Here, software development frameworks and components are delivered as a service, to be consumed by application developers. This is probably the least understood form of cloud computing, with examples including Google App Engine, DotCloud, and Microsoft Azure.

■ **Infrastructure-as-a-service (IaaS):** In IaaS, compute, network, and storage infrastructure resources are delivered as a service, to be consumed by IT system administrators. Using the least amount of abstraction, this form of cloud computing is readily understood, with offerings including Amazon EC2 and S3, Savvis Symphony, SunGard Availability, and Rackspace Open Cloud.

This model of separating cloud services into software, platform, or infrastructure is popularly known as the SPI model, and is depicted in the stack shown in Figure 3-1. Although there are several other service models, such as network-as-a-service (NaaS), unified communications-as-a-service (UCaaS), identity-as-a-service (IdaaS), and desktop-as-a-service (DaaS), the SPI model can be thought of as encompassing all of them. The SPI model is now widely accepted for classifying cloud services and helps cloud providers and consumers in understanding and discussing their scope and control of the cloud's computational environment.

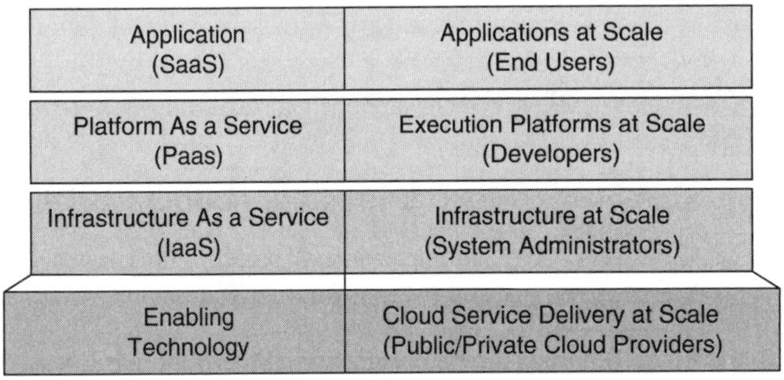

Application (SaaS)	Applications at Scale (End Users)
Platform As a Service (Paas)	Execution Platforms at Scale (Developers)
Infrastructure As a Service (IaaS)	Infrastructure at Scale (System Administrators)
Enabling Technology	Cloud Service Delivery at Scale (Public/Private Cloud Providers)

Figure 3-1   *Cloud Services Classification: SPI Model*

The relationship between SaaS, PaaS, and IaaS is not mutually exclusive, though. In fact, as illustrated in Figure 3-1, they can build on top of each other. A SaaS offering could, beneath the covers, utilize platform and infrastructure services from a cloud, although those platform and infrastructure resources might be available only internally and not offered to the end user as a PaaS or IaaS offering. Similarly, a PaaS offering might rely on the infrastructure from the IaaS layer below. Underneath the three service category layers is an enabling technology layer, which provides the IT foundation that ultimately enables all these services.

The sections that follow examine each of these three service types in a little more detail.

Software-as-a-Service

In the SPI model, SaaS provides the highest level of abstraction, delivering applications running on a cloud infrastructure to the end user over the network. The consumer typically accesses these applications through a thin client interface, such as a web browser. In the SaaS model, the consumer has hardly any control over the cloud service, and can customize only certain user-related application parameters. The cloud provider manages almost all aspects of the service, including the infrastructure, the operating system, the database, and the application itself. Even the security of the service is mostly considered the provider's responsibility. This frees up the consumer, who now does not have to manage any aspect of the cloud service and can instead focus on using the application toward achieving business objectives.

SaaS offerings are seeing rapid growth in adoption and are changing the way software is delivered to users. In addition to the factors driving the adoption of cloud computing in general, certain trends are driving the popularity of SaaS:

- Purchasing licenses for every computer in the organization is proving cost-prohibitive for many organizations and is fueling a paradigm shift toward pay per usage or subscription models for software.

- SaaS applications can now provide a more desktop-like experience over the web. This has been enabled by the increasing penetration of broadband and other cost-effective high-speed access to the Internet and the enhanced interactivity and user engagement brought about by innovative technologies such as AJAX.

- The arrival of web application frameworks have simplified and accelerated the development of SaaS applications

- Evolution from the *application service provider* (ASP) model, where third-party applications were maintained by the ASP vendor, to the SaaS model, where the application is developed and maintained by the SaaS vendor themselves.

However, data privacy and security concerns weigh against the rapid adoption of SaaS, especially by larger enterprises. Multitenancy offered by SaaS applications means that comprehensive data separation is required between tenants. This is all the more important because tenants today are putting business-critical and sensitive information in their SaaS applications. Such data isolation needs to happen not just in the databases but also across all components of the SaaS stack, including billing and subscription management. A properly designed SaaS stack can help provide comprehensive per-tenant isolation and alleviate such concerns.

SaaS Stack

Figure 3-2 shows a SaaS offering based on dynamic and scalable infrastructure (server, network, and storage) and platform technology (operating system, database, application runtime environments, and so on) layers. The SaaS functionality layer sits atop these foundational layers, performing critical activities such as the following:

- Per-tenant customization, configuration, security policy and audit trails

- SaaS operational aspects such as subscription management, billing, metering, analytics

- SaaS plumbing, including performance instrumentation, notification, and caching

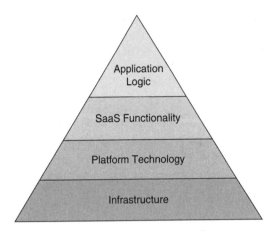

Figure 3-2   *SaaS Multitenant Stack*

Finally, the application's business logic sits on top of all these layers.

SaaS applications typically support web services *application programming interfaces* (API) based on standard technologies such as REST, SOAP, or JSON. This allows one SaaS service to be invoked by others or for a mash-up application to invoke multiple SaaS applications to create a unique new service. This provides a huge amount of potential for service reuse and for applications to leverage the functionalities of already developed applications, instead of re-writing code.

SaaS vendors usually offer only a single version of an application at a time to consumers to lower the maintenance and upgrade costs associated with supporting multiple software versions. However, an increasing amount of customization is being offered to tenants, allowing them to change the look and feel of the application or specify policies. This ability to customize some aspects of the application, when combined with the core advantages (significant cost benefits while bypassing service delivery and management overhead), makes SaaS an attractive proposition.

PaaS

In the preceding SaaS section, you saw how application software can be delivered as a turnkey service to the end user, who then does not have to be concerned with developing, maintaining or operating the software and hardware resources. This seems pretty convenient to the end user, and so why should anyone bother with PaaS (or even IaaS for that matter)?

For enterprise IT, the answer to that question lies in the reality that organizations have unique business processes and the software they use needs to be in sync with the way the business operates. PaaS allows these organizations to build and deploy their own niche or custom applications, which are unlikely to be available as a SaaS offering from a cloud provider. PaaS can thus enable competitive advantage for a business. With SaaS, everyone has access to the same software and can use it the same way, which doesn't allow much scope for differentiation, as illustrated in Figure 3-3.

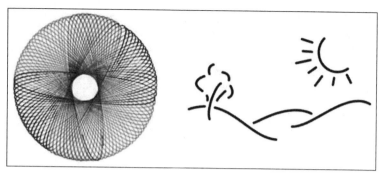

Figure 3-3   *Flexibility: SaaS (Stay Within Boundaries) Versus PaaS (Draw with Free Will) (Source: Samisa-abeysinghe.blogspot.com)*

The PaaS model is primarily targeted at developers, enabling them to rapidly develop scalable applications for their end users. The cloud consumer (the developer, in this case) has complete control over the application and some aspects of the platform, typically related to setting the application environment. The cloud provider, in contrast, has admin control over the development platform and total control of the software and hardware infrastructure underneath. But the provider lacks any control over the application itself. Security functions are shared between the provider and the consumer.

The growth of PaaS offerings is, in part, driven by cost savings and other factors contributing to the adoption of cloud computing in general. Here are a couple of trends specifically driving the adoption of PaaS:

- **IT as competitive advantage:** Organizations are increasingly looking toward IT as a business differentiator and expect new services and applications to be customized to the unique business processes of the organization and to be rolled out rapidly. PaaS platforms offer an attractive solution for such organizations, facilitating rapid development by offering application development tools, frameworks, databases, runtime, and more. Unlike SaaS, these platforms allow the flexibility to create custom or niche applications that can help differentiate the business from its competitors.

- **Need for elastic scalability:** With the advent of social networking and the huge number of potential users with access to the cloud, cloud applications need to be prepared to handle rapid spikes in load. PaaS platforms have been developed with such elastic scalability in mind. Application developed on these platforms can be rapidly deployed at scale, leveraging the dynamic multitenant infrastructure beneath. Typically, once developers learn and adapt to the rules of the particular platform, they can develop applications that take advantage of the elastic scalability offered by the platform.

On the flip side, fear of vendor lock-in has become the primary barrier to adoption of PaaS. Applications developed on the platform of a particular PaaS leverage the services and APIs of that platform to enable rapid development and scalable deployment. Another PaaS provider with a similar platform might not have those services or may have a different API for interacting with those services. This means that applications may not be easily portable across PaaS providers, leading to a fear of lock-in among organizations that are looking to adopt PaaS.

Another effect that contributes toward a higher "escape velocity" in changing cloud providers, is *data gravity*. With organizations accumulating data over time in the cloud, moving such large amounts of data between cloud providers becomes an inhibitor to changing cloud providers. If an organization's chosen PaaS provider goes out of business or if the relation with the provider sours for some reason, the organization might not be able to easily move to another PaaS provider.

What Is Data Gravity?   In general, *data gravity* is a term used to indicate that data, analogous to a planet, has mass. And because of this mass, data has gravity and can attract more data (in addition to services and applications), which leads to accumulation of large amount of data over time.

PaaS Components

PaaS offerings typically consist of a computing platform and a solution stack, offered as a service. The compute platform provides an environment where software can be launched and run, but the capabilities provided by the solution stack vary significantly from provider to provider. The services and APIs provided by the solution stack facilitate the rapid development and deployment of cloud applications (applications that scale elastically and are highly available). Examples of such services and APIs cover distributed caching, queuing and messaging, file and data storage, security, identity, usage-based billing, and performance monitoring and management.

In addition to these services, some of the modern PaaS offerings include services for activities beyond application development and deployment. Such services include project management, team collaboration, application design, and testing. This allows organizations to perform the complete application life cycle management on the PaaS cloud, without requiring any on-premise or local infrastructure.

An elastically scalable multitenant PaaS offering is typically supported by a dynamic virtualized infrastructure layer beneath. Some PaaS providers such as Microsoft Azure, Google App Engine, and Force.com build their PaaS platforms atop their own infrastructure. Others, such as Heroku, Engine Yard, and DotCloud, utilize the infrastructure provided by IaaS providers such as Amazon AWS.

Targeting developers at enterprise IT and *independent software vendors* (ISV), PaaS platforms today offer support for a wide variety of programming languages such as Ruby, Python, PHP and Node.js. These platforms enable, at an attractive price point, rapid development and deployment of scalable applications.

IaaS

IaaS makes up the lowest layer in the SPI stack, offering infrastructure resources such as servers, storage, and network as a service. Compared to IaaS, PaaS provides a higher level of abstraction, hiding the infrastructure from the consumer and enabling the rapid development and deployment of elastically scalable applications. So, just as we asked the question earlier about why PaaS is needed when we have the ease of SaaS, a similar question arises here. Why should anyone use IaaS and deal with all the complexity of infrastructure when PaaS can hide all that away and let you focus on rapid application development?

The answer to that question is twofold. First, the development of certain applications needs special features not available on any PaaS platform. PaaS environments can be fairly restrictive, and applications that need anything different from the offered features are simply out of luck. Second, when legacy enterprise applications need to be ported to the cloud, it is quite difficult, if not impossible, to modify them to fit the restrictions of the chosen PaaS platform. In both these scenarios, IaaS is a natural fit.

IaaS is primarily targeted toward the IT administrator and ISVs. The admin uses IaaS to augment or replace the organization's on-premise servers, storage, and networking resources. ISVs rely on IaaS for a dynamic scalable infrastructure on top of which they can develop, test, and deploy their software offering. Although the IaaS provider controls the facilities and the infrastructure hardware, the consumer has control over pretty much everything else, including the operating systems, the development platforms, the deployed applications, and networking features such as firewalls and load balancers. The IaaS providers are responsible for providing a secure infrastructure, but the consumer is responsible for securing everything above it.

Let's examine a couple of IaaS-specific trends that are helping to drive its continued adoption.

- The ongoing paradigm shift from infrastructure ownership to infrastructure-as-a-service is the primary driver for IaaS adoption. The resulting cost and flexibility benefits brought about by phenomena such as *cloud bursting* can be powerful motivators for organizations looking toward the cloud, as discussed in Chapter 2.

What Is Cloud Bursting? Enterprises have to incur huge amounts of capital expenses to equip themselves with sufficient infrastructure capacity to handle their peak load. During the rest of the time, these servers are sitting idle, running at less than 10 percent load. Cloud bursting can help eliminate such wasteful spending. Cloud bursting is the process of offloading workloads to the cloud during periods of peak infrastructure demand, paying only for the duration the infrastructure from the cloud was used.

■ Another driver that has been gaining in importance has been the impact of cloud computing on the environment. The increased utilization of infrastructure, coupled with the higher energy efficiency of that infrastructure in cloud data centers (compared to an enterprise's on-premise infrastructure), mean that greater amount of work is done per unit of energy consumed. So, along with the cost savings, IaaS consumers can tout the "green" benefits of their move to the cloud.

IaaS inhibitors typically include concerns around virtualization security, availability, and the ability to adhere to regulatory compliance in an IaaS cloud environment.

IaaS Components

The three key components of an IaaS cloud are compute, network, and storage. Chapter 1, "Virtualization," discussed how these three components could be virtualized, allowing them to be dynamically offered to multiple tenants. In an IaaS offering, the compute, networking, and storage resources are interrelated and need to be managed and orchestrated together rather than as separate and independent resources. There would not be much benefit to allocating a VM to a tenant when there are no network resources available to provide connectivity or mandatory firewall-based security for that VM. Figure 3-4 illustrates virtualized shared resources that are orchestrated together to fulfill the consumer's service request, received over an API or through a portal. Operations and business support systems are part of this IaaS stack built on the data center and IP/MPLS-based *Next Generation Network* (NGN) infrastructure. (The management and orchestration of cloud services is discussed in more detail later in this chapter.)

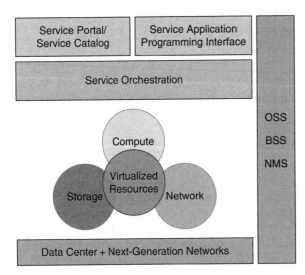

Figure 3-4   *IaaS Stack*

Comparing IaaS, PaaS, and SaaS

The preceding sections explored several aspects of SaaS, PaaS, and IaaS. The sections that follow now contrast these three service types in a couple of different ways, each offering a unique perspective at understanding their relationship.

Scope and Control

Figure 3-5 contrasts the varying degree of scope and control of the cloud environment presented to the cloud subscriber and the cloud provider for the three service models. Clearly, SaaS allows minimum amount of control to the consumer (only settings to personalize or customize certain aspects of the application), and this control increases in the PaaS model and is the highest for IaaS, where the consumer can even select the operating system and the development environment. They could even be allowed to configure network services such as the load-balancer and firewall settings between the VMs of their multitier application.

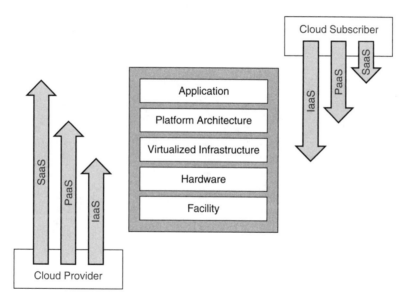

Figure 3-5 *Scope and Control in the SPI Model (Source: NIST, SP-800-144)*

For the provider, in general, the scope and control relates inversely with that for the consumer. Although the provider is responsible for the facilities and hardware infrastructure (the lowest layers in the cloud stack) in all three models, their support above these layers varies with the service model. In IaaS, the provider's scope and control is limited up to the virtualization infrastructure layer, consisting of elements such as the hypervisor and VMs. This scope and control increases in PaaS and is the highest in SaaS, where the provider is responsible for everything up to and including the application itself.

Evolution

Service providers offering collocation and hosted services have been facing declining margins and are looking to expand into cloud services as a way to lower their operational costs and gain more efficient use of the infrastructure. IaaS allows them an easy way to offer higher-value services, increasing their revenue and profits per square foot of their data center facilities. Compared to PaaS and SaaS, which require a deeper software focus and expertise, IaaS provides a natural entry point for these service providers, which are already experienced in the infrastructure business.

IaaS provides a platform offering elastically scalable infrastructure, which can be used for various applications, such as compute-as-a-service, cloud bursting, disaster recovery, and more. As shown in Figure 3-6, PaaS and SaaS platforms can build on top of such an IaaS platform, thus allowing them to leverage an efficient and flexible infrastructure underneath. Therefore, IaaS can be considered a foundation for all cloud services. It is also the service we focus on most throughout the rest of this book.

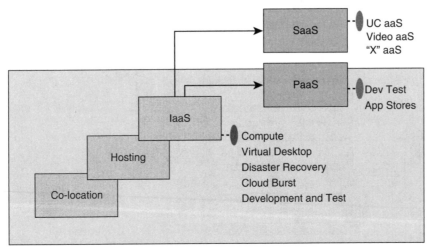

Figure 3-6   *SPs Moving Up the Value Chain to Cloud Services*

Deployment Models for the Cloud

So far, this chapter has extensively discussed how clouds can be classified based on the type of services they offer. Another way of classifying clouds is based on how they are deployed. Depending on the purpose or the nature of how the cloud is located, *National Institute of Standards Technology* (NIST) has defined four deployment models:

- Public cloud
- Private cloud
- Hybrid cloud
- Community cloud

The sections that follow delve deeper into each of these types.

Public Cloud

Public clouds are openly available for use by the general public. They are typically owned, managed, and operated by an organization selling cloud services. Amazon's AWS, Salesforce.com, Terremark/Verizon Enterprise Cloud, and Microsoft Azure are examples of public cloud services, which are available to enterprises, *small and medium-size businesses* (SMB), and individuals who have access to the Internet. Public clouds are usually located in the premises of the service provider organization.

Private Cloud

Private clouds are operated for the exclusive use of an organization. Within the organization, there are usually multiple consumers of the cloud service, such as departments or business units. A private cloud may be owned, managed, and operated by that organization or a third party, and may be located either on- or off-premises.

Enterprises with significant IT needs could benefit from private clouds, which allow them to address concerns associated with public clouds, such as privacy, control, and compliance. Such corporate clouds would be run with the same philosophy and attributes as public clouds (self-service, pay-per-use chargeback, on-demand scalability, and multitenancy) with authorized access over the network.

Consider the case of a retailer expecting a spike in its e-commerce systems during a promotion. The marketing team responsible for the promotion would go ahead and book an internal cloud via a web-based portal. Resources from the internal cloud would be rapidly made available to handle spikes in demand during the promotion period, and the corresponding usage would be metered with appropriate granularity and billed to the marketing department driving the promotion.

Building and operating a private cloud does need a significant amount of IT expertise, but once one is available, business users can tap into the services offered by the cloud without much technical know-how.

Hybrid Cloud

A hybrid cloud is a combination of two or more distinct private, public, or community cloud infrastructures. Although each constituent cloud in the hybrid cloud retains its unique identity, they are bound together with technologies (standardized or proprietary) that enable application and data portability across them, as illustrated in Figure 3-7. This enables constituent clouds to load balance and seamlessly move workloads to each other.

Public clouds are operated by service providers at huge scale with high efficiency, which enables them to offer their customers unmatched cost benefits with access to nearly infinite pool of resources. Enterprises considering the public cloud are concerned about security and the privacy of their data in the public cloud, along with unease about losing control of IT infrastructure. In addition, in certain industries, moving data outside the corporation could possibly result in violation of regulatory compliance.

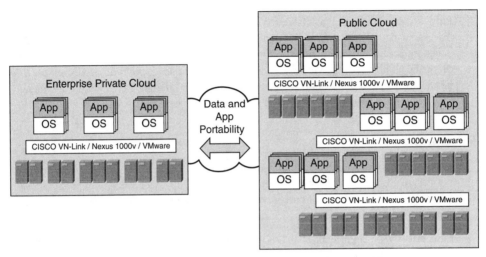

Figure 3-7   *Hybrid Cloud: Bringing Together the Best of Both Worlds*

Private clouds help address the security, compliance, and loss-of-control concerns associated with public clouds by keeping the application and data within the organization. But they are unable to match the efficiency, cost reductions, and near-infinite scale of public clouds. Hybrid clouds bring together the best of both worlds. Enterprises can maintain control of their sensitive data and mission-critical workloads, which would run in their private cloud, while still leveraging the cost benefits and scale of the public cloud to offload other workloads to public clouds.

There is increased focus on the role of the network in hybrid clouds. This is not only for ensuring workload migration between enterprise private cloud/data centers and public clouds but also to maintain appropriate and consistent quality of experience when an enterprise cloud user in a branch is accessing applications either in public clouds over the Internet or in a private cloud, typically over the WAN.

Several cloud providers today offer *virtual private clouds* (VPC), a specific example of the hybrid cloud model. Here the provider offers the same degree of security and private IP addressing that an enterprise would get in its own data center, but as a service. Enterprises essentially are being allocated a slice of the provider's cloud where they can host applications or components of applications sharing the same IP address space as applications running inside their own data center networks and can apply their custom management, routing, and security policies. A VPN can help secure the enterprise connectivity to their VPC. This secure and familiar environment increases confidence as these businesses increasingly look to leverage the public cloud (for use cases such as cloud bursting or disaster recovery).

Community Clouds

Community clouds serve a common function or purpose. They are operated exclusively for a specific community of consumers, belonging to one or more organizations that share common concerns such as mission, policy, and compliance or security requirement. Such clouds may be owned, managed, and operated by a third party or by one or more of the organizations in the community.

At first glance, community clouds seem like adding yet another *cloud deployment* definition. But a closer look reveals an important type of cloud that may get more and more common in the years ahead. A couple of examples here will help illustrate the potential of community clouds.

Consider a cloud designed specifically for a specialized and highly regulated industry (for example healthcare or investment banking). Such a cloud would be purpose built to handle security and regulatory compliance requirements of that industry. In addition, it could offer services such as an industry-specific database and analytics service to its users on a pay-per-use basis; this is much more efficient and cost-effective than each user maintaining his or her own copy of this common database. Instead of each organization in that industry trying to use commodity IaaS clouds and fitting security and compliance requirements to it, a community cloud for that industry may make much better sense (both for the organizations consuming services and for the third-party cloud provider offering them).

Apps.gov is an example of a community cloud, with the government being the community. This portal provides common cloud services, including business, productivity, and social media applications to various U.S. government agencies. By leveraging a common cloud infrastructure built specifically for the government, higher levels of efficiencies can be achieved, helping drive down costs.

Open Clouds: Toward the True Intercloud

We started off with stand-alone data centers, which progressed to the emergence of public and private clouds. Hybrid clouds form the next step in this evolutionary journey, allowing private and public clouds to start becoming interoperable and share workloads. While such type of federation among clouds is just beginning, we believe the development and maturity of cloud standards will eventually bring about ubiquitous connectivity, allowing private clouds to obtain service from any number of public clouds, or for public clouds to offload to other public clouds during peak periods. Such a mature marketplace, based on open standards and interoperability, can be thought of as the *Intercloud*.

Figure 3-8 illustrates the timeline for the journey toward the Intercloud. In a sense, the Intercloud is an enhancement and extension of the Internet itself. In much the same way as the Internet decouples clients from content—you don't have to have a preexisting agreement with a content provider to find and access their website in real time—the *Intercloud* will decouple resource consumers from resource providers, allowing the consumers to find resources on demand and without preexisting agreements with providers. Such an open market would have naming and discovery mechanisms, just as we have *Domain Name System* (DNS) on the Internet. Trust standards would be established, just like HTTPS on the web today. The Intercloud is explored further in Chapter 13, "Peeking into the Future."

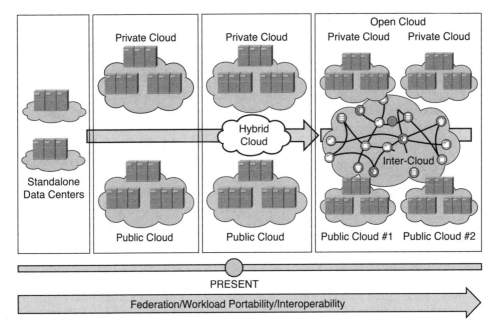

Figure 3-8   *Timeline of Cloud Deployment Models*

Cloud Actors

Having discussed the classification of cloud services (IaaS, PaaS, and SaaS) and cloud deployments (public, private, hybrid, and community), let's turn our attention to the cloud ecosystem and understand the various actors involved, the role they play, and the activities and functions they perform. Figure 3-9 illustrates five actors as defined by NIST and their relationships: cloud consumer, provider, broker, auditor, and carrier.

The *cloud consumer* is the entity (individual or organization) that selects, uses, and pays for the cloud service. The consumer obtains the service from either a cloud provider or a cloud broker. A *cloud provider*, in contrast, performs services to support the business of consumers, at the agreed upon security, service levels, and cost. *Cloud brokers* provide additional value on top of services from providers, or they combine and integrate multiple services into one or more new services. *Cloud auditors* are third parties that independently assess cloud services and their performance, privacy, and security. Finally, *cloud carriers* are the entities that provide connectivity and transport of cloud services between the providers and the consumers and play an important role in security, *service level agreement* (SLA) management, and interoperability.

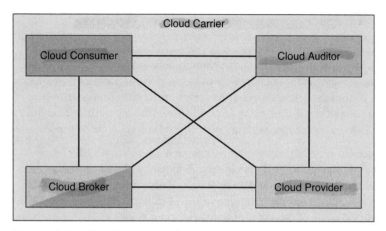

Figure 3-9   *Cloud Actors and Their Interactions (Source: NIST)*

Figure 3-10 takes a closer look at the functions of the cloud provider. Typically, the provider's activity includes service deployment, cloud service management, and service orchestration, with security and privacy functions pervasively spread across all the activities. Security and privacy tasks include authentication, availability, confidentiality, identity management, integrity, security policy management, and the proper collection, use, and disposition of the consumer's *personal information* (PI) and *personally identifiable information* (PII).

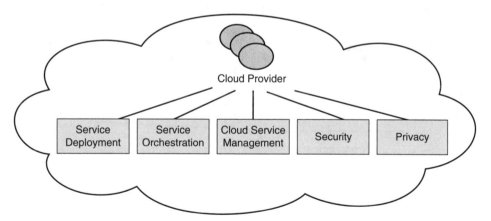

Figure 3-10   *Functions of the Cloud Provider (Source: NIST)*

Service deployment covers operating the cloud in one of the defined deployment models: public, private, hybrid, or community (all of which were discussed earlier in this chapter).

The remainder of this chapter focuses on the other two provider functions: cloud service management and orchestration. These are exceedingly critical to a successful cloud offering, and yet they are usually the least-understood functions, as well.

Cloud Service Management and Orchestration

Cloud service management helps both consumers and providers. Consumers benefit because it provides them an effective means to contract services with a certain service level, modify those services and service levels, and measure the performance, availability, and consumption of those services. Providers, however, are looking to monetize their cloud assets, get a competitive edge by providing a flexible offering to their customers, and offer certain SLAs to consumers, while monitoring and enforcing those service levels.

Traditional management systems cannot usually scale well enough to handle the cloud. The management system needs to be dynamic enough to handle the elastic nature of the cloud. In addition, automation is key, and pretty much all the provisioning needs to be zero touch. Figure 3-11 illustrates the *Cisco Intelligent Automation for Cloud* (CIAC), a cloud management and automation software solution that includes self-service provisioning and orchestration.

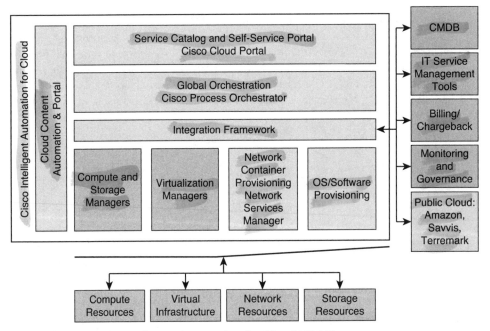

Figure 3-11 *Cisco Intelligent Automation for Cloud (CIAC)*

Let's examine the key building blocks:

- **Self-service portal:** An intuitive and easy-to-use portal enables the cloud user to perform functions such as service ordering, looking up consumption data, or monitoring the SLA for subscribed services. Policy-based controls guide the behavior of the portal. Differentiated access is provided for customer IT Admin, Partner, and User roles. In addition, instead of using a portal, automated systems and processes at the consumer could request services via the provider's API.

- **Service catalog:** A service catalog provides an abstracted standardized set of services that are easy for consumers to understand and order. From a monetization perspective, the service catalog is a key element and provides opportunity to sell premium services and to create additional revenue streams for the cloud provider. Here are some examples of services and associated options that a provider could offer in their service catalog:

  - VM options such as size

  - Network options around segmentation, security, and optimization

  - Storage options around file/block, RAID level, replication, minimum *input/ output operations per second* (IOPS)

  - Multisite options for application around mobility/burst and disaster recovery

  - Applications and application development stack options

  - Environmental options related to power, cooling, rack, real estate, and so on

The service catalog and the self-service portal enable increased flexibility and efficiency in ordering services. As soon as those services are ordered, they need to be delivered rapidly. To avoid slow and error-prone manual provisioning, the catalog needs to tie into the orchestration unit.

Service Orchestration

Orchestration is a fundamental capability of the cloud. The *orchestrator* automates the delivery of the service, ensuring appropriate service levels and configuration. The consumer starts by requesting a service from the service catalog (via the portal or through an API), which then feeds into the orchestrator. The orchestration engine converts that service request into multiple provisioning requests, coordinating across multiple resource domains (for example, the compute, storage, and networking domains in the case of IaaS) while taking into account the interdependencies between them. The Cisco Process Orchestrator in Figure 3-11 leverages adapters to connect to heterogeneous server, network, storage, virtualization, and application domain managers.

The orchestration system collects the status of the provisioning requests from individual domains, and only after it can accurately verify each of them for success does it reply back with a positive acknowledgment toward the consumer-facing layer above. Consider the case of a consumer requesting for a VM with network services and storage. Although the compute service is able to bring up a VM and the storage service is able to allocate appropriate storage, the network service cannot provide the requested connectivity. It is important for the orchestration layer to fail this request; otherwise, the consumer could end up with a VM that is not of much use because it cannot be accessed. Or worse still, if it lacks the requested network isolation, we could end up with a security breach!

Automation of the manual tasks involved in the service enablement process is critical for a successful cloud service offering (successful, not only in terms of the reduced time for delivering services, but also from the cost point of view). With the scale involved in cloud services, having human involvement in handling each order not only increases the time for delivering services but also proves cost-prohibitive for the provider. Such automation needs to be pervasive throughout the service management framework: starting from the portal that allows the consumer to select services without having to interact with a provider employee; to the abstraction of services in the service catalog, which makes it easy for the consumer to order and customize services; to the automated provisioning across multiple domains, taking into account the interdependencies between the domains.

Summary

This chapter explored the cloud taxonomy, covering classifications of clouds based on the type of services offered (IaaS, PaaS, and SaaS) and based on their deployment model (public, private, hybrid, and community). It also discussed the different entities in the cloud ecosystem (provider, consumer, broker, auditor, and carrier) and their interactions. You also learned about the functions of the cloud provider, in particular cloud service management and orchestration.

So far in this book, we have focused on virtualization, the journey toward the cloud, the classifications of clouds, and the building blocks of a cloud offering. With the next chapter, we turn to the central theme of this book: the role of networks and network services in enabling business-grade cloud services. That chapter, along with subsequent chapters in this book, covers networks inside the cloud data center, between clouds, and beyond clouds to the end users.

Review Questions

You can find answers to these questions in Appendix A, "Answers to Review Questions."

1. Which of the following is not a cloud deployment model?
   a. Private cloud
   b. Hybrid cloud
   c. SaaS cloud
   d. Community cloud

2. Which type of cloud service provides the maximum amount of flexibility and control to its tenants?
   a. IaaS
   b. PaaS
   c. SaaS
   d. UCaaS

3. Typically, which entity's role involves providing connectivity and transport for cloud services?

   a. Cloud broker
   b. Cloud carrier
   c. Cloud provider
   d. Cloud consumer

4. Which of the following functions enable standardized services to be offered for consumption?

   a. Billing
   b. Service catalog
   c. Incident management
   d. Customer management

References

■ NIST Cloud Computing Reference Architecture, SP-500-292

■ Analyst White Paper from Enterprise Strategy Group, Enabling IT as a Service: http://www.cisco.com/en/US/prod/collateral/netmgtsw/ps6505/ps11869/esg_enabling_it.pdf

■ SaaS Platform Characteristics: http://blog.sciodev.com/2009/03/27/saas-all-paas-are-not-created-equal/

■ http://cloudminds.wordpress.com/2011/06/29/the-cloud-spi-model-part-1-software-as-a-service-what-you-really-want-from-the-cloud/

■ Samisa Abeysinghe blog, PaaS vs SaaS: http://samisa-abeysinghe.blogspot.com/2011/08/cloud-computing-why-paas.html

■ Mccrory's blog: http://blog.mccrory.me/

■ Cloud Service Management: http://www.cioupdate.com/trends/article.php/3868701/Service-Management-is-an-Imperative-in-the-Cloud.htm

Chapter 4

Networks and Services in the Cloud

In this chapter, you learn about the following:

■ Networks helping to overcome barriers to cloud adoption

■ Increased relevance of the network and network services

■ Monetization of network services

■ Evolution of networks toward meeting the challenges of the cloud model

■ Map of the subsequent sections of the book

The CIO's Dilemma

The cloud has created a paradigm shift in the way IT resources are provided and consumed. The previous chapters discussed how virtualization has proven to be the disrupter that has accelerated the journey to cloud. Cloud deployments have brought about game-changing benefits for both the providers and the consumers but continue to be challenged by certain inhibitors to adoption. Consider the case of an enterprise's *chief information officer* (CIO) contemplating a move to the cloud. The cost and agility benefits offered by cloud deployments make it an attractive option for the organization. It allows the IT group to focus its limited resources on the core business of the company, enabling it to fund and undertake new projects with business impact. Figure 4-1 illustrates how the majority of IT budgets are spent on maintenance, resulting in unfunded new projects, which ultimately result in missed business opportunities.

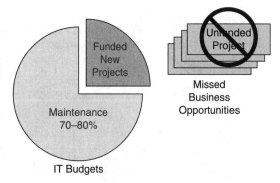

Figure 4-1   *CIO's Dilemma*

The elastic nature of the cloud allows IT to rapidly respond to changing business conditions, scaling up and down on demand. The cloud can help the IT department to cater to demand elasticity and avoid outages/unavailability of business-critical resources such as the company's e-commerce website during the crucial holiday shopping season, for example. The resulting loss of revenue and negative customer sentiment could be avoided by leveraging the nearly unlimited scale offered by the cloud. Clearly, CIOs have a lot to gain by moving workloads to the cloud and enabling IT to focus on providing competitive differentiation for the organization.

However, the CIO has several concerns that impede the migration to cloud. Security and privacy of the organization's data in the cloud is a primary concern for CIOs. The multitenant nature of cloud deployments come with intricate concerns about competitors running workloads on the same shared infrastructure and potentially gaining access to proprietary applications or sensitive data belonging to other tenants. Organizations have different regulatory requirements to comply with depending on their industry and the jurisdictions under which they perform business. CIOs need assurance of compliance to internal and external regulations as they move workloads into the cloud. Can the IT organization still have the ability to run audit reports on their cloud assets? In addition, CIOs need visibility of their workloads in the cloud. Can the cloud resources consumed by the organization be accurately measured?

Service level agreements (SLA) are another key area of concern for the CIO, who is responsible for ensuring a certain level of performance and availability for the organization's service consumers.[1] IT organizations in over two thirds of enterprises provide some form of internal SLA to their customers (the various business and functional units within the company). Can the CIO continue to offer equivalent SLAs after migrating to the cloud? What is the impact to the uptime metrics for the organization's mission-critical applications? And how will performance metrics such as latency, jitter, and loss affect the end user's quality of experience when delivered from the cloud?

How can cloud providers assuage such concerns from the CIO and enable the organization to migrate to the cloud with confidence? The network is uniquely positioned to help address these challenges and accelerate the adoption of cloud services toward fulfilling the mission-critical needs of the organization. Let's take a look at how networks and network services enable the cloud provider to address each of these inhibitors:

- **Security:** Today's multitenant cloud deployments leverage shared infrastructure, causing most organizations to have concerns about securing their data and isolating it from other tenants of the cloud. The ubiquitous nature of the network and its role in connecting physical and virtual cloud resources—inside data centers and beyond—positions it appropriately for providing comprehensive security, from the infrastructure all the way to the application. The network provides an ideal platform to consistently enforce security policies from physical to virtual stacks, from local data center to remote virtual data centers.

- **Visibility and compliance:** The network is inherently aware of user interactions, connected resources, and data traversing service provider networks or the Internet, and even inside and between cloud data centers. This awareness, combined with the powerful capabilities of network analytics, positions the network as an ideal platform for monitoring and providing visibility into the cloud service and infrastructure. Cloud providers could then make relevant pieces of information available to the tenants, allowing them visibility into their current share of cloud resources. Cloud consumers gain deep insights into their services, such as performance statistics, accurate resource use, and location information.

  In addition, this tenant-level visibility enables the generation of event logs and the production of audit reports. This is particularly useful toward verifying compliance with regulations such as *Health Insurance Portability and Accountability Act* (HIPPA), *Payment Card Industry* (PCI), and others, which still need to be adhered to as organizations move to the cloud.

- **User experience/SLAs:** Cloud consumers, especially enterprises, are looking for cloud providers to offer certain levels of availability and performance SLAs. As described previously, the network is naturally suited to monitoring cloud services and infrastructure. This allows the network to intelligently re-orchestrate resources and redirect workloads in the event of failure or performance degradation. Such actions based on policy-driven automation allow the network to improve the resiliency and as a result the availability of the cloud service.

  It also allows protecting the user experience with the cloud service, which is dependent on the latency, jitter, and packet loss that the distributed cloud service is subjected to. In this regard, cloud service providers who also own or have access to IP *Next Generation Network* (NGN) assets are uniquely positioned to offer end-to-end cloud SLAs to their customers, providing them significant differentiation. (Chapter 12, "End-to-End Cloud SLAs," explores these end-to-end SLAs in detail.)

Increasing Relevance of the Network

The network provides the capabilities and analytics that allow the cloud provider to allay the fears of the CIO. So far, this chapter explored the network's pivotal role in spurring the adoption of the cloud, enabling organizations to migrate more and more of their core workloads to the cloud today. And as we look ahead, the network is poised to play an even more crucial role in future clouds.

World of Many Clouds

A variety of clouds exist today: public, private, and hybrid clouds, along with community and specialty clouds to address the needs of different business verticals such as healthcare, media, finance, or government. As illustrated in Figure 4-2, we are moving toward a world of many interconnected clouds, serving the needs of users who want to experience cloud services anywhere, at any time, and on any device, and of businesses, which want IT to be delivered as a service.

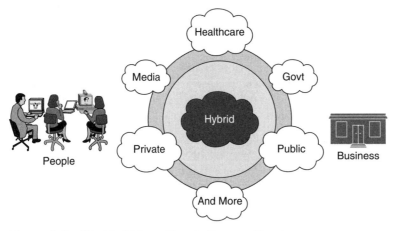

Figure 4-2   *World of Many Clouds (Source: Cisco)*

In this multicloud world, the network's role is significantly expanded because these clouds need to securely connect to each other. In addition, massive amounts of infrastructure resources, along with applications and content, need to be combined and delivered on demand, to provide a secure and consistent user experience regardless of the user location and number of cloud platforms involved. The network fabric enables bringing together these capabilities dynamically, virtualizing connections within the cloud, between clouds, and beyond the clouds to the consumers.

An Even Larger Cloud

Over the past few years, there has been an explosion in the number and types of consumer and business mobile devices, sensors, and actuators, many of which are now connected to the network. Although we tend to think so, clouds are not limited to the servers in data centers. In fact, the cloud extends out to all these network-connected electronic devices, smart meters, and other sensors, as illustrated in Figure 4-3. When you put it all together, it is easy to see that this is an even larger cloud on the horizon, with billions of network-connected components.

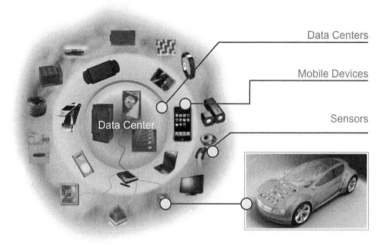

Figure 4-3   *Cloud of Mobile Consumer Devices and Sensor Devices (Source: J. Rabaey, "A Brand New Wireless Day")*

Consider the dozens of sensor devices running inside modern cars today. With 3G/4G mobile data connectivity enabling *machine-to-machine* (M2M) communications, sensor devices can monitor and share vehicle performance data with the car manufacturer, who can then use it to suggest appropriate maintenance or repairs. Or consumers might want their car to communicate with other cars around them, over an ad hoc local network, and learn about road and traffic conditions up ahead. Security is obviously critical here. After all, we would not like untrusted parties gaining access to these devices, with perhaps the ability to start interfering with brakes or other vehicle safety features. The possibilities are endless, and as you can see, dynamic, scalable, and secure networks have an increasingly vital role to play in the cloud in the years ahead. These futuristic clouds are further explored in Chapter 13, "Peeking into the Future."

Growth of Cloud Data Traffic

Consumer and business cloud services, including rich-media services, keep growing in popularity, leading to an explosion in data center traffic. According to Cisco's Global Cloud Index, cloud IP traffic is expected to grow at 66 percent *compound annual growth rate* (CAGR) from 2010 to 2015, which is twice the 33 percent CAGR expected for overall data center IP traffic during the same period. As illustrated in Figure 4-4, overall data center traffic volume is expected to reach 4.8 zettabytes in 2015. And cloud traffic is expected to be over a third of that pie (1.6 zettabytes). (A *zettabyte* is a billion terabytes; the number 1 followed by 21 zeros!)

Note   Cisco's Global Cloud Index considers all provider and enterprise data centers, and includes the following traffic categories:

1. Traffic that remains inside the data center

2. Traffic between data centers

3. Traffic from data center to end users over the Internet or IP WAN

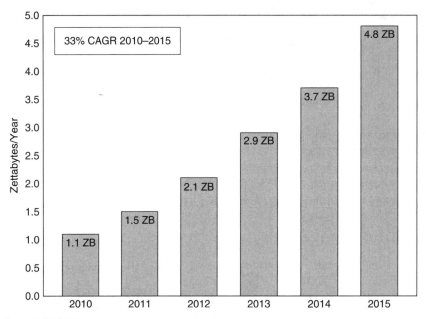

Figure 4-4   *Data Center Traffic Quadruples from 2010 to 2015. Cloud Traffic Is Expected to Be Just over One Third of the Data Center Traffic in 2015. (Source: Cisco Cloud Index)*

Let's try to put 1.6 zettabytes in perspective. This is the equivalent of 5 trillion hours of business web conferencing or 1.6 trillion hours of HD video streaming. Another interesting comparison is with the overall global Internet traffic, which in 2015 is expected to be just under 1 zettabyte, according to the Cisco *Visual Networking Index* (VNI).

In addition to the mind-boggling growth in traffic volumes, cloud applications, services, and infrastructure are responsible for transforming the pattern of data center traffic flows. Cloud-ready networks inside data centers, between data centers, and from data center to users will play an increasingly crucial role in terms of scaling efficiently to handle this growth in cloud data traffic and maintain profitability for the cloud providers without compromising the end-user experience.

Monetization

Earlier in this chapter, we discussed the role of the network in speeding up adoption of cloud services, providing solutions to the fundamental concerns that businesses have about wholeheartedly embracing the cloud. Cloud providers can leverage their network assets to enable their customers to confidently start moving more and more of their critical workloads to the cloud. On top of this, what if cloud providers could also directly monetize their network assets? What if networks and network services could be offered by the provider as a service; that is, *network-as-a-service* (NaaS)?

Along with compute and storage, networks and network services can be offered as a service, to be consumed, metered, and billed, based on usage. The economics of this model provide network vendors and cloud providers with strong incentives to innovate on compelling network services that add significant value for their customers.

The following are methods to offer networks and services for consumption.

Service Catalog

The discussion on cloud service management in Chapter 3, "Cloud Taxonomy and Service Management," explained how cloud services, defined in the service catalog, are offered to customers through self-service portals or via *application programming interface* (API) access. In addition to including various predefined cloud services, the service catalog enables the flexibility to add or modify optional features for those services. The same service catalog provides a means to define and offer networking for consumption (ranging from a basic VLAN service to a complex network service that provides security across multiple data centers).

To include network services in the service catalog, they need to be abstracted and presented in a simplified manner to the customer who may not be a networking expert. The intricacies and complex operations involved in enabling the network service must be hidden from the customer. Simplification is key, and ordering NaaS should be as easy as a few clicks on the cloud portal or a small number of intuitive API calls.

Here are a few examples of data center networking services, both basic and premium, that a provider could offer in their service catalog:

- Traffic isolation between tenants
- Access control between *virtual machines* (VM) of three-tier apps
- Load balancing across tiers of the three-tier apps
- *Virtual private network* (VPN) termination to isolated segments
- *Quality of service* (QoS) inside the data center fabric

The service catalog does not need to be restricted to network services inside the data center. After all, the end user consumes the cloud service from across the WAN (Provider IP NGN) or Internet. Cases where the cloud provider owns or controls network assets in the IP NGN present an opportunity to abstract network services available in the IP NGN bring it up to the service catalog. Examples of such services include the following:

- *Virtual Private LAN Service/Multiprotocol Label Switching* (VPLS/MPLS) VPN for private access to cloud

- WebVPNs for public access to cloud

- App performance enhancement with WAN acceleration, web caching

- Security through firewall, *deep packet inspection* (DPI), and distributed threat detection services in the NGN

- Optimal cloud services placement based on network proximity and performance

Not only do these NGN services open up additional revenue streams for the cloud provider, they also enable the provider to offer end-to-end security and performance capabilities. Certain network services such as firewall, QoS, and WAN application acceleration could potentially be distributed across the NGN and data center networks.

Network Services à la Carte

One option for monetization is to offer network services à la carte. Here network connectivity and services can be individually ordered by the consumer. The exact needs are conveyed as part of the API call or via a portal. For instance, if the developer needs to simply connect the database VM to an isolated virtual network segment that is not routable from the Internet but reachable from the web servers, those network attributes would be specified as part of the API invocation, as shown in the following pseudo API example:

1. Create a DB network, specifying the following address range:

```
create_network(name="db-net", cidr="10.0.1.0/24")
```

2. Attach the DB VM to the network created in Step 1:

```
attach_vm(vm=vm_uuid, network="db-net")
```

3. Create a route to allow web servers to access the DB servers:

```
create_route("web-net","db-net", "local")
```

A well-designed API enables the users to easily describe what they want out of the network: for example, a network that supports a certain amount of bandwidth, a network with QoS, or perhaps a network with monitoring services. The APIs represent a contract to provide a certain service. While the underlying networking devices may differ, the functionality delivered by the API call is expected to be the same. In essence, a network hypervisor is needed. Analogous to the compute hypervisor, the network hypervisor would provide the ability to abstract the underlying networking hardware into services that can then be consumed by the user.

Not too long ago, though, developers did not have any visibility or control over the network, with *infrastructure-as-a-service* (IaaS) offerings focusing primarily on compute and storage, as illustrated in Figure 4-5. The network was there only to provide connectivity. Each VM would have a very flat view of the world, and there would not be any topology at all. Obviously, network services would not be available for consumption in such architectures.

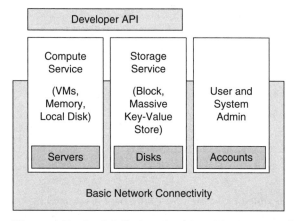

Figure 4-5 *IaaS Offerings Lacking API Access to the Network (Source: Cisco, Lew Tucker)*

OpenStack Quantum

OpenStack is open source software that enables any organization to build their public or private cloud stack. It aims to deliver a massively scalable cloud operating system, along the lines of the software that powers colossal clouds such as Amazon EC2 today. OpenStack has been gaining momentum, with contributions from a growing global community of developers, vendors, and service providers helping it grow in functionality and maturity.

Initially, OpenStack started off as a platform underpinned by three major services: the Nova compute service, the Swift storage service, and the Glance virtual disk image service. The OpenStack development community has been actively engaged in developing additional services, some of which are shown in Figure 4-6. One such service, named Quantum, aims to provide network connectivity as a service. Along with requesting VMs and storage, developers can now request network connectivity, as well, using the Quantum API.

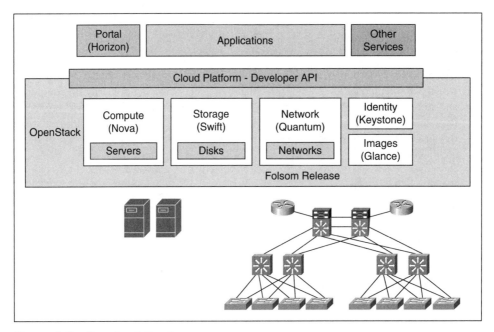

Figure 4-6   *OpenStack Services*

Figure 4-7 shows how Quantum has a pluggable framework with plug-ins offered by multiple networking vendors, including Cisco and Nicira/VMware. This is key to adoption; customers do not have to fear being locked into a particular vendor. The plug-ins map the API abstractions to the actual networking device underneath. In addition to offering basic Layer 2 virtual network segments, the Quantum API has an extensible architecture allowing advanced network services to be offered through the API extensions. And this extensible architecture is important, as the Quantum API is still evolving, and new network features such as firewalls, VPNs, and load balancers can be offered through the extensions first, before they get baked into the core Quantum API over time. Cloud providers have an opportunity to differentiate themselves by offering advanced networking features via the extensions.

Services such as OpenStack Quantum represent a fundamental shift in cloud networking. Networks are no longer hidden beneath the hypervisor, and network services are no longer limited to providing basic connectivity for the VMs. Applications can interact with network services via the API, bypassing the hypervisors.

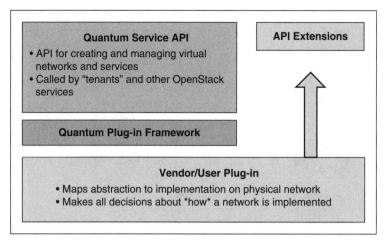

Figure 4-7 *Quantum API Architecture*

Network Containers

Network containers provide a representation of the data center network infrastructure that is dedicated to a tenant for the provisioned time. As compared to ordering individual network services, containers enable a higher level of abstraction, encompassing the set of network connectivity and network services allocated to a tenant service. Figure 4-8 shows an example of a tenant network container for a three-tier web application. Separate network containers have been created for the Web, App, and DB tiers, nested inside the tenant network container and separated by firewall services. External connectivity is provided for the container to be reachable from the corporate VPN for management purposes, while the Web container is reachable from the Internet through a load balancer.

If the entire topology in Figure 4-8 can be saved as an abstract model, it could be offered through the services catalog for consumption. That would significantly ease the deployment of the tenant's application, freeing the tenant from the lengthy process of individually ordering these network services and managing the interdependencies. A sophisticated network abstraction system such as the Cisco *Network Services Manager* (NSM) enables such use of network container models to define the behavior of the network services as a holistic virtual network infrastructure.

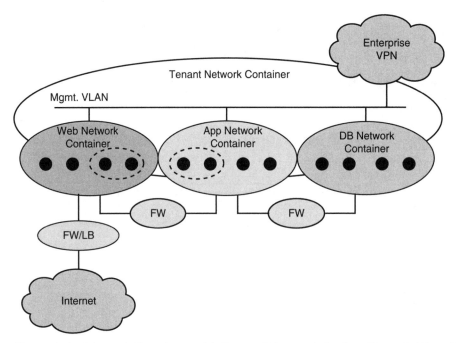

Figure 4-8 *Network Containers with External Connectivity for a Tenant's Three-Tier App*

Cisco Network Services Manager

Cisco NSM provides model-based policy-driven abstraction and orchestration of the cloud network environment, leading to increased flexibility in terms of what can be done in the network, what services/capabilities can be exposed from the network, and what tenant container environments can be provisioned on the network. A REST-based API allows orchestration and other systems to interact with NSM and access the abstractions.

Comprehensive network container models, such as the three-tier web application in Figure 4-8, can be instantiated on diverse cloud network infrastructures, with NSM abstracting away the platform-specific behaviors of the underlying networks. Figure 4-9 shows an NSM system managing three cloud infrastructure stacks or pods. One of the pods could be based on Nexus networking platforms, the other may be leveraging existing Catalyst-based networking, and the third may be based solely on virtual network services. The NSM service controller associated with a pod understands the specific devices and platforms in the pod, and when it receives a directive to instantiate a particular abstract topology model, it interacts with the networking devices in that pod to stitch that topology together.

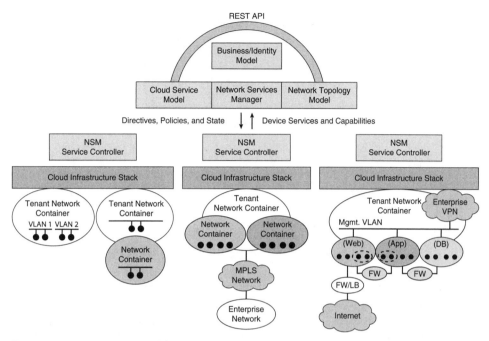

Figure 4-9 *Cisco NSM and Instantiated Network Containers for Multiple Tenants*

In addition to the abstraction, this model enables the mobility of network containers. Instantiated network containers, including the application and data residing in them, can be moved from one cloud pod to another, as needed, without any changes.

Various types or tiers of container model can be included in the service catalog, addressing different requirements such as security, performance, or application delivery. The customer can then pick one or more of these containers, and then select the VMs, which will be placed inside the container. The cloud administrator designs these container models to address the varied network service needs of their customers and enable the provider to offer differentiated pricing on these containers based on the density, complexity, and perceived value of the included network services.

Even though the service catalog allows the tenant to easily pick and choose from a variety of network services and predesigned topologies, tenants might need to customize and fine-tune their logical network in the cloud to meet their goals. Providers that can offer the tenant admin increased flexibility on day 2 operations, such as runtime configuration and modification of network services, will be able to further differentiate their offerings from the competition.

Through our discussion about OpenFlow Quantum service and the Cisco NSM system, you saw how network services can be offered in a simplified manner to spur consumption (either as individual network connectivity services or as network containers). These offerings enable cloud providers to gain access to additional revenue streams, realizing improved returns on their infrastructure investments.

Evolution of Network Services for the Cloud

To fulfill their role in the adoption and monetization of cloud services, networks need to adapt to the cloud environment. The rise of cloud models is changing what is happening on the network:

- Change in traffic patterns caused by increasing server-to-server traffic and the location-independent endpoints at both sides of a service.

- The new infrastructure is highly virtualized and programmable; servers and applications have become increasingly mobile.

- Change in access patterns for applications and services, predominantly through mobile devices.

- New applications are more data intensive, collaborative, and media rich.

These changes are driving the rapid evolution of networks. But not everything about the network has to change. Its foremost purpose still remains the same. The network still has to provide transport for the movement of data between the various components of an application, its storage, and the end user. It still has to provide security for access to applications and data. And it is still responsible for delivering a certain level of application performance to the end user. What changes is how these jobs are to be performed (with automated provisioning and management, with support for virtualization and multitenancy, and with location independence).

Automation

Automation is one of the most important areas of evolution for networks. And APIs are a fundamental means of enabling automation. One of the biggest impacts of the cloud on networks is the sheer scale and the frequency of change. And APIs allow us to address both of them. When network and network services can be provisioned and managed with well-designed APIs, such as those exposed by the network hypervisors discussed earlier in this chapter, the cloud network can scale efficiently from one rack to a whole data center to collections of data centers. At the same time, frequent changes brought about to the network, as tenants allocate and de-allocate cloud services, can be handled without any human touch. The economics of the cloud make such zero-touch operations mandatory.

Virtualization Awareness and Multitenancy

A couple aspects of virtualization are relevant to the evolution of networks. First is the network's awareness of server virtualization, which was introduced in Chapter 1, "Virtualization." Such virtualization-aware networks can identify and treat each VM as a separate networking endpoint. In addition, such networks can attach security and other policy profiles to VMs in a sticky fashion. As VMs migrate from one physical host to another, or one data center to another, these profiles move along with them.

The other aspect relates to networks themselves: that is, network virtualization. Also discussed in Chapter 1, virtualization of networks and network services enables the end-to-end isolation required to allow multiple tenants to securely coexist on the same shared underlying infrastructure. Advanced network abstractions such as containers can build on top of this virtualization and provide the flexibility of carving up the infrastructure into network containers. Such containers, described earlier in this chapter, would be completely isolated from the network containers of other tenants, enabling multitenancy.

Location Independence

Networks today support user and device mobility in various ways. With the advent of cloud, network capabilities around mobility need to evolve further. The virtualization and resource pooling aspects of clouds means that servers and applications are no longer tied to physical infrastructure either. In fact, applications can be thought of as floating over a pool of infrastructure resources, seamlessly extended within and between clouds.

With the mobility of applications and data in addition to the users themselves, networks can no longer depend solely on their location to make policy decisions. These modern networks, shown in Figure 4-10, gather and rely on context information in this borderless world, ensuring that users can access only those applications and that data to which they are entitled. In addition, these networks strive to achieve a consistent level of user experience, irrespective of the location of the user, application, and data in the cloud.

Figure 4-10   *Application/Data Mobility*

Quick Guide to the Rest of This Book

The network fabric is the glue that securely binds together heterogeneous resources inside clouds and between clouds and delivers them beyond the cloud to the end users. Based on requirements, characteristics, and administrative domains, cloud networks can be divided into three distinct entities:

- Data center networks

- WAN/IP NGNs

- Enterprise/consumer networks

How are these networks evolving to support cloud models? What is the role played by these networks in enabling business-grade cloud services? And how do we instantiate these concepts in deployment use cases? What end-to-end considerations apply for the secure delivery of cloud services with an SLA? These are some of the questions we explore in the rest of this book. The three parts of this book that follow are organized along the lines of the network sections listed here. The first one delves into data center networks. The next one explores the network between the data centers and from the data centers to cloud users. And the final one covers cloud consumer/enterprise networks, and then brings it all together with an end-to-end view of cloud service delivery. Here's a reader's map to these three sections.

Part II: Inside the Data Center Networks

We begin in Chapter 5, "Role of the Network Infrastructure in a Virtualized Environment," by examining the changes in networking infrastructure required to adapt to the virtualized environment of today's cloud data centers. What trends are driving the data center network design? How are virtual network services hosted on this network fabric? Next, in Chapter 6, "Securing and Optimizing Cloud Services," we examine the design of secure, multitenant data center networks. How can virtual security services be enabled inside a tenant's network container, and then across tenants? How can predefined instances be used to provision security compliant frameworks for PCI-DSS, HIPAA, and other regulations? Then, Chapter 7, "Application Performance Optimization," delves into optimization of cloud services and enhancing the end user experience. How do virtual application delivery solutions work?

Part III: Inside the SP Next Generation Network (WAN)

Cloud service providers that own or control WAN/IP NGN assets are able to mobilize their cloud resources between data centers and are also able to securely deliver and optimize the cloud service all the way to the customer edge. Chapter 8, "NGN Infrastructure That Supports Cloud Services," discusses *Data Center Interconnect* (DCI), the drivers, and the technologies. We also explore exciting changes that allow the cloud network to automatically adjust and optimize to account for such mobility. Chapter 9, "Securing Cloud Transport and Edge Using NGN Technologies," explores advanced security technologies in the NGN that protect the cloud edge and enable secure access to cloud services and applications. Then, we wrap up this section with acceleration technologies for cloud services over the WAN, in Chapter 10, "Optimizing and Accelerating Cloud Services." In addition, we explore how network intelligence, exposed by innovations such as the Network Positioning System, facilitates the optimal placement and selection of cloud services.

Part IV: Putting It All Together—Cloud Services Delivered

Enterprise networks are adapting to this new world order and playing a critical role as a control point in the consumption of cloud services. Chapter 11, "Connecting Enterprises to the Cloud," covers the architecture of cloud connectors and explains how advanced branch networks enable survivability, optimization, security, and performance of cloud services. We then discuss the all-important topic of cloud SLAs and how distinct networks can be stitched together to enable end-to-end cloud service delivery in Chapter 12, "End-to-End Cloud SLAs." Finally, in Chapter 13, "Peeking into the Future," we look at future trends as related to the cloud and what they mean for networks and network services.

Summary

This chapter began with a discussion about the CIO's dilemma in moving to the cloud and how the network can catalyze the confident adoption of cloud services by enterprises. However, the role of the network does not stop here, and in fact it is poised to become even more critical as we enter the world of many clouds and the bigger cloud brought on by the rapid growth of the Internet of Things. In addition, we explored how providers can monetize their investment in the network and offer network services in the service catalog for consumption through an API or a web portal. These services can be ordered individually or via abstracted network container models. Finally, we discussed how today's networks are evolving to meet the challenges of the cloud model.

This chapter explored the role of the network in enabling the success of business-grade cloud services, which is the central theme of this book. Subsequent chapters in this book build on the concepts discussed here and extend them to the different areas of the network involved with the cloud (DC networks, the WAN/NGN, and the enterprise network) and tie them together end to end, from the production point all the way to the consumption point.

Review Questions

You can find answers to these questions in Appendix A, "Answers to Review Questions."

1. What are the enterprise's areas of concerns about migrating to the cloud that the network helps to address?

   a. Compliance

   b. Security

   c. SLA

   d. All of the above

2. How can cloud providers better monetize their network investments?

   a. Offer advanced network services through a service catalog

   b. Protect network assets by not exposing their services to tenants

   c. Offer basic network connectivity for VMs

   d. Embed network services inside orchestrator

3. Which of the following is an open source cloud platform offering networking as a service?

   a. OpenFlow

   b. Amazon EC2

   c. OpenStack

   d. OpenOffice

4. Which of the following are key areas of evolution for networks in the cloud?

   a. Automation/API

   b. Flexible Multitenancy

   c. Location independence

   d. All of the above

References

1. Cloud Networking Report, Ashton, Metzler and Associates: http://www.webtorials.com/content/2010/12/2010-cloud.html

- OpenStack – Open Source Cloud Operating System: http://www.openstack.org

- Cisco White Paper - Cloud: Powered by the Network: www.cisco.com/en/US/solutions/.../white_paper_c11-609220.pdf

- Cisco CloudVerse: Enabling the World of Many Clouds: http://www.cisco.com/en/US/solutions/collateral/ns341/ns991/solution_overview_c22-693654.html

- Cisco Global Cloud Index: http://www.cisco.com/en/US/solutions/collateral/ns341/ns525/ns537/ns705/ns1175/Cloud_Index_White_Paper.html

- Cisco White Paper - Networking and Cloud, An Era of Change: http://www.cisco.com/en/US/solutions/collateral/ns340/ns517/ns224/ns836/ns976/white_paper_c11-677946.html

Chapter 5

Role of the Network Infrastructure in a Virtualized Environment

In this chapter, you learn about the following:

- Trends influencing the data center
- Network segmentation strategies
- Virtual networking and virtual network services
- Service overlay architecture

Traditionally, the network has been a seamless fabric within the data center, connecting the campus and branch to the resources and services within the data center. As the data center evolves, the fabric needs to adapt to new requirements. These new requirements are characterized not only by economically scalable models but also by operational and management simplicity. What are these network models? How do they fulfill the requirements of this new fabric?

This chapter defines the trends and tenets of these models. Each tenet is explained with examples to establish a foundation to understand real-life, complex, and intricate data center deployments.

Typically, applications drive data center architectures and resource requirements. These applications include mission-critical, real-time, resource-intensive software stacks characterized by their distributed nature. As these applications begin scaling to support growing business models, the traditional data center designs, which were typically silo based, prove to be bottlenecks to growth. Compute and storage resources are deemed to be underutilized, and this warrants a major redesign and re-architecture of the data center.

Virtualization enables the data center to evolve into a scaled multitenant-capable infrastructure where the application is no longer dependent on the physical nature of the hardware (that is, application-specific hardware). As the load on the application scales, strategies such as virtualization, load balancing, and workload mobility enable the application to serve its clients with better metrics such as lower latency, flexible *service level agreements* (SLAs), and elasticity. These strategies can be implemented in the software stack or in hardware. Choice of implementation is determined based on scale, flexibility, and performance requirements. Whereas software delivers capabilities tuned to specific software stacks, a hardware-based approach delivers them in an accelerated and scalable manner.

The new fabric needs to evolve to support these characteristics and metrics of the virtualized data center. This chapter begins with a discussion of the trends influencing the data center, followed by evaluation of technologies available to address these changes.

Trends Influencing the Data Center

The design of a data center depends on the applications and services hosted by the data center. It is bound by business objectives to be accomplished by the hosted service. Therefore, a business decision on the data center infrastructure relies on the economy of the data center elements used and maximizing the return on investment (ROI) on the infrastructure. In addition, a reliable disaster recovery plan is critical to the business continuity. These business strategies drive technical requirements and subsequently technical decision making. The technical decision process ultimately determines the technologies and products that will be used to build the data center.

What are the trending technologies within the data center? How do they accomplish the business and technical objectives to sustain a profitable business?

The chapter explores the following five trends:

- Virtualization and consolidation

- Cloud enablement

- Power and cooling considerations

- Return on investment

- Economy of scale

The sections that follow provide a few real-world examples within the scope of these trends to validate the strategies being considered.

Case 1: Acquisition of a Community Bank

Besides the business challenges typically involved in an acquisition like that of a community bank, one of the key technical challenges for data center architects is to consolidate infrastructure and provide seamless access to products and services of the financial institution to maintain business continuity. These products and services include desktop services, customer-facing banking applications, and the applications typically used in conducting everyday business or self-help kiosks and other business applications. Also, IT organizations usually standardize the hardware, including workstations and servers.

This case represents one of the applications of private cloud computing in the enterprise. Adopting a private cloud philosophy, this enterprise can consolidate the data center resources to provide a unified access to the branch office, as shown in Figure 5-1. Besides this, the data centers can mobilize the applications depending on the load at each data center using CPU burst techniques and load-balancing strategies with different scopes: local, site, global.

The sections that follow examine these cloud computing trends in more detail.

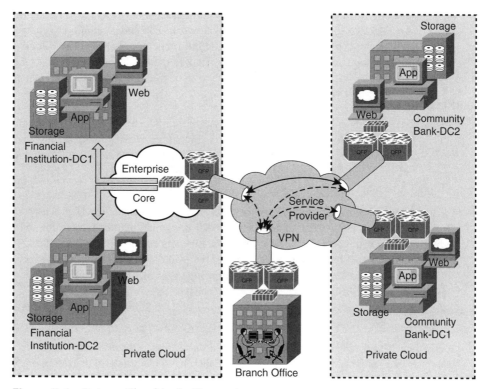

Figure 5-1   *Private Cloud in the Enterprise*

Virtualization

The key to keeping business continuity here is to enable access to the software applications that will sustain the business while the acquisition process progresses. Virtualization can help in addressing the hardware and software concerns. To begin with, virtualizing the service interface using *virtual desktop infrastructure* (VDI), including applications of the two financial institutions typically used in executing business. This strategy would help in standardizing the user interface so that the employee of either institution can access the respective applications from all locations, as shown in Figure 5-1. Furthermore, this would alleviate the dependence on the workstation or the operating system standardized by each institution. Finally, the services being hosted within the data centers can be consolidated across the data centers to support the new scale and elasticity requirements.

These requirements imply that the network fabric identifies the virtualized compute element and enables intelligent and efficient use of these compute elements. The network typically supports virtualization via a segmentation mechanism, which could be a *virtual local-area network* (VLAN), *virtual private network* (VPN), or a combination of the two. This also implies that a data center interconnect mechanism such as an optical (*dense wavelength-division multiplexing* [DWDM]) interconnect *Layer 2 virtual private network* (L2VPN)/*Layer 3 virtual private network* (L3VPN) is required to enable *virtual machine* (VM) mobility. Chapter 8, "NGN Infrastructure That Supports Cloud Services," covers the *Data Center Interconnect* (DCI) in detail.

Cloud Enablement

A cloud-enabled data center is an umbrella architecture of which virtualization is a component. Cloud computing defines a framework encompassing sharing hardware resources, virtualization, intelligent services, management, rapid elasticity, and flexible SLAs. These elements of the cloud architecture are discussed in more detail in Part I of the book (Chapters 1 through 4).

Cloud-enabling the data center benefits the enterprise by simplifying the IT processes. IT services can be omnipresent, and the service delivery would be much faster due to the reduced operational process, such as automation. Business can benefit from the cloud-enabled infrastructure by enabling on-demand services and development of new revenue streams on top of existing services. This might include typically renting out excessive compute capacity (*infrastructure-as-a-service* [IaaS]) or the services (*platform-as-a-service* [PaaS], *software-as-a-service* [SaaS]) to subscribers. Subscribers, in turn, benefit from the concept of pay per use and reduce their capital costs.

A cloud-enabled data center also provides ubiquitous access to these services and resources in a secure and scalable manner. The fabric has a major role in delivering this access. A policy defines the roles of fabric elements and its characteristics, including capabilities, resources, and their availability. For example, the applications used in financial institutions are heavily transaction based and require low latency. The fabric needs to provide a latency-optimized network slice to address the demands of the data center.

Power and Cooling Considerations

In its simplified form, efficiency of a data center is a measure of resources consumed to deliver the core business application to the end user. A data center typically includes compute storage and network elements to deliver the core business application or service ubiquitously and in a scalable manner. Power and cooling are consumed to deliver these services. As a result, the *power-usage effectiveness* (PUE) is a major consideration in data center design. PUE is a ratio of power required by the data center to the power required to deliver IT services. A PUE value of 1.0 is a theoretically perfect measure of effectiveness; however, this is practically unattainable. Ideally, a PUE rating of 1.5 or less indicates a well-designed data center.

Hardware equipment used in building data centers generally exhibits a common characteristic in that it draws power even when idle. In addition, a disaster recovery solution requires maintaining redundant equipment to enable business continuity. A few strategies to consider here include the following:

- Mobilizing workloads to create a dense and consolidated workload footprint while maintaining the appropriate SLAs. This allows controlling the amount of power drawn by servers that are not being used by reducing the clock cycles of the idle CPUs. This is more efficient than completely switching power off to the server, because server boot introduces delay in a mobile workload environment. This also reduces the cooling requirement for the servers.

- An innovative technology such as Energywise enables optimized power and cooling management in a cloud environment. It allows an energy policy defined per unit of the cloud instance (rack, pod, and so on) and an interface that can provide trending information of energy utilization for analysis.

- Virtualization ensures granularity in hardware usage, which enables controlling the amount of power drawn by the virtualized hardware; for example, storage virtualization enables thin provisioning and oversubscription of storage, which allows controlling the amount of power drawn by the storage disks. Using a blade server chassis allows consolidation of workloads and an oversubscription of compute resources. which in turn improves the power and cooling characteristics (PUE) of the data center in general.

Return on Investment

Return on investment (ROI) is a significant metric to determine the sustainability of the IT organization based on the revenues generated by the services and applications hosted in a data center. As such, it measures the *capital expenditures* (CapEx) and *operating expenditures* (OpEx) required to maintain the data center and the time taken to recover these costs incurred to create the services and applications. OpEx is clearly the area where most optimization is engineered to maximize the data center ROI; however, a few cases influence the CapEx as well.

First, consider the items that contribute to the CapEx:

- Converged network interfaces and *network interface card* (NIC) virtualization are major contributors that enable "cable-once" architectures. The physical interface is responsible for delivering raw bandwidth, and the virtual NIC enables payload definition: Ethernet or Fibre Channel.

- Oversubscription enabled by virtualization allows maximizing savings on compute and storage hardware.

- Network virtualization technologies such as *virtual routing and forwarding* (VRF)/VPN and contexts/zones enables network service elements such as firewalls/*Network Address Translation* (NAT) devices to be shared across the data centers, thus maximizing the existing hardware utilization.

- The biggest impact cloud enablement has is on IT CapEx. Traditional IT CapEx, including hardware (compute, network, storage) for each service or application, is virtualized for the workloads. These workloads can be consolidated or distributed, based on SLAs, using automation. This drives down the CapEx and converts it into an OpEx. However, the automation is key in keeping the OpEx to a minimum.

Next, consider the items that contribute to OpEx:

- High-availability and disaster recovery strategies require maintaining idle equipment constantly powered so that workload mobility can be initiated in cases of workload bursting or an actual disaster.

- Energy consumption for the power and cooling needs of the components within the data center are major contributors to the OpEx. Controlling PUE enables efficient operational metrics.

- Data center analytics provides critical information such as load and utilization of the hardware resources. This enables the data center administrator to predict and define strategies to automate recovery procedures to address overload and disaster recovery conditions; for example, year-end accounting is a major event and stress on the data center resources of the financial institution. Using analytics can automate and trigger the exact time of redirecting workload toward the cloud or the redundant site based on thresholds rather than manually triggering a script to include additional compute in the load balancer or storage blocks.

Economy of Scale

In a silo-based model, the cost of growing the business is usually linear to the cost of equipment required to host the services and applications. Although this was sustainable in the past, physically such a model is bound by space and power/cooling constraints, which limit the growth that can be achieved, something most big enterprise customers are facing today.

One of the biggest factors influencing the data center architecture is the commoditization of the data center components. If the data center is designed based on the principle that none of the electronic components are reliable and that they are prone to failure, the hardware can be made with less-reliable and cheap components, thus reducing the overall cost of the hardware and contributing to the economy. However, this strategy needs to be properly balanced with innovation required in creating efficient low-power scalable architectures, which are typically not possible with commoditized hardware.

Case 2: Service Provider Enabling New Services and Content to Its Customers

This use case category includes typical mobile, wire-line, content, and application service providers. Platforms delivering these new services usually have a prolonged process of development, testing, and onboarding of applications to the production environment. Challenges include variations in development and production environments, validating security policies, and simplifying development platform, all of which need to be addressed to simplify and streamline the process. Service providers are also constantly evolving the service architectures to deliver better services, such as transitioning from 2G to 3G to 4G or adopting the *IP Multimedia Service* (IMS) architecture model to deliver ubiquitous services for their clients.

To address these concerns, the service providers deploy *black-box* racks, which have been prequalified by the application developers, resulting in huge data centers, which are underutilized. To address business continuity, these black-box architectures are provisioned in active/standby redundancy mode, thus increasing the number of unused components within the data center. Adding new services to an existing service portfolio involves implementing additional architectures, which might not use the existing infrastructure because of limitations of the current design.

Figure 5-2 depicts a typical service provider environment where each block represents the services hosted or partner services offered via a unified service delivery mechanism. The clients (enterprise, residential, or mobile) can access these services ubiquitously.

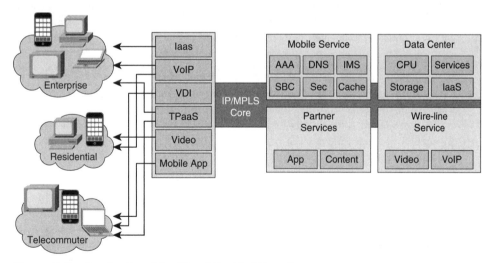

Figure 5-2   *Service Provider Cloud-Enabled Data Center*

As you can see, services hosted in each block (for example, IMS, VoIP, video) can be consolidated within a virtualized data center, and the respective services can be enhanced by service specific devices such as *session border controllers* (SBC) for voice and video services, load balancers for compute, and so on to meet the service-specific SLAs. To achieve these optimizations, the following concepts need to be deployed.

Virtualization

The key to simplifying this business model is to reduce the time taken to develop, test, and onboard applications onto the production environment. To begin with, virtualization can enable simulation of the production environment as a sandbox to develop and test the applications in a secure and controlled environment. This allows an efficient and simple application onboarding or sandboxing process. Furthermore, virtualization can consolidate the services hardware requirements by efficient allocation of compute, storage, and network resources to respective applications. Growth of these IT and service instances can be managed and predicted precisely in units of each resource instead of adding black-box racks. Finally, compute clustering and load-balancing strategies can be deployed to maximize the hardware utilization as an alternative to active/standby redundancy strategy.

Cloud Enablement

A service provider is a classic example of a typical multitenant environment where resources and services are shared. The consumers of these resources and services could be developers, end customers, or internal organizations, which sustain the business. A diverse set of consumers demands different services and SLAs, such as development platforms, collaboration suites, and content and applications services. Although building a consolidated architecture to host these diverse applications is a significant task, managing this architecture becomes an increasingly complex task because of the different user interfaces to manage elements and services of the infrastructure.

Virtualizing the infrastructure requires a fabric that can scale the services seamlessly and integrate the service-specific components. The fabric might have to scale geographically while trying to localize traffic as much as possible to optimize the bandwidth costs and application latency. With such a distributed infrastructure, DCI is a significant piece of the architecture that will enable any type of communication (Layer 2 or Layer 3) between the data centers.

Cloud-enabling the infrastructure allows not only building a multitenant-capable infrastructure but also managing the infrastructure to build and break down services on demand. Each service can be predefined as an instance of the infrastructure with relevant infrastructure components and appropriate SLAs that can be used as a self-served service catalog coupled with the ability to automate SLA management. This enables the service provider to open up the black-box architecture and virtualize these resources for additional services. It is important here to recognize the significance of the SLAs that are associated with each service, because an SLA determines the quality of experience and the effectiveness of cloud enablement of the infrastructure. Cloud SLAs are explored in further detail in Chapter 12, "End-to-End SLAs."

Power and Cooling Considerations

Service providers generally deploy multi-megawatt data centers to deliver services based on current silo-based architectures. This quickly limits that amount of growth a data center can achieve. Virtualization enables the service provider to realize immediate savings by sharing the data center infrastructure, with much of the previously underutilized hardware now available for sharing with other services and applications. Studies have revealed that virtualization can achieve anywhere between 50 percent to 80 percent or more efficiency in hardware utilization. An innovation such as interface virtualization enables oversubscription of physical interfaces while allowing different payload types to be carried by the physical interface. These techniques enable the conservation of power by maximizing the available resources.

In a service provider environment where workloads are diverse and complex, estimating power requirements of hardware can be a complex task. To simplify this process, units of the infrastructure, which typically can host all the services, are defined. This is typically referred to as a *point of delivery* (PoD). Each PoD has fixed-scale, capacity, and power characteristics such that a predictable performance unit can be provisioned on demand.

Return on Investment

In a service provider environment where business is based on volume, the scalability of the solution deployed is a significant criterion for investing in any technology or product. Virtualization delivers a scalable solution for the compute and storage needs. Scalability of the fabric includes control and forwarding plane capabilities. Control plane features are primarily associated with software, and the forwarding features are associated with hardware. As a result, the ROI depends on both hardware and software elements of the data center.

CapEx items include the following:

- The control plane scale in the service provider environment is limited by current protocols, such as *Spanning Tree Protocol* (STP), which yields less than 100 percent bandwidth efficiency to create a loop-free Layer 2 topology. This is extremely expensive to maintain because higher-speed ports such as 40G/100G ports are required. Technologies such as *Transparent Interconnect of Lots of Links* (TRILL), FabricPath, and *Provider Backbone Bridging* (PBB) are protocols to consider to address this issue.

- The data plane scale is dependent on the table size management of MAC (Layer 2) and IP (Layer 3) addresses. Distributed architectures typically deliver higher scale of these tables. Besides these, the physical port density and speeds are also significant contributors to the CapEx; for example, when considering scalable architectures beyond 10G speeds, Ethernet has the capability to deliver 40G/100G speeds with a lossless fabric implementation via *data center bridging* (DCB), which also supports Fibre Channel traffic for storage needs.

- As the data center grows, the requirements on the bandwidth provided by the fabric become a critical consideration. 40G/100G interfaces with terabit-per-slot capacities for switches and routers become important drivers to protect the CapEx on the network. This translates to investment in scalable platforms optimized for high-speed interfaces enabling fabrics to cater to the data center requirements for its life cycle.

OpEx items for consideration include the following:

- Data center orchestration and management is a major contributor to OpEx costs. Ideally a single management plane to communicate and program the elements of the data center simplifies the operational process within a data center. A standard *application programming interface* (API) on the platforms within the data center enables faster integration in a cloud ecosystem.

- Cloud analytics associated with the trends and patterns of the resource utilization provides important data points to how hardware resources and services are utilized. This information can be used to automate compute, storage, WAN, and energy resources. Typically, this helps in determining the gravity of a service and determines the optimizations to be made around this "sweet spot."

- Billing, reporting, and auditing for the services offered in the data center are complex tasks that require automation in a dynamic and elastic environment such as a cloud-enabled data center. This implies that current techniques used for these applications such as NetFlow need to evolve to provide more granularity and scalability. *Internet Protocol Flow Information Export* (IPFIX) enables collection intervals in milliseconds and granular flow definition to monitor flow information accurately.

- Maximizing infrastructure utilization enables a power-efficient data center. This is typically achieved using oversubscription. Pay as you grow or pay per use is a common oversubscription strategy used that provides mutual cost benefit to the subscribers and the service provider.

Economy of Scale

As discussed earlier, scale is a significant driver in the data center design in a service provider environment. The cost of scaling the data center is influenced by three main factors:

- **CapEx:** Scaling data centers in a service provider environment poses a cost challenge. Therefore, every attempt to minimize the CapEx of the solution is considered. One of the most attractive propositions is the use of commoditized hardware. *Commoditization* refers to hardware such as servers, storage, and network equipment built with generally available components (off-shelf), including CPUs, storage disks, network processors, and such. The benefits commodity components provide are development flexibility, features velocity, and substantial cost reduction. In contrast, application purpose-built components (*application-specific integrated circuit* [ASIC]) provide performance at scale with innovative technologies that are usually targeted to overcome current limitations. Clearly, there are trade-offs to either approach. The best fit for the cloud data center requirements depends on the SLAs being associated with the services being hosted and the scale required.

■ **Unit of scale:** As the data center scales to accommodate growing business, it is imperative to be able to quantify growth in a predictable manner. This quantification helps in determining a unit of the physical infrastructure that will enable incremental capacity. It also aids in determining the incremental CapEx and OpEx associated with turning on more units of such infrastructure. These units are termed as *PoD* units. The container units consume a fixed amount of power and cooling and deliver a fixed cloud capacity in terms of compute, storage, and network services. Containers simplify the scaling of data centers while providing a seamlessly integrated resource pool. These containers are physical containers, which contain the resources so that they can be moved easily. Such containers are suitable for applications like restoration of services in disaster-struck regions, quickly increasing capacity of an existing data center for a short period or reducing real-estate requirements by distributing these containers over a region.

Figure 5-3 shows a Cisco data center container deployment. The container is fully customizable, has capacity to hold 16x44RU racks, and drives a PUE of 1.05 to 1.3 depending on the cooling resource available. They can be rapidly deployed within 90 to 120 days and come with a complete management solution.

Figure 5-3 *Cisco Data Center Container*

Similar to the Cisco data center container solution shown in Figure 5-3, a network container instance definition simplifies the provisioning process. Network containers, and their provisioning through network hypervisors, such as the Cisco Network Services Manager (NSM), were introduced in Chapter 4, "Networks and Services in the Cloud." Figure 5-4 illustrates three examples of software container instances (bronze, silver, and platinum) representing units of network services that can be subscribed to by a tenant. These container instances shown in Figure 5-4 include typical IT services, including compute, storage, and network services. Each container instance defines a logical slice of the shared infrastructure in the data center.

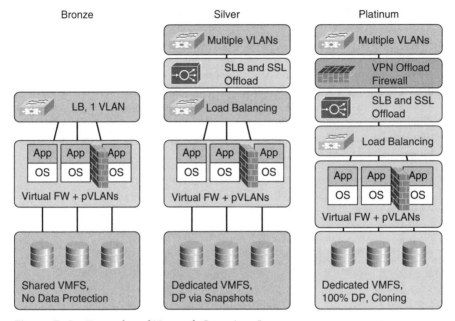

Figure 5-4   *Examples of Network Container Instances*

Predefining a container instance usually reduces the provisioning process from days to minutes depending on the complexity of the container instance definition and simplifies the planning, sizing, and management of the data center infrastructure.

■ **Power and cooling:** A major part of the data center design and expense includes providing power and cooling to the data center components. Although every device consumes power in a similar manner, determining a mechanism to provide a redundant supply to each device, adoption of a DC or AC strategy, and driving an optimal PUE within the data center are some of the challenges with designing a power strategy. Similarly, heat-emitting characteristics of these devices determine the strategy to provide a cooling solution. Because every device emits heat differently, a fully functional data center has heat spots where the maximum heat is being dissipated. Maintaining a consistent temperature is key to protecting the devices from "burning out." Several cooling strategies, such as air cooling, liquid cooling, spray cooling, or seawater cooling, can be considered depending on the geographic location and the availability of such resources in abundance.

Case 3: Public Utility Companies Offering Smart Technologies to Address Power and Energy Requirements in a More Reliable, Economic, and Sustainable Manner

Current models of centralized power generation and distribution are similar to the mainframe era of computing. These models depend on a few utility providers, and the distribution is unidirectional (that is, from the provider to the consumer). Without intelligence in the distribution layer, resource utilization cannot be controlled or managed efficiently or securely. With the advances in public utility resources, such as solar, wind, and water energy, the traditional consumer can now be a provider of energy back to the central grid that feeds communities. Again, some intelligence in the utility grid is required to be able to account for this new provider model.

Virtualization

The first step toward improving energy utilization is to educate the consumer on the energy consumption per device in the residence or commercial property. For example, if a commercial property manager can view and control the precise time of switching electrical devices such as lights, air-conditioning units, or computer monitors on or off within the property, the amount of power utilization can be better managed. With technologies such as smart metering, the amount of energy consumed by various devices within a property (residence or commercial) can be controlled and managed more effectively. Technologies such as smart metering require a secure, multitenant-aware, massively scalable virtualized data center environment to accurately record, monitor, and bill energy utilization along with the subscriber information.

As shown in Figure 5-5, the smart meter control node in the data center manages the smart meter installed in individual properties. The smart meter records the energy-consumption levels periodically and transmits the information to the smart meter control node in the data center. This data is analyzed to extract information such as the period during which energy is consumed the most, the appliances consuming this energy, or the cost of energy consumed. Using these analytics, information can be sent to the consumers about minimizing costs, replacing old appliances with new Energy Star-rated appliances, and controlling the use of appliances during certain times of the day. The consumers can access this information from their computers or mobile devices. In addition, intelligent controls can be installed to control the appliances so that the power utilization might be optimized.

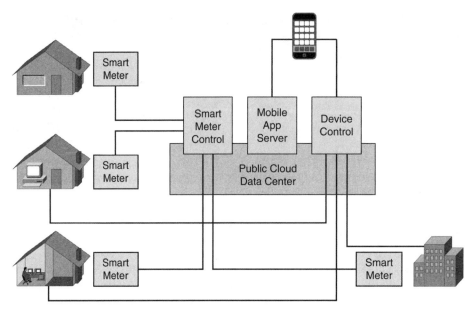

Figure 5-5   *Public Cloud Application: Smart Meter*

Cloud Enablement

A public community cloud implementation includes small records of a large number of community members. Therefore, it is important to automate the process of recording the subscriber information and secure the information from attacks. The subscriber can use this information to remotely control or program the energy-consuming devices such as the HDTVs, air-conditioning units, or the heater units in the residence. In a multitenant dwelling unit, where common resources such as lighting, water, and heating are maintained, power to these resources can be controlled to suit the tenant usage and can be shut down thereafter. However, security compliance is critical to the success of a public cloud deployment.

Cloud enablement not only brings the capability to virtualize the subscriber records for ubiquitous access and control of the energy policy for utilization but also enables subscribers to become an energy supplier by sharing any excess energy they might generate. Typically, solar-powered units reduce the consumption of energy from the provider, but any excess energy can be fed back to the "power grid."

Return on Investment

A number of public community cloud deployments have enabled innovations in services delivered via the Internet; however, most of these applications are aimed at delivering services to the public and not use the public resources or capabilities. Because these types of cloud systems are still in a premature state of adoption, the ROI estimation is not easily measured. Following are some applications:

- **Instant voting:** Traditional methods of public voting incur a huge cost on the public. A number of controversies and issues about vote counting, duplicate votes, and citizens being remote at the time of voting and generally increasing the election participation may arise with a public cloud. Although online voting is a popular method in many polling and voting exercises, securing the voting system for public elections is one of the major challenges. When these challenges are addressed, an instant voting system can simplify and quicken the process significantly. Cloud concepts of trusted zones and virtualization could address some of these issues. However, a more elaborate evaluation is required to address all the security concerns to make this concept a reality.

- **Community services:** New visitors to a city or region often spend a lot of time researching points of interest or locating them. These services can be made available via a community portal to mobile devices as soon as the visitor enters the region. Besides this, information about weather and travel conditions can be delivered to the visitor upon registration. Alternatives suggesting detours to a neighboring city that shares a relationship can be recommended as a potential destination, and an itinerary can be updated.

Economy of Scale

Public community cloud deployments require a significant investment, primarily because of the scale requirements. Besides scale, security is a major concern because of the sensitive information that public clouds usually deal with. A simple web application delivering compute service has fewer security concerns than the case of instant voting discussed earlier. Cities could consider pooling resources to deploy common infrastructure to build highly reliable and efficient community clouds to cater to local communities.

Case 4: High-Performance Computing and Low-Latency Applications

High-performance computing (HPC) is primarily used in industrial applications, such as finite element analysis and gene research, research applications, such as astronomical studies, and 3D imaging. Low-latency applications, such as financial market analysis, university research applications, and gaming, are sensitive to latency in data analysis and rendering. Depending on whether the application is resolving mathematical, graphical, or string calculation or analysis, the application could use distributed/grid computing. HPC leverages parallel computing concepts, as illustrated in Figure 5-6.

A user program or application triggers a job, which is managed by a master job scheduler. Depending on the complexity and distribution of the compute instances, there could be one or more such job schedulers that proxy the function of the master. The job scheduler is responsible for assigning enough compute instances to process the data. This assumes that the job can be split into multiple chunks that can be processed in parallel. Similarly for data-centric processing, the map-reduce function employs map and reduce functions to process data simultaneously.

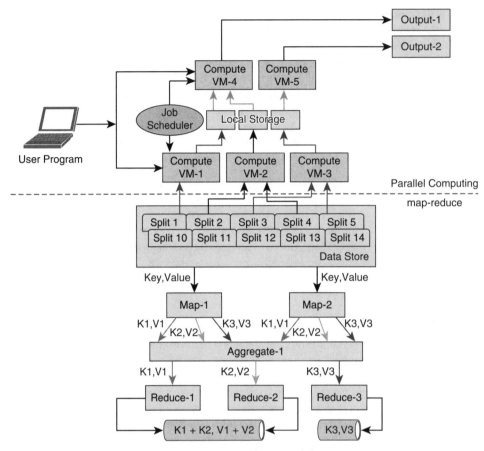

Figure 5-6 *Parallel Computing and Map-Reduce Models*

Low-latency computing requires that the data be accessed, processed, and rendered in the least possible time. Latency in computing depends on memory speed, network bandwidth, transport latency, and storage *input/output operations per second* (IOPS). Minimizing each of these attributes requires innovations in the respective areas to deliver a complete low-latency solution; for example, high-speed memory technologies such as *Double Date Rate 3* (DDR3), extended memory technologies like on the Cisco *Unified Computing System* (UCS), high-speed network capability, low-latency switching elements, and high-speed storage network options. In many data-centric processing operations (for example, web searches, analytics, and research applications), it is important to reduce the latency in data access and processing.

Virtualization

Because compute virtualization is derived from parallel computing, applications that typically use parallel computing can almost invariably benefit from virtual computing. Virtual computing has the possibility of increasing the computing power beyond the constraints of parallel computing. The major difference between parallel computing and virtual computing is that virtual computing spans servers, whereas parallel computing is driven by a powerful multicore and multi-CPU (or GPU) architecture. Furthermore, compute virtualization can also reduce cost by using off-the-shelf hardware. As shown previously in Figure 5-6, the map-reduce approach enables virtualization of the process and enables distribution of the job across a large cluster of CPUs.

Cloud Enablement

Whereas HPC models are traditionally closed systems and are an extremely expensive investment, cloud models for HPC propose to introduce a pay-per-use model that allows sharing this expensive resource and reducing the investment required by using off-the-shelf hardware. Besides that, the cloud model simplifies the management of such HPC clusters by enabling a template-based configuration of resources and the SLA required for an application. This eliminates complex evaluation, qualification, and setup processes typically involved in HPC deployments. The cloud model also enables compliance mechanisms required to meet the performance and security guidelines set by HPC users.

Power and Cooling Considerations

With HPC, because the applications are usually compute and memory centric, the heat emitted by these devices create larger hotspots than other implementations. This is due to the high density of compute, memory, and storage resources within a fixed area to maintain latency and performance constraints. Therefore, the typical cooling mechanisms may not suffice. Liquid cooling and spray cooling are usually preferred over air cooling. As mentioned in Case 3, containers can be deployed across the campus to distribute the power and cooling requirements. This strategy also helps in reducing the hotspot concentration in particular regions.

Economy of Scale

As discussed previously, HPC usually requires a concentrated resource pool that is bound by latency requirements, which is in nanoseconds to a few microseconds ranges. This implies that compute and memory are packed as close to each other as possible. Although DDR3 technology provides the speed, it limits the number of channels available to the CPU cores to access the memory. Cisco UCS extended memory technology helps here in scaling the *Direct Memory Access* (DMA) channels to render a multiple of memory modules accessible to the CPU core complex; however, this comes at the cost of increasing the power consumption and heat emission of the server.

Another consideration in HPC models is the ability to scale the storage IOPS. This directly depends on the storage speeds that can be enabled. Fibre Channel and InfiniBand provide the advantages of storage speeds of up to 40G; higher speeds such as 100G become cost-prohibitive. An alternative to InfiniBand is *Fibre Channel over Ethernet* (FCoE). With Ethernet speeds scaling to 100GE and innovations such as *data center bridging*

(DCB), which allows implementation of a lossless fabric for storage applications, it is simpler and easier to consolidate storage networks into a single fabric. These innovations enable building highly scalable, low-latency, and cost-effective HPC solutions.

Summary of the Use Cases

Each of the preceding use case discussions reveals that virtualization is a key technology enabling consolidation of hardware resources, resulting in new requirements on the fabric, such as VM-awareness, elasticity (that ability to provision or deprovision a resource), power efficiency, and multitenancy.

To deliver these services, the network fabric needs to adapt to the segmentation rules of the respective data centers, maintain VM-awareness, and provide a multitenant-aware and elastic mechanism to enable or disable these services on demand. In addition, the fabric needs to be aware of virtualization in storage hardware and network services such as load balancing, application accelerators, and security to efficiently utilize the resources across the data centers.

A cloud-enabled data center delivers to each tenant an instance of the virtual data center with a choice of services and elements integrated together by a fabric. The section that follows explores the characteristics of the fabric.

Network Segmentation in the Data Center

As demonstrated in the chapter so far, the fabric is a key component of a cloud-enabled data center. Designing the fabric for the data center is primarily about predefining network segments and their roles (for example, trusted and untrusted zones, service segments, and storage segments). Predefining the segmentation strategy allows containing the scale of specific functions independent of the other segments. Finally, it is important to integrate these segments via a unified fabric to create a seamless connection between the various components of the data center.

Because the cloud-enabled data center is a shared resource, the fabric needs to host multiple tenants and enable a simple mechanism to operate the data center. Because the data center now has a denser workload footprint, the segmentation scale required pushes the current limit of segmentation. Segmentation techniques used today include the following:

- VLAN-based framing, including dot1q, q-in-q, and *provider-based bridging* (PBB)

- Layer 3-based segmentation, including VRFs, MPLS, or IP VPNs

Although there could be many possibilities to the design of a data center fabric based on Layer 2, Layer 3, or a combination of the two types, there are two main goals to achieve in designing the fabric:

- Multitenancy (secure isolation between tenants)

- Network containers (virtual segments for each tenant)

Segmentation alone does not address the scale requirements of the data center. The MAC table size on each switch also increases exponentially as the data center grows. Hence, a new control plane capable of scaling the cloud-enabled data center is required to overcome the limitations of the legacy protocol, such as STP and its variants.

This new control plane needs to provide the following:

■ Equal-cost multipathing

■ MAC learning optimizations

■ *First-Hop Redundancy Protocol* (FHRP) multipathing

■ MAC scaling strategy

The Cisco FabricPath technology innovation enables these characteristics in a Layer 2 fabric, as shown in Figure 5-7.

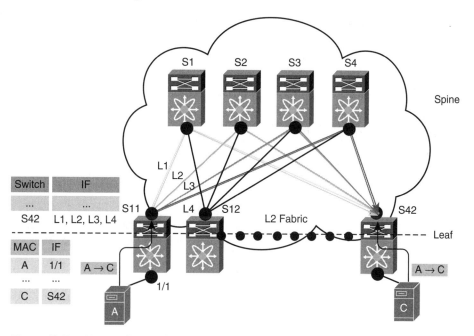

Figure 5-7 *Cisco FabricPath*

Cisco FabricPath defines two layers (spine and leaf) that separate the core switching functionality from the edge switch. The edge switch (leaf) alone does MAC learning, while the core switch (spine) forwards traffic based on the edge switch MACs, as illustrated in Figure 5-7. FabricPath allows the simplicity and plug-and-play nature of traditional Layer 2 fabrics and enables *equal-cost multipath* (ECMP) routing and hierarchical MAC learning function within the core. This hierarchical MAC learning function refers to the capability of the spine to use switch IDs of leaf switches to switch traffic instead of using the host MAC addresses. FabricPath also allows efficient link utilization in the fabric, because all links can participate in forwarding traffic in an ECMP scenario, unlike blocked links in an STP scenario.

Traditionally, storage networks were built independent of the data network. So, the data center fabric would appear split. Unified Fabric integrates storage network seamlessly using FCoE, which uses DCB to enable a lossless fabric required to transport storage traffic. DCB is a set of standards under the 802.1 working group that define requirements to transport Fibre Channel traffic over Ethernet. Figure 5-8 lists the standards involved, which are further described in the list that follows.

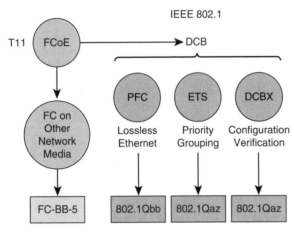

Figure 5-8   *Data Center Bridging*

DCB defines three standards:

- **Priority-based flow control (802.1Qbb):** To guarantee a lossless fabric, Ethernet uses pause frames to control ingress and egress queues to avoid dropping frames within the fabric.

- **Enhanced transmission selection (802.1Qaz):** To guarantee bandwidth for applications sharing a link, priority queuing is used to ascertain performance requirements of the applications. For example, if three applications—high performance computing (high priority), LAN traffic (low priority), and storage traffic (medium priority)— share the same link, bandwidth for the applications is allocated based on the guaranteed values configured.

- **Data center bridging eXchange (802.1Qaz):** Uses *Link Layer Discovery Protocol* (LLDP) to negotiate the quality metrics, including PFC, ETS, and application priorities, across a fabric link. In addition, there is a provision to exchange the metrics (capabilities) of individual platforms to implement the highest quality of transport to address application requirements. LLDP could also be used to exchange partial or full configuration to simplify operational tasks

FCoE is a layered protocol and closely resembles the OSI stack, as shown in Figure 5-9.

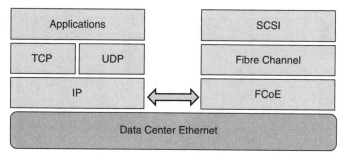

Figure 5-9   *FCoE Protocol Stack*

FCoE uses a Layer 3 lookup to forward frames and rewrites source and destination addresses of the FCoE frame and hence resembles the IP layer in the OSI stack. FCoE uses source and destination *Fibre Channel identifiers* (FC-IDs)—S_ID and D_ID—to identify Fibre Channel hops. These frames are encapsulated in a standard Ethernet MAC to be transported over regular Ethernet ports. The Fibre Channel forwarder does an FC-ID lookup to determine the next hop toward the destination.

Unified fabric leverages FCoE to integrate the storage network into the data center fabric as shown in Figure 5-10. This in turn provides three benefits:

- Simplifies and accelerates the provisioning process.

- Reduces the number of adapters required because the storage and LAN interfaces can be virtualized. The physical interface is shared between the two forwarding paradigms. The Ethernet frame itself carries the intelligence to differentiate the payload as storage or data. As a result, Ethernet cabling is all that is required to connect the server chassis to the network.

- Eliminates the requirement for new hardware to enable the FCoE function. Traditional routers or switches can host the *Fibre Channel Forwarder* (FCF) function to forward Fibre Channel traffic. Therefore, the storage hosts can be directly connected to the Ethernet network.

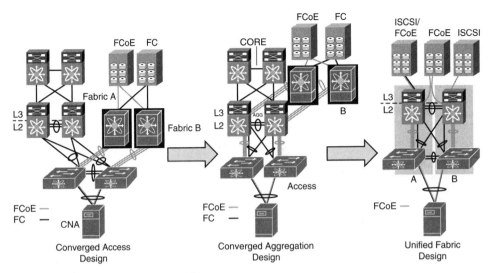

Figure 5-10 *Unified Fabric Evolution*

Multitenancy

The definition of a tenant and its scope is an important step in the construction of an instance of the virtual data center. A tenant could simply be associated with a telecommuter or a branch office requiring virtual desktop instance. Alternatively, a more complex definition of a tenant could be an enterprise application with multiple tiers scaling independent of each tier with a scope from a region to the entire globe with multiple network segments separating a *demilitarized zone* (DMZ) segment from the private/internal segment. A multitenant-capable data center is required to guarantee the resource availability for the duration of the tenant subscription and is unaffected by conditions of other tenants. Multitenancy is enabled typically by separating the forwarding and control planes in the network fabric by using a Layer 2 (dot1q, q-in-q, mac-in-mac) and Layer 3 (VRF) segmentation techniques. Network services such as firewalls, load balancers and NAT, storage capacity, and compute instances within the context of a container instance comprise the resources consumed by a tenant, as illustrated in Figure 5-11.

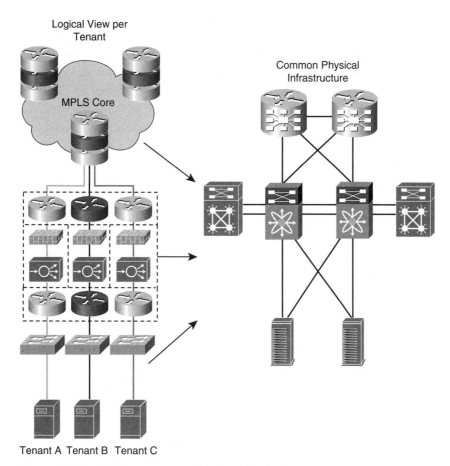

Logical View per
Tenant

Common Physical
Infrastructure

MPLS Core

Tenant A Tenant B Tenant C

Figure 5-11   *Multitenancy on Cloud-Enabled Infrastructure*

Network Containers

A virtual instance of the data center basically consists of defining the elements that
constitute a cloud service. The cloud service provider will have defined a few types of
instances of the cloud service that can be enabled on their infrastructure. These instances
are referred to as *network containers*, as illustrated previously in Figure 5-4. Each network container type can be viewed as a type of IaaS service tier that tenants can choose
based on their application and other requirements. The types of service instances that
can be spawned and the space and power constraints dictate the container sizing. The
cloud service provider offers these containers and other options like disaster recovery or
application onboarding through a service catalog to the customer. The customer chooses
a type of service from the cloud portal, and the services are enabled on demand. In

addition, the service catalog could include SLA definitions, which could define the QoS metrics and other service guarantees. Cloud SLAs are discussed in detail in Chapter 12. When the container definition is finalized, the next important step is to orchestrate the end-to-end provisioning. This involves not only keeping track of the resources available to determine whether the requested service can be provisioned but also being able to validate the end-to-end configuration.

Virtualization-Aware Network

The network has always been a shared resource, and therefore different forms of virtualization already exist; however, virtualization of the compute and storage resources imposes scale requirements on the segmentation mechanisms and requires the capability to switch at a VM level. This implies that the virtualization needs to start at the NICs used in the server hardware and extend into the physical network elements that are part of the fabric.

Virtual Switching

As virtualization of the compute layer separates each instance as a unique self-contained VM with all the characteristics of a physical machine, the network interface provides network-level separation for each individual VM. So, a single physical server could be host to multiple virtual server instances and hence multiple virtual interfaces. Traditional network switching is not capable of switching between virtual interfaces; communication between these VMs or servers can be enabled via one of two methods:

- **Port extension:** A slight modification to the bridging component in the physical switch to identify the virtual interfaces via the physical interface enables traditional switching to be applied to these virtual interfaces. This usually involves using another tag identifier within the frame to indicate the virtual interface the traffic originates from, as illustrated in Figure 5-12. This implies that there could be some issues with backward compatibility with traditional switches.

  The Cisco UCS M81KR *virtual interface card* (VIC) and UCS P81E implement the VM-FEX technology that enables up to 128 virtual interface instances within a single physical NIC. VEPA is an alternate technology and enables similar virtualization available on HP NICs.

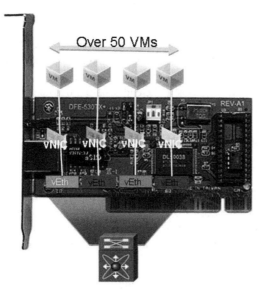

Figure 5-12   *Virtual Port Extension*

■ **Virtual switch:** An alternative to the port extension mechanism is to create an instance of the switch itself on the physical server that enables communication between the VMs. Communication between external servers occurs via traditional network switching and routing techniques without any changes required. One benefit of a virtual switch is that all the feature-rich capabilities and optimizations of a network switch can be easily made available via a virtual switch to the VMs. Figure 5-13 illustrates this concept using Cisco Nexus 1000V (N1kv).

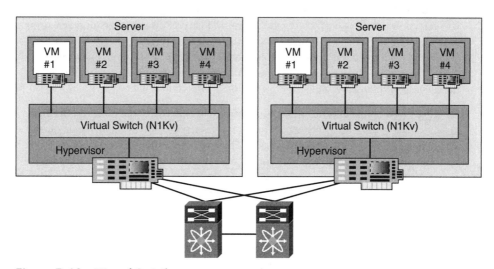

Figure 5-13   *Virtual Switch*

Network Policy

The process involved in provisioning a cloud service includes not only configuring the compute instance but also network characteristics, network services, SLA attributes, and storage requirements. However, these resources are usually under different administrative domains and thus prolong the time required to complete the end-to-end provisioning of the service. In a cloud environment, where service elasticity is a primary requirement, the provisioning and deprovisioning tasks need to be dynamic and quick. Besides, depending on the scale of subscribers requesting the service, the provisioning task cannot be a prolonged process.

One of the benefits of virtualizing a network interface is the capability to define the interface characteristics independent of the physical interface. This enables the capability to pass diverse payload types via the physical interfaces, including Ethernet and Fibre Channel. Another benefit of virtual interfaces is that network policy can be predefined as a template and attached to a VM. This network policy can include detailed network characteristics, including Layer 2 and 3 capabilities, security policies, and QoS policies.

Defining a network policy enables a predefinition of the data and storage network characteristics, QoS, and security policies based on subscriber SLAs. Based on the definition of the network policy, it is now possible to estimate the number of instances that can be hosted on the cloud infrastructure and enable a level of admission control on the infrastructure. Because a network policy is independent of the interface type, it enables application of this policy to physical and virtual interfaces alike. This allows differentiation of services and the ability to monetize the infrastructure.

VM Mobility

Traditionally, mission-critical applications were impacted by disaster recovery situations, which include power outage, hardware failure, and natural disaster. Therefore, ensuring business continuity was a difficult but significant task. A typical disaster recover plan involves cloning the infrastructure required to sustain critical business operations. This strategy is service impacting and requires a continuous evaluation process to ascertain the success of the recovery plan.

Creating a VM template enables you to record the stateless characteristics of the compute, storage, and network elements. This simplifies the cloning of the instance on any other virtualized host in a remote location. Thus, virtual mobility enables agility of the business that complies with the best common practices of a data center design. Besides agility, VM mobility also enables consolidation of VM instances within a cluster to minimize the energy utilization in a data center. Maintenance cycles typically cause a downtime in the service. VM mobility allows zero-impact maintenance cycles, thus enabling new services within the data center without impacting existing ones.

The capability to define network policy templates aids in moving the network characteristics along with the VM, simplifying the network provisioning process. Cisco Nexus

1000v implements the port profiles. Innovations in optimizing the routing for the moved VM can be enabled through technologies such as *Location ID Separation Protocol* (LISP). Chapter 8 discusses LISP in detail.

Virtual Network Services

Network services within a data center enhance the services hosted by implementing advanced algorithms to improve the experience and quality of the service. These services include load balancing, firewall, security, NAT, application accelerators, and so on. Each of these services is available on appliances and service modules from different vendors. Appliances deliver performance and scale but typically are required to be collocated with the network devices. To scale the network services, these appliances are stacked up and consume additional ports on the network devices. This restricts the access to these services geographically because the physical appliances are not "movable." However, physical appliances do provide hardware acceleration and hence are well suited where peripheral services are required, as in the case of peripheral security and global load balancing or site selection.

Virtualizing the network services enables hosting these services on virtualized hardware, including servers or generic hardware on network equipment (service on a blade). A cloud service is typically a dynamic instance, which includes a set of network services that should be able to "move" along with the cloud service. Also, the subscriber may choose to have a third-party network service implementation that the cloud service provider may not support.

The concept of a virtual network service addresses these challenges. It enables flexibility of network service implementation, choice of implementation, and greater agility.

Fabric Intelligence for Virtual Services

Virtualization of network services allows the possibility of hosting them on the same hardware as a compute instance. Therefore, practically, a network service instance behaves the same as a compute instance. Hence properties such as network, security, and QoS policies typically applied to a compute instance can be applied to a network service instance as well. In addition, because the network service primary function is to enhance the cloud service, it needs to be tightly integrated with the compute instance. The network fabric that integrates the compute instance and the network service instance might simply provide a transport path or be enhanced to optimize the path between the compute and network service instances.

Optimizing this path between the compute instance and the network service instances implies that the fabric be able to chain the network services to be applied in the path of the traffic to or from the compute instance. Cisco's implementation of vPath on the Nexus 1000V virtual switch is an example of the path optimization.

Service Overlay

Virtualized network services provide an option to implement a feature-rich cloud service, but appliance-based network services are still the platform to deliver performance and scale. Therefore, you cannot ignore them in a cloud data center. However, to enable the agility and flexibility characteristics of the cloud data center, there needs to be an evolution of the fabric to enable access to the network service from any part of the network. This implies that the network services be "routable." This is delivered with the service overlay model.

The service overlay model enables the network services to be routable by providing a mechanism to discover the network service appliances and to divert user traffic via the service chain as required.

In Figure 5-14, the service network refers to the domain that enables a routable service using appliances connected by switches or routers. The device (switch or router) connecting the data network with the service network has the intelligence to define the service chain and a mechanism to translate the encapsulations between the two networks.

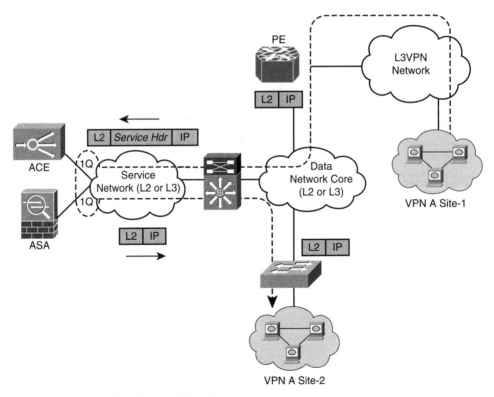

Figure 5-14   *Service Overlay Model*

Summary

Factors influencing the design of a data center include a need to scale, simplify the operations and management plane, and embrace green technologies. Cloud-enabling the data center allows the system to scale quickly and on demand and reduce power consumption. Operations are simplified by adopting wire-once technology, which is enabled by innovations in network interface technology using virtualization. This allows abstraction of the physical interface from the payload type (Ethernet and Fibre Channel). A physical and software container model enables simplification of the orchestration and management process. High density of services instantiated within an area allows continuous operation of essential hardware as needed only and maximizes their utilization. This, in turn, optimizes the power and cooling requirements. Finally, the key to deliver business-grade, scalable cloud services includes the integration of network services efficiently and in a scalable manner. Securing and optimizing the cloud services is a significant next step addressed in the subsequent chapters.

Review Questions

You can find answers to these questions in Appendix A, "Answers to Review Questions."

1. The power usage effectiveness of a data center should ideally have a value of which of the following?

   a. 0.5

   b. 1.0

   c. 1.5

   d. 50

2. Which of the following are major contributors that enable "cable-once" architectures?

   a. Dynamic NICs and virtual cables

   b. Converged network interfaces and NIC virtualization

   c. Server virtualization and Ethernet cables

   d. Interface multiplexing and dual-homing

3. FabricPath is characterized by which of the following features?

   a. ECMP

   b. Use of switch IDs for MAC learning

   c. MAC routing

   d. STP

4. Unified fabric includes which of the following technologies?

   a. CFS

   b. NFS

   c. FCoE

   d. SCSI

5. FCoE is equivalent to which layer of OSI?

   a. Layer 1

   b. Layer 2

   c. Layer 3

   d. Layer 4

Reference

Controlling Corporate Energy Consumption via the Enterprise Network: http://www.cisco.com/en/US/prod/collateral/switches/ps5718/ps10195/lippis_energywise_external_final.pdf

Chapter 6

Securing and Optimizing Cloud Services

In this chapter, you learn about the following:

- The motivation for securing data center resources

- Regulatory standards for securing tenant data

- Techniques for providing multitenant-aware security for cloud services

- Management and auditing of security services

It is evident that the data center is one of the most critical parts of any business, hosting not just the applications and information but also any intellectual property and the entire business process of a company. It is therefore imperative to secure and optimize access to the data center physically and virtually. Chapter 9, "Securing Cloud Transport and Edge Using NGN Technologies," and Chapter 11, "Connecting Enterprises to the Cloud," cover these topics in detail.

If you look beyond the technicalities of the data center and consider the need for a data center infrastructure and its relevance to a business, you can understand the elements of the data center that you need to secure and optimize. A business usually requires a set of applications to streamline the business process and ultimately deliver a service. Every element of the data center directly or indirectly contributes to enabling a service, thus generating revenue and the growth of the business. Idle elements or an attack on the data center—physical or virtual—could affect the productivity and prove detrimental to the business. Securing the infrastructure is therefore an essential part of the data center design strategy. Chapter 9 covers aspects of securing the cloud (that is data center) infrastructure from the *Next Generation Network* (NGN) point of view.

The performance and scale of an application are bound by the compute, storage, and network elements within the data center. Therefore, an attack on the data center usually targets one or more of these resources. Protocol attacks exploit the application protocol stack, and brute-force attacks attempt to degrade the performance and stall the application. Attacks are also devised to steal application data such as subscriber records, including credit cards, Social Security numbers, bank accounts, and critical applications (such as sales forecasting) that are offered as Software as a Service (SaaS). Some attacks are devised to steal Internet time or bandwidth with botnet-based attacks.

It is almost intuitive here to compare the layered data center security strategy to the principle used in developing bullet-proof glass, as illustrated in Figure 6-1. Bulletproof armor is a significant part of physical defense and security strategies against bullet attacks.

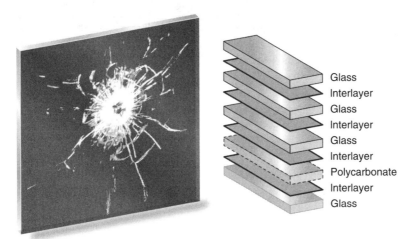

Figure 6-1   *Bulletproof Glass and Armor*

Theoretically, bulletproof glass or armor is based on the principle of refraction—a solid material can alter the direction of the bullet or halt penetration. Glass, being transparent, is suitable for bullet proofing vehicle windows or creating a transparent bullet-proof perimeter for securing an area, while maintaining visibility inside the protected area; the thicker the glass, the greater the refraction. However, the bigger the bullet, the more refraction is required, and beyond a point the economics of manufacturing a thick-enough glass in the required form factor becomes too heavy to be operationally viable. Another factor limiting the thickness of the glass is that if multiple distributed attacks were to be made, the glass could ultimately shatter and cause more harm to the person inside the protected area than the bullet itself. Hence, another technique involving layered panes of transparent material, including glass and plastic, is used to slow down, distribute, and refract the attack. So, in principle, a layered approach reduces the impact of the attack by absorbing the impact itself.

If you apply this principle to the context of data center security, it yields a security strategy for each layer—Layer 1 to Layer 7—with each layer representing some hardware in the data center, such as a *network interface card* (NIC), switch, router, storage, compute, and network. Together, they constitute a defense system that can thwart a range of attacks. More specifically, the security layers are as shown in Figure 6-2 and described in the list that follows.

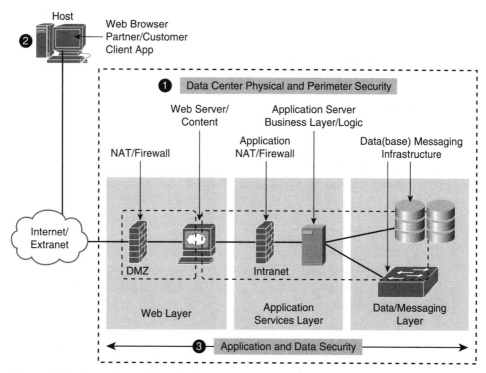

Figure 6-2 *Data Center Security Layers*

■ **Physical security:** This layer addresses the security of the physical location and the data center facility. Placement of the data center facility and hardening the structure against attacks—*electromagnetic pulse* (EMP) and warfare (chemical, blast, radiation)—or natural disasters are significant criteria for physical security. The data center entrance is restricted to authorized personnel and monitored at all times. Keycard and biometric scanning protocols with round-the-clock video surveillance are typical strategies implemented today. Within the data center, you can ensure security of the infrastructure by using caged racks and video cameras. Detailed logs of the access to the infrastructure and periodic auditing of these logs help ensure that breaches, if any, have been identified and recorded.

■ **Host security:** Typical source of attacks on the data center infrastructure include hosts with little or no security. Malicious users and programs use hosts to attack the data center infrastructure to bring down the service or impact business. Therefore, it is imperative to equip trusted hosts accessing the data center services with security. These security measures include configuring the host OS built-in firewall and security features, antivirus, antimalware software to thwart any attack on the data center via the host. Besides, necessary software patches (especially security patches on the OS and applications) are mandatory for a robust host security.

■ **Application and Data security:** This layer is probably the most important of a security strategy because it is completely under the control of IT. Protection of the data center infrastructure and services serves as the final defense against any attack. Server OS hardening and security patch management is critical. Besides, a robust security layer, including a firewall, and an intrusion protection system are key to the security of the application and data. Rules defining access to the data and policies enforced on the web and application tiers ensure security of the data. Data encryption and transport layer security mechanisms are tools used for securing data.

In the context of the virtualized data center, in addition to a layered approach, the security strategy needs to be aware of virtualized and multitenant environments. This implies that each tenant could have a different security policy that might have to be enabled by the virtualized infrastructure. To control the explosion of these security requirements, regulatory authorities have defined certain security standards that set a benchmark for infrastructure to guarantee security.

The rest of this chapter deals with the methods available to secure the data center infrastructure and tools available to validate the implementation. This chapter takes a holistic approach to security at different layers of the cloud to provide the most scalable solution to the customer.

Motivations to Design Secure Multitenant Networks

A security strategy adopted within a data center is usually based on the applications and the information hosted. The applications define the information flow and the logic used to map the information. Within an enterprise, these applications store business intelligence and customer-sensitive information that is critical for establishing a trust relationship with the customers. This could escalate to national significance if the information stored is sensitive, mission critical, or of national significance. Therefore, it is not only important to secure the data but also the information flow, because an attack on the flow could compromise the information or data as well. So, it is imperative to have knowledge of these attacks to create a counterstrategy to protect the data and the information flow.

Broadly speaking, attacks are classified into soft and brute-force attacks. Soft attacks target the protocol stack and usually exploit the vulnerabilities in the protocol or application/OS stack. Brute-force attacks are usually *denial of service* (DoS) attacks targeted toward stalling the application or security stack. In either case, the goal of the attack is to deny access to the application or service for legitimate users or steal information for unethical use. A general knowledge of application flow—in the cloud application stack—helps in understanding the appropriate security strategies available. The types of applications usually hosted by service providers and primary candidates for cloud-enabled service models are briefly discussed here A few typical information flow models and the attacks designed to compromise the information and the relevant flows are also explained.

Figure 6-3 illustrates a simple web application implementation. The figure also depicts the information flow model. The information flow can be described as follows:

1. Information is generated and stored in the form of HTML files. These files are managed using a file system.

2. A web server defines methods and processes to access this information.

3. A web client (browser) defines information access methods via a legitimate interface, usually referred to as *application programming interfaces* (API).

4. The Internet provides a transport mechanism (TCP/IP) to carry the web traffic between the web client and server. Similarly, a network enables a communication mechanism between the web server and file system or storage arrays.

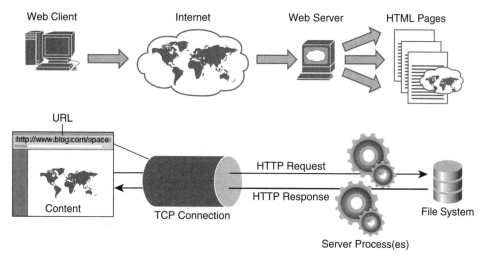

Figure 6-3   *A Simple Web Application*

Some web and peer-to-peer applications use more advanced techniques described in the sections that follow to enhance performance, latency, and availability of the application. These advanced techniques are usually implemented at Layer 6–7 of the IP stack.

HTTP Tunneling

HTTP tunneling is a technique used to tunnel application payload over a network. HTTP here is used as a transport protocol to tunnel an application through firewalls and *Network Address Translation* (NAT) appliances that primarily protect TCP/UDP ports. These HTTP tunnels originate and terminate on the HTTP clients and servers. Some typical reasons to use HTTP tunneling include the following:

- Private or secured Internet browsing

- Secure online transactions

- Internet traffic encryption

- Protect online subscriber identity

- Some instant messaging applications

- Gaming and peer-to-peer applications

Consider a mobile worker who executes business on the fly. This requires the worker to access corporate resources or collaborate with subject matter experts located in the central office. Figure 6-4 illustrates some typical applications using an HTTP tunneling solution for a mobile worker accessing corporate resources securely over an Internet connection. This enables the mobile worker to have ubiquitous access to corporate resources without having to depend on the local firewall configurations, which might be beyond the control of the worker. HTTP tunneling leverages the fact that TCP port 8080 is usually left open in a firewall, thus allowing HTTP traffic to pass. With a secure HTTP session, the user traffic can be encrypted while traversing the Internet.

However, this flexibility can be easily abused to direct an attack toward the service hosted behind the firewalls because the tunnel bypasses all network layer security.

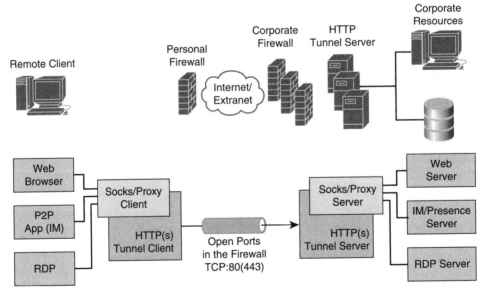

Figure 6-4 *HTTP Tunneling Example*

Web Proxy/Caching

Web services usually rely on multiple transactions between a client and server to post content on a web client (browser). Depending on the proximity of the client to the server, the transactions may introduce variable delays if the content is sourced from geographically dispersed servers. Web proxy and caching techniques help to speed up the web experience. Web proxy servers are usually deployed at the client site (forward proxy) or server side (reverse proxy), as shown in Figure 6-5.

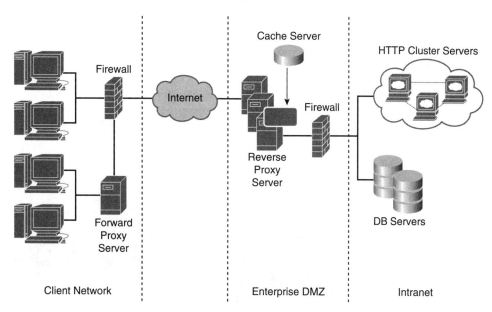

Figure 6-5   *Proxy and Caching Server Examples*

A forward proxy server is usually deployed in the client network. It primarily addresses the following use-cases:

- Hide the internal network topology

- Use common security policies for each proxy connection

- Share an Internet connection between multiple users

A reverse proxy server is deployed on the *demilitarized zone* (DMZ) network and addresses the following use-cases:

- Hide the true server identity.

- Perform load balancing on servers.

- Acceleration—encryption/*Secure Sockets Layer* (SSL), compression, and security.

■ **Caching.** Offload web servers by caching static content, including pictures and graphics. In addition, proxy caches can reduce server resource usage by buffering content to serve slow clients (such as mobile devices) accessing dynamic web content.

All the elements in the preceding list form service stacks categorized broadly as software, database, and network stacks. Each stack is a potential target for an attack that could degrade service—in this case, delay or complete loss of access to the information stored. Although you can assume that some security mechanisms are in place, such as network access lists, password-based user access, and secured protocol stacks, the nature of attacks is such that they evolve to overcome all these basic security mechanisms.

A web hacking incident database (WHID) tracks web-based attacks in real time. Figure 6-6 shows a snapshot of this information.

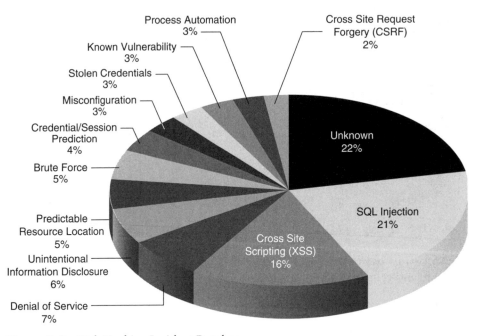

Figure 6-6 *Web Hacking Incident Database*

Unknown attacks form the majority of attacks, which should be interpreted as an active community of attackers constantly devising new methods of compromising a protocol stack. Some examples of known attacks are as follows:

■ An attack directed toward the web server could include a high rate of TCP (Open/Syn) establishment sessions, which could stall the network stack on the web server.

- SQL injection refers to the vulnerability of unverified or unsanitized user input that allows SQL queries that were not intended to be executed by the original application. This could result in brute-force password guessing, identity forgery, and other exploits associated with a database.

- *Cross-site scripting* (XSS) refers to an attack in which malicious scripts are injected into an unsuspecting user, allowing the attacker access to sensitive information capable of modifying the content on the website.

- *Cross-site request forgery* (CRSF) is an attack in which an authenticated end user is forced to execute unwanted actions on the web application (or SaaS application), resulting in compromise of the end user data. If the administrator account is compromised, the website could be completely under the attacker's control.

- Stolen credentials are a type of attack that leverages insufficient authentication or authorization enforced on the servers.

- (Distributed) DoS attacks overload a service with a number of requests such that the service cannot distinguish between legitimate traffic and attacks and thus stalls the service.

With dynamic, rich, media-based applications becoming the trend, the number of web transactions has substantially increased, often blurring the distinction between an attack and legitimate traffic. This necessitates more robust security architecture in the application tier. Moreover, if these applications are cloud enabled (that is, virtualized and distributed), the complexity of the security architecture increases linearly or exponentially. Figure 6-7 shows an example of a complex rich-media client application and the vulnerability points.

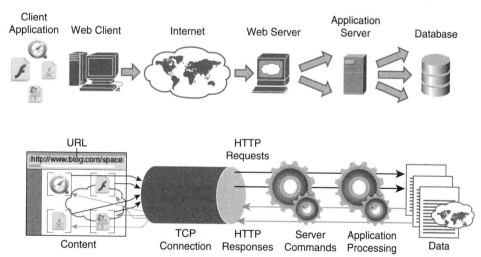

Figure 6-7 *Rich-Media Web Application*

Figure 6-7 illustrates the various states of data in a web transaction. Data is generated in the client application transferred via a web client using a network connection to a database maintained by the application server. The web server defines a process to store and retrieve the data. More generically, data exists in one of the states: in use, in flight, and at rest. You must understand each of these states to be able to create a security strategy around them; for example, you need to authenticate source data, you need to encrypt data in flight, and you need to secure stationary data.

A cloud-enabled application usually includes all the elements in Figure 6-7 in a virtualized and distributed environment. Although it might seem that providing a security mechanism could be a more complex task for a cloud-enabled application, cloud enablement can actually create an intelligent distribution process for an application. Security itself should be an intrinsic layer that can be attached and can shadow the real application and the overall web transaction itself.

Design Considerations for Securing Multitenant Data Centers

The data center design depends largely on the applications hosted in the data center. Similarly, the security design strategy depends on the applications hosted in the data center. These applications are categorized into relevant industry verticals such as healthcare, finance, e-commerce, and any Internet business that requires storage of customer information that includes credit cards, health records, and other confidential information. Storage of this information for conducting business with the customer is usually not, by itself, a threat. However, if this information is stolen or shared with business partners without proper authorization, there is a breach of trust and security of the customer information. The sections that follow provide a few examples of possible threats to information and the relevant techniques that you can use to secure the information.

Threat: Identity Theft

Bill Thor decides to apply for an ASIV credit card via Bells Dargo Bank. The bank requests that Bill provide his personal information, including name, date of birth, address, and Social Security number. Once the online account is set up, Bill has a credit line of up to $100,000. Bill decides to make his first purchase using the card at an online store—Fraudheaven—and makes a payment for $500. Bill is happy with the ease of shopping and is lost in his daily routine. When Bill gets his first month's bill, he gets a rude shock when he sees the amount he owes to the bank is $50,000 (in addition to the $500). Bill calls the bank and asks about the charges to his account. The bank tells him that the $50,000 charge came from a luxury vacation resort in Bali. Bill is dumbfounded. He has been working hard for the past month to meet deadlines at work, and a vacation was out of the question. Clearly, Bill is a victim of identity theft, and his personal information with the bank was compromised.

What really happened was that there was an online attack on the Fraudheaven service, and information (names, dates of birth, and addresses) of around 5 percent of the customers was stolen. Bill was one of those unfortunate customers. A closer inspection of the data center that hosted Fraudheaven's website reveals that it was not *Payment Card Industry-Data Security Standard* (PCI DSS) compliant. Therefore, a hacker compromises the web application with ease and stole vital information from Fraudheaven's service.

Solution: PCI DSS Compliance

Understanding the payment transaction process will enable you to recognize vulnerabilities and mitigations to such.

Figure 6-8 illustrates a typical credit card transaction. Although each entity listed in the figure could be a separate institution, to enable a secured transaction each entity is required to be PCI DSS compliant. Each entity could be running different applications to service their clients on hardware from different vendors. When a cardholder makes an online purchase, the transaction involves sharing the cardholder data with each of the entities until the issuing bank approves the payment.

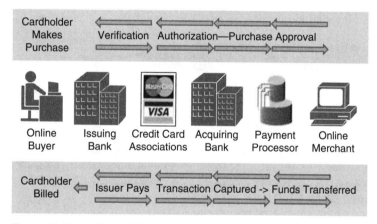

Figure 6-8   *A Typical Payment Transaction Process*

The *Payment Card Industry Security Standards Council* (PCI SSC) issues a PCI DSS every 3 years to enhance the security and integrity of customer information that is stored or processed by merchants (such as Fraudheaven), payment card issuing banks (Bells Dargo Bank), processors (ASIV), and developers (Fraudheaven's web application for online purchases). The PCI DSS defines best practices to provide isolation, encryption, and monitoring tools to protect the customer information during any payment card transaction.

Note   The current version of PCI DSS is 2.0.

As Figure 6-9 illustrates, the PCI SSC has defined three scopes of requirements to ensure a secure payment transaction: the payment card, devices, applications, and infrastructure. *PCI PIN Transaction Security* (PCI PTS) defines security requirements on the characteristics and management of devices used in the protection of cardholder PINs and other payment processing activities. *Payment Application Data Security Standard* (PA DSS) defines application security requirements used to initiate or process a payment transaction. PCI DSS defines security requirements of the infrastructure that hosts the application and website of the service provider.

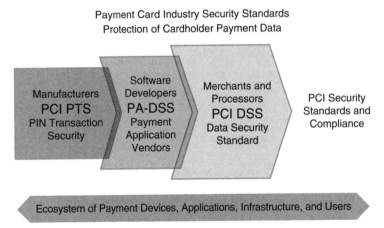

Figure 6-9   *Scope of PCI-DSS*

Securing hardware and applications is critical, but it is still incomplete without appropriate user security. Some discipline and policies on the user front, such as storing of payment card numbers and details on a nonsecure device, not changing online passwords regularly, not logging out from websites, and so on, are examples of user-driven security holes that can only be restricted but not eliminated by a system. Table 6-1 outlines the goals and requirements set by PCI DSS for infrastructure.

Table 6-1 *PCI DSS Goals and Requirements*

Goals	PCI DSS Requirements
Build and maintain a secure network	Implement a process to validate security configurations on network devices periodically.
	Deny traffic from all untrusted networks and hosts, except for cardholder access.
	Use personal firewalls on mobile and employee computers with connectivity to the Internet.
	Prohibit access to the system components directly from the Internet.
	Use nonstandard or vendor-supplied passwords.
	Encrypt administrative access, including web-based management tools.
Protect cardholder data	Limit the time for which cardholder data is stored.
	Prohibit storage of authentication data even if encrypted.
	Mask PIN when displayed.
	Document, implement, and protect all cryptographic keys and encryption procedures in the infrastructure, including the network.
Maintain a vulnerability management program	Apply and regularly update security patches on system components and antivirus software.
	Implement a process to regularly update new security vulnerabilities information.
	Secure web applications using protection mechanisms and secure coding guidelines.
Implement strong access control measures	Restrict access to the cardholder data by business need to know.
	Assign a unique user ID for each individual with computer access.
	Restrict physical access to cardholder data.
Regularly monitor and test networks	Track and monitor all access to network resources and cardholder data.
	Regularly test security systems and processes.
Maintain an information security policy	Maintain a policy to address information security for employees and contractors.

Operational Challenges

Security policies included in PCI DSS are not exclusive to payment card transactions, but they provide a benchmark for secured infrastructure for transaction processing. As previously stated, PCI defines security requirements for storing and using customer information and also includes the hardware and applications involved in the payment transactions. While security mechanisms are in a perpetual catch-up mode with new types of attacks and threats, it is imperative that a periodic security audit of the infrastructure be done to update the security policies and strategy.

Compliance with PCI standards is a complex and involved task and requires substantial effort to implement and maintain PCI-compliant business models. The PCI organization provides some guidelines to help businesses with implementation and maintenance of the PCI compliance. First, depending on the number of transactions, there are four levels of compliance. The higher the number of transactions, the more stringent compliance checks required. Second, PCI provides a list of approved companies and providers—*Qualified Security Assessors* (QSA), *Payment Application Qualified Security Assessors* (PA-QSA), *Approved Scanning Vendors* (ASV), *Internal Security Assessors* (ISA) and *PCI Forensic Investigators* (PFI)—to assist businesses with the compliance requirements. Figure 6-10 depicts the areas of PCI addressed and qualified with third-party approved vendors within this architecture.

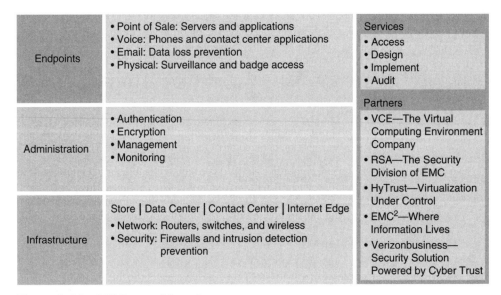

Figure 6-10 *PCI Scope of Security*

As shown in Figure 6-10, the PCI security objectives apply to every piece of hardware and software used in the business premises and can therefore easily add to the operating expenditure (OpEx) and capital expenditure (CapEx) of the business.

Penalties

Complying with PCI security standards is not only a security measure; its violation could result in penalties from the payment card issuing authority to the bank, which ultimately gets passed on to the merchant. This could result in increased transaction fees or a lump-sum penalty of up to $200,000. In addition, noncompliance could affect the trust between the service providers and prove detrimental to the business. Therefore, investment in PCI DSS compliance can help create a successful long-term business model for the customers as well as business partners.

How the Cloud Model Can Help

The cloud model brings in an element of virtualization and distribution to the architecture that enables instantiation of the PCI DSS workflow. This means that you can instantiate the functions defined in the PCI DSS-compliant workflow on any virtualization-aware hardware and thus inherit the distributed scale properties typical of a cloud model. Besides this, if the functions can be exported to a public cloud that is PCI DSS compliant, much of the CapEx costs involved can be controlled without affecting the service when an occasional increase in demand is required—usually seasonal sales events, mobile sales enablement, temporary point-of-sales, and so on.

In the example, Fraudheaven could use a PCI DSS-compliant cloud service to deliver security and integrity to its customers while having options to integrate with other compliant cloud vendors to scale rapidly. If Fraudheaven could actually regain a reputation for their security services, they could offer their own PCI DSS-compliant infrastructure services, thus opening new revenue opportunities.

Information Confidentiality

Cloud service providers usually collect and generate information based on the services rendered to their clients. The healthcare industry is a typical example where patient information is collected and the patient health records are generated. These records often include intimate and private information about the medical conditions of a patient. This information is shared with essential people and organizations, including doctors, nurses, billing clerks, specialists, and so on, but it is still important to protect the confidentiality and privacy of the patient. These records—*personal health records* (PHR)—are usually stored as paper documents or an electronic document (*electronic health records*). The *Health Insurance Portability and Accountability Act* (HIPAA) defines methods to secure these records and restrict the information that can be shared without compromising privacy. HIPAA is implemented as policies regulating the information exchange between elements of the information systems defined for medical institutions; for example, *hospital information systems* (HIS). Figure 6-11 outlines the reference architecture for the HIS.

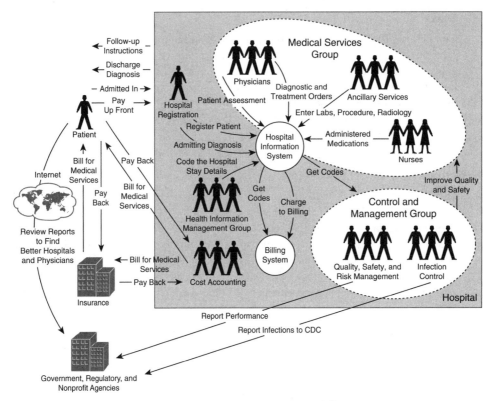

Figure 6-11   *Hospital Information System Business Workflow*

Figure 6-11 depicts a typical flow of patient information from the time of admission to discharge, and all the processes in between. Every time a patient signs the consent form at the time of admission to a healthcare facility, he agrees to the exchange of information between the different entities that are involved in delivering the healthcare service. Not all the entities in the figure access the same type of information, but HIPAA lays down the specific information elements that "should" be shared to complete the specific process. In this way, HIPAA defines security and privacy rules for consumers and covered entities.

Implementation of these rules requires a framework that you can implement in software so that the health information management systems can have a common interface to exchange information. HL7-international is an organization that standardizes these interactions between the healthcare workflows.

As Figure 6-12 illustrates, several messaging standards apply to the health information systems and the various entities of the healthcare chain.

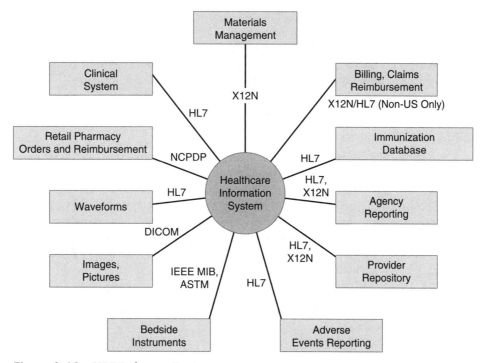

Figure 6-12 *HL7 Reference Design*

Similarly, there are policies and rules defined for the underlying infrastructure to securely host the health information systems. HIPAA, along with HITECH Act, defines the guidelines for securing the infrastructure and the tools used for exchanging the patient records. Network security requirements under HIPAA require organizations to employ data encryption, firewall protection, and email protection as a means of protecting confidential patient information. Further, the HITECH Act advises organizations to implement data encryption technology within their networks. Firewall protection requirements are designed to prevent the likelihood of a system security breach. Email security requirements, though partially handled by a reliable firewall system, can further be secured through encryption software.

To prevent unauthorized access to PHR, network system requirements under HIPAA mandate the use of a medical billing system that provides a standardized method for recording services rendered and transacting patient billing information between health-related organizations and third-party payers. Organizations handling patient information are also required to maintain updated patient authorization forms that permit organizations to store, record, and transmit patient information. In terms of patients being able to gain access to their own records, HIPAA requires organizations to take measures to ensure patient information is available in the event of a fire or a system failure. Compliance with this provision requires organizations to have a reliable backup system capable of storing patient information and recovering lost data. Finally, the organization needs to implement an auditing system that allows monitoring of the information flow of a patient record offline. To do this, the network is required to define role-based access for any entity that needs to access the patient information. In addition, a role-based user-level access control on the patient record is required to avoid unnecessary exposure of the patient records to the entities.

Operational Challenges

The *hospital information system* (HIS) is a complex architecture that involves information flow based on service rendered by different operational units within the hospital. Figure 6-12 captures the protocols used in the information workflow management of a patient's case. For every hospital to implement the HIS, involving a hardware qualification process would drive up CapEx and OpEx costs, and maintaining and upgrading the infrastructure to the latest standards would become prohibitive. Besides, it is very difficult to control the confidentiality of the patient information if multiple business partners of the hospital render services.

HIPAA compliance encompasses training of the personnel using the system to feed or pass information; however, this is a mandatory and standardized process for any certified medical practitioner.

Penalties

HIPAA violations and noncompliance could lead to penalties in the range of $100 to $1.5 million depending on the severity and frequency of the violations. This is detrimental to the hospital and its partners' business. In addition, the risk of knowingly or unknowingly exposing patient information to irrelevant parties could jeopardize patient privacy.

How the Cloud Model Can Help

The cloud model can simplify and centralize a HIPAA-compliant HIS using a public cloud service model. A public cloud service model delivers a data-centric approach, wherein the user-information is stored in the public cloud and is accessible by authorized medical professionals via a service policy configured in the HIS. If the patient chooses to change the service provider or is transferred to another facility, the policy model enables the patient to make the necessary choices. Privacy and confidentiality of this patient information need to be maintained at the cloud service provider even though the healthcare providers for this patient changed.

The cloud model involves creating instances of the HIS that can be customized for each hospital-specific workflow and adding services (security and extranet with other service providers) to create a differentiated model based on the specific services rendered by a hospital. As an additional benefit, a single type of attack cannot bring down all HIS instances if the services models vary considerably. You can encrypt the patient information using a storage-as-a-service type of distributed model to create a resilient HIS architecture.

Besides the security requirements previously discussed, other considerations while designing a secure data center include the following:

- **Degree of confidentiality:** Customer information generated as part of service delivery is for the most part relevant to the workflow of a specific service provider. A service provider usually partners with other service providers to offer a complete service package to its customers. This requires the service provider to share relevant customer information with its partners. So, the information system of the service provider needs to have policies in place to regulate the access to customer data for its business partners. These policies need to provide time-based access and limits to the data retention to ensure that the customer data cannot be compromised. This defines the degree of confidentiality between a customer and the primary service provider.

- **Span of control and accountability:** Storing and sharing of customer data is inherently a security risk. The cloud service provider is responsible for the security and integrity of the customer data that is retained to deliver the service and for the duration of the service. A security strategy enables the service provider some control over customer data against known threats. A first step toward securing the customer data is to define *role-based access control* (RBAC) profiles and maintain records of the workflow followed by the specific user. This enables the service provider to audit how the data was accessed and back trace any security breaches if they happen.

- **System performance:** Deploying a security strategy or complying with any of the regulations (PCI, HIPAA, *Graham-Leach-Bliley Act* [GLBA]) requires a lot of traffic inspection and treatment depending on criteria defined. Traffic inspection and treatment requires multiple memory lookups and processing at the packet level, which increases the latency and *quality of service* (QoS) metrics, thus affecting the system performance. To optimize the system performance while not compromising security, QoS profiles associated with the RBACs should be predefined so that the appropriate resources can be dedicated to meet system SLAs.

- **Intranet and extranet:** Business expansion, consolidation, and mergers usually involve consolidating compute, storage, and network (and services) resources such that additional resources are made available to the business as a whole. This requires extending the segmentations used across the data centers where the resources reside, also called an intranet. Similarly, integrating business partners within the workflow requires exposing relevant resources to the partner infrastructure to conduct business seamlessly, also called an extranet. Each of these examples requires sharing network information in a secure manner so as to allow service/application interaction. You should implement these controls in the intranet and extranet based on the trust models between the peering entities.

How Virtual Security Is Enabled: Solutions and Architectures-Based Approach

As discussed earlier, security traces the entire workflow of a business, and therefore it is imperative to understand the workflow elements and the data transition states to be able to secure the data in each stage. The first section of this chapter described a typical workflow implemented in most enterprises and businesses, which is a web-based application with a number of components delivering a service/application portfolio. Broadly, these components include storage, compute, network (including services), and data transition states (static, in flight).

Security has evolved over the years, and many solutions are available today to counter threats to a data center. Virtualization enables security to be mobile, portable, and omnipresent, thus arming the data center with the necessary tools and knobs to be able to counter any threat. Multilayered elastic security architecture can be quickly enabled to provide a robust and timely defense against even the most brutal attacks.

The sections that follow look at the current security solutions available and their evolution to address a virtualized data center.

Traditional Security Approaches as Applied in Virtual Environment

Current implementations of security assume an appliance-based model collocated within the network where virtual infrastructure is deployed. Security policies are managed and applied at different points in the network to secure the data center. This approach separates the management domain of security from the network layers while enabling an integrated forwarding plane, which allows a flexible and dynamic definition of the security policy and scope.

Security Containers: Contexts and Zones

Security appliances use contexts/zones to partition the appliance resources to deliver multiple security functions. These functions could define a multilayer security design or multitenant security contexts or define trusted and untrusted zones. These containers provide the necessary separation in a virtualized multitenant environment and the guarantees required to build robust security layers.

Segmentation and Access Control Lists

Segmentation usually defines separation used within a container to identify path, trust zone, and multilayer separation. Segmentation can be implemented in Layer 2 (dot1q, q-in-q, PBB) or Layer 3 (VRF, MPLS) or overlays (VXLAN, NVGRE). Choice of segmentation depends on application and scale requirements.

Access control lists (ACL) define network security policies. These security policies can then be used to perform an action, including QoS—queuing, policing, shaping, dropping traffic; *policy-based routing* (PBR); *control plane policing* (CoPP); and more generically securing control and data planes.

Secured Access

Secured access can be broken down into multiple layers, including access to the data center, storage, and servers. This includes securing the edges of the network connecting to the Internet and other private domains such as extranet and server farms. IPsec and SSL are some of the most popular protocols used to secure the network layer. Storage security is usually implemented as an encryption technology that secures the data stored and physical separation of the interfaces serving data networks and storage networks.

Application Security

Applications used in an enterprise environment often include productivity and collaboration tools, email, and web services. To secure these applications, you must understand the semantics of the protocol stacks used by these applications, to differentiate between authorized and unauthorized flows generated. Application and content signature identification is a major task in determining whether the application is authentic or compromised. Special appliances perform these tasks to identify potentially harmful content or application. These appliances can scan email and websites for viruses, malware, phishing sites, and other well-known threats that can cause serious issues in an enterprise network. Once these are detected, the appliances enable a configurable action to be taken, such as quarantining the infected host, throttling the bandwidth or QoS, or redirecting the traffic to a more intelligent device to further analyze the harmful content or application pattern.

Virtual Appliance Approach

The traditional security model does not address the requirements of a cloud-enabled data center because the capabilities of the appliance limits its applicability at scale and varying environments (for example, PCI, HIPAA, GLBA). Moreover, multitenant security requirements can vary so drastically as to void a single model of implementation. It is intuitive to devise a virtualized security model to mimic the characteristics of a virtualized application or instance to address the cloud-enabled application requirements. A virtualized approach not only allows the capability to port current security implementation to a virtualized environment but also adds additional security capabilities instantly.

The following sections describe some of the products currently available that enable virtual appliance-based security solutions. Nexus 1000v is the base platform on which Cisco virtual *Adaptive Security Appliance* (ASA) and Cisco *Virtual Security Gateway* (VSG) are enabled. So, a quick overview of Cisco Nexus 1000v follows.

Nexus 1000v (N1kv) is primarily a virtual switch that enables communication between VMs. It also enables services insertion and chaining in the data path using vPath. Figure 6-13 illustrates an N1kv model.

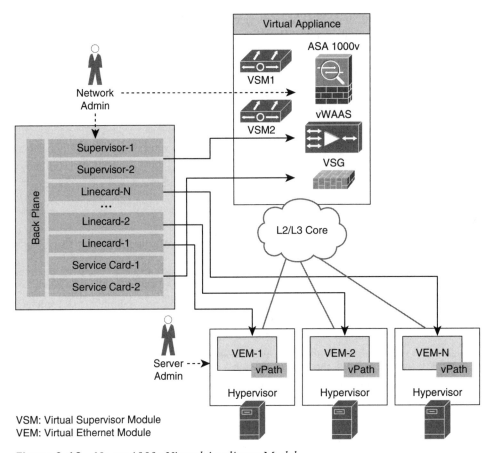

Figure 6-13   *Nexus 1000v Virtual Appliance Model*

As Figure 6-13 illustrates, N1kv can be considered an equivalent of a modular switch. *Virtual Supervisor Modules* (VSM) and a *Virtual Ethernet Module* (VEM) in the N1kv are the equivalent of a supervisor engine and linecards or service modules in a modular switch. vPath integrates Layer 2–7 services to the VEM forwarding logic. vPath is the protocol between service nodes and the N1kv that caches logic to service packets on the VEM as it were on the service nodes. This allows simplicity in deployment, capacity planning, and administrative tasks.

Cisco ASA1000v Tenant Edge Security Solution

ASA appliances offer a feature-rich security platform to protect the network access to data center services or enterprise resources. The challenge posed by a cloud-enabled infrastructure is multitenant capability across physical and virtual environments, scaled-out architecture, and simplicity of management. ASA 1000v is a virtual security appliance that enables the same functionalities as a physical appliance.

Figure 6-14 illustrates a security solution based on the Cisco Nexus 1000v virtual appliances. The ASA 1000v provides edge security capabilities, including IPsec VPN, NAT, DHCP, default gateway, static routing, stateful inspection, and IP audit.

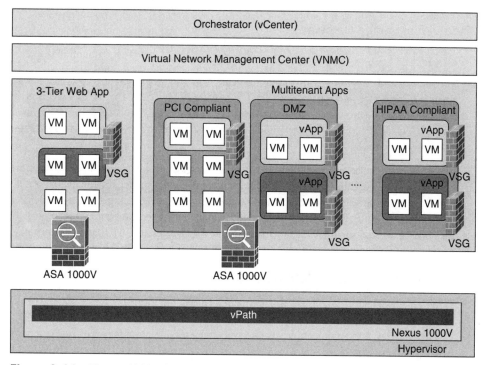

Figure 6-14   *Nexus 1000v Security Architecture*

The main components illustrated in Figure 6-14 are described as follows:

- **Virtual Network Management Center (VNMC):** A centralized management plane. Its functions include security policy management, vCenter integration, and a northbound API. It can manage multiple service devices or appliances and is multitenant aware.

- **Virtual service node:** A distributed service plane. It can maintain the runtime state of the service, service processing (policy engine), and stateful firewall. It can run multiple instances of the same service or a single instance spanning multiple hosts.

- **vPath:** The distributed forwarding plane embedded in the virtual switch (Nexus1000V). It intercepts and redirects the initial traffic to the service node. Once the service node performs its security policy lookup function, the result is cached in the vPath for that flow, and the local virtual switch module treats the subsequent packets accordingly.

This approach optimizes the forwarding path such that irrespective of how many services are to be applied to the traffic there is a single pass via the vPath rather than traffic being punted sequentially to each service appliance.

Cisco Virtual Secure Gateway

Cisco Nexus1000V *Virtual Security Gateway* (VSG) is Cisco's zone firewall. When combined with edge firewall (Cisco Nexus 1000v ASA), this is another approach to address the firewall and admission control requirements in virtual deployments. VSG enables insertion of service in the path of the traffic to/from VMs. Thus, the traffic flow is not hair-pinned via the service node, but rather the resultant decision is cached on the virtual switch (such as Cisco Nexus1000V). This model enables introduction of any service into the forwarding path.

VSG enables rules based on network such as IP address and application (TCP/UDP) port number and VM attributes such as instance name, guest OS name, zone name, parent app name, port-profile name, cluster name, or hypervisor name. The scope of these rules can be defined using RBAC, allowing strict control over the servers and hosts that these policies can be applied to.

Deployment Considerations

Deployment of security architecture is dictated by the requirements being addressed; for example, compliance with a security standard (including PCI DSS, HIPAA, GLBA, Sarbanes-Oxley, and so on), enterprise security, and service provider security. Depending on the business workflow, there could be a need to enable communication between one and more of these security zones. Within the cloud-enabled data center, the processes between applications and storage need to be secured so that multitiered applications such as web-based applications are secured at each tier.

Virtual data center defines an instance of the tenant business/process workflow. Security in the virtual data center involves securing the following:

- **Access to the virtual data center:** This secures the perimeter of the virtual data center and includes authentication and encryption of sessions from the Internet to the virtual data center. IPsec- or SSL-based VPN access are the options considered for access via Internet. In hybrid cloud models, VPNs (Layer 2/3) extended from the enterprise data center provide the secured access. A firewall instance defines the security policy rules for protecting the data center resources.

- **Communication between the different tiers of the application:** Usually an application defines the exact flow from one application tier to the other. Creating rules to enable the authentic flows and block the others maximizes resource utilization and *Federal Information Processing Standard* (FIPS) compliance when required.

- **Storage security:** Securing storage differs substantially from network security and primarily includes separating storage paths, zoning, and encrypting the data on storage devices. Zoning provides security on top of path separation by restricting the devices accessible from the hosts. Encryption provides confidentiality to the user data. In a cloud-enabled data center, one of the important properties that a security framework needs to support is mobility (application or VMs). This implies that the security policies and rules need to move with the application or the VM.

- **Multitenant firewall:** When the business workflow includes partners, the security strategy needs to extend beyond the tenant virtual data center. Moreover, some security gateway function needs to enable compliance with the partner security framework. This is enabled again by a firewall, which defines security policy rules that allow authorized flows and block others. These firewalls usually need to be aware of sessions (such as HTTP, SIP, video) and be able to perform some amount of policing on confidential data crossing the borders. These policies, along with access control, based on the role would restrict the exposure of the data center resources and content from outside its domain.

- **Data leakage protection (DLP):** As mentioned earlier in this chapter, data exists in one of three states:

  - *Data at rest* refers to stored data (usually via a database application). Examples include credit card numbers, Social Security numbers, and insurance records, to name a few, stored in a database.

  - *Data in flight* refers to data being transported over a network. This is usually an HTTP session, TCP/UDP port, or source/destination IP addresses. Examples include raw data being transported via an email application or data snippets shared via an instant messaging application;

  - *Data in use* refers to an endpoint (a client application) accessing or processing data. This refers to copying or duplicating sensitive data in a user-generated document and storing it in an untrusted device such as a USB drive.

  Raw data is usually wrapped in layers of protocol encapsulations spanning the seven layers of the OSI model. Besides these encapsulations, a software stack could have its own encapsulations too. This implies that a data loss/leakage protection strategy requires components that are capable of deep packet inspection with a scope defined by the data state as defined earlier.

  A DLP solution ideally analyzes context (protocol wrappers) and the content (raw data) and uses tools in the network, storage, and compute layers to plug data leakage or loss. Contextual analysis usually includes evaluating the following:

  - File ownership and permissions

  - Use of encrypted file formats or network protocols

- User role and business unit (through directory integration)

- Specific web services (such as known webmail providers and social networking sites)

- Web addresses (not just the session content)

- USB device information, such as manufacturer or model number

- The desktop application in use (for example, something copied from an Office document and then pasted into an encryption tool)

Content analysis uses one or more of the following techniques:

- **Rules based or regular expression:** A simple technique used to search for simple strings or digits such as credit card numbers, medical billing codes, and other textual analyses.

- **Database fingerprinting:** A slightly more complex technique used for exact matches on a combination of data. This technique uses policies to define multiple match criteria with the ability to restrict the scope of the search.

- **Document matching:** A technique used for unstructured content or sensitive data within a document. Unauthorized copy or duplicating of this content onto a USB drive or sharing it over an instant message is monitored and blocked.

- **Statistical analysis:** A technique used to detect policy violations in a huge number of documents (for example, marketing plans and engineering specification documents) that resembles the protected content.

- **Lexicon:** A complex technique that tries to analyze content and protect a concept or an idea. This is done using a combination of dictionaries rules and policies.

- **Predefined categories:** A set of predefined rules and dictionaries for common data types such as credit card numbers, medical billing codes used in PCI and HIPAA, and other such categories. Because these are predefined, compliant infrastructure can easily provide protection for customer-sensitive data.

Each of these specialized techniques could be delivered over a cloud as a service, thus enabling the customer to build a best-of-breed security solution for their data center. Examples of these services include DLP for email, content discovery, and DLP for web filtering. Each of these examples uses some agent in the customer data center to scan or discover content (in case of email) and match with a central dictionary and rules that define treatment of suspect content.

- **Zones:** Virtual data centers use zones to define logical domains within a data center. These logical domains could represent trusted-untrusted communication boundaries or application boundaries. Communication boundaries are typically deployed via DMZ policies. Application boundaries are deployed using firewalls and security gateways.

Summary

Security is one of the most important services of any data center architecture. An understanding of business and application workflows is key in designing a security framework. In a cloud-enabled data center, you can use predefined instances to provision security-compliant (PCI DSS, HIPAA, GLBA, SOX, and so on) frameworks. Virtualizing the services enables a multitenant-capable security deployment model while retaining VM characteristics such as mobility, elasticity, and manageability.

Because the nature of an attack is largely unknown, a good security strategy is one that can evolve over time. A cloud security model makes such an evolution possible and provides a plug-in type solution, while keeping operations simple. Finally, security of data in its three states—at rest, in motion, and in use—is of paramount importance to protect and guard a service.

Review Questions

1. Which of the following are known attacks on an application?

    a. TCP/IP Syn attack
    b. Web client spoofing
    c. Wiretapping
    d. Root password hacking

2. Which of the following could be penalties of not complying with PCI DSS?

    a. Fines up to $200,000
    b. Imprisonment
    c. Exile
    d. Permanent ban from Internet access

3. HIPAA compliance is to protect user data in which of the following?

    a. Hospital and medical systems
    b. Financial institutes dealing with the stock market
    c. Enterprise cloud-enabled systems
    d. Service providers dealing with hospital business

4. VMware vShield suite includes which of the following?

    a. Network security
    b. NAT
    c. Application security
    d. Load balancers

References

- Payment Card Industry PIN Transaction Security (PCI PTS): https://www.pcisecuritystandards.org/approved_companies_providers/approved_pin_transaction_security.php

- Payment Application Data Security Standard (PA-DSS): https://www.pcisecuritystandards.org/security_standards/index.php

- Cisco compliance solution for PCI-DSS 2.0 design and implementation guide: http://www.cisco.com/en/US/docs/solutions/Enterprise/Compliance/Compliance_DIG/Compliance_DIG.html

- Data Loss Prevention: http://www.cisco.com/en/US/netsol/ns895/index.html

- Secure data center solution: http://www.cisco.com/en/US/netsol/ns340/ns394/ns224/ns376/index.html

- HER related healthcare solutions: http://www.cisco.com/en/US/products/hw/vpndevc/services.html

Chapter 7

Application Performance Optimization

In this chapter, you learn about the following:

- Application architectures and performance in the cloud

- Strategies for managing application performance

- Cloud model challenges and application delivery

Application performance is a measure of the response time of the application. The response time depends on proximity and bandwidth attributes of the transport channel used to access the application. *Application layer traffic optimization* (ALTO), as covered in the "Network Positioning System" section of Chapter 10, standardizes the framework and the protocols to optimize application performance across the Internet. This chapter explores methods used to optimize the transport protocol and thus render a geographically consistent user experience.

Research has shown that aside from security, application performance is one of the biggest concerns of a cloud model and would influence an organization's decisions as to whether to adopt the cloud model. Reasons for this include customer experience (primarily) along with automation of complex operational tasks, quicker turnaround of customer issues, and *service level agreement* (SLA) measurement capability. Enterprises have realized the significance of application performance in maintaining business metrics and hence success.

Imagine the following scenarios: on-time arrival of flights with greater than 99% accuracy, the operations teams on the trade floor resolving trouble tickets within short time frames (15 to 30 minutes), a single tool to manage application performance that can be extended to private or hybrid cloud models. All these scenarios illustrate some of the requirements, with no clear solutions, that enterprises experience with application performance.

To influence application performance, it is important to understand the interactions within and between applications in greater detail. This implies an understanding of the business logic and process. After that, tools to monitor and derive analytics to create quantifiable actions aimed at influencing application performance can be used. This, in turn, improves the end-user experience.

What are the application tiers and the interactions? What are the monitoring and analytical tools available to measure and benchmark the application performance? How does this in turn affect the end-to-end SLAs described in Chapter 12? The rest of this chapter answers these questions.

Application Architectures in the Cloud

Typical enterprise applications are productivity or sales tools that enable business processes. These applications include email and calendar services; collaboration tools, including wiki, video/audio conferences, and instant messaging; business applications, including *enterprise resource planning* (ERP), CRM and HR applications; engineering applications, including terminal services, *Network File System* (NFS), shell, *File Transfer Protocol* (FTP); and other web applications, including Internet and intranet/extranet access.

All the office and collaboration applications in the preceding list are multitiered applications. Multitiered applications enable a task-oriented approach to solve complex business or service requirements. Each tier assumes a certain role and responsibility, thus creating an end-to-end workflow. The workflow ultimately delivers a service that fuels a business. A three-tier architecture is one of the most common implementations of a multitier architecture. This is easily illustrated by an email service. The first tier (client) provides the front end to the user. The user can view email via this front end, which could be a special desktop client or the web interface. The middle tier is where the application server is instantiated. The application defines specific *application programming interfaces* (API) for the client to access the email. The application server also performs necessary authentication and security checks to make sure that the receiver is authorized to receive the content. In addition, the content being viewed is checked for any viruses or worms that could potentially compromise the service itself. Finally, the database tier is where the content resides. The database creates keys to enable the application tier to sort, search, and retrieve data relevant to a specific user.

The key to enable communication between all these tiers is the network fabric and the protocols used to exchange data. Table 7-1 lists some of the most commonly used enterprise applications and the transport protocol used for client-server communication.

Table 7-1 *Transport Protocols for Commonly Used Enterprise Applications*

	Application	Transport Protocol (Port Number)
Office	Mail (SMTP)	TCP (dynamic port, 25)
	LDAP	TCP/UDP (389)
	IMAP4	TCP (143)
	POP3	TCP (110)
	DNS replication	UDP (53)
	CIFS	TCP (149, 445)
Collaboration	WebEx	TCP (1270), HTTP(80)
	VNC	TCP (5900–5906)
	Terminal Services	TCP/UDP (3389)
	SIP	TCP/UDP 5060/5061
	Jabber	TCP 5222/5223
	RTP	TCP/UDP 5004/5005
Business	Business continuity software	TCP (10566)
	DB server	TCP/UDP (3180, 1433)
	NFS	UDP (2049)
	SSH	TCP (22)
	Shell	TCP (514)
	FTP	TCP (20)
	Internet/intranet	TCP (80, 8080, 443, 911)

It is evident that most of the applications use TCP/UDP to access the service. This table reflects the transport used by the client tier to access the application or service. Because the application performance depends primarily on the user perception of the responsiveness of the application, it is an important layer to optimize, to deliver immediate performance improvement.

The following sections explain in more detail the characteristics of the three-tier architecture and the methods to optimize the transport between the tiers to improve application performance as a whole.

Three-Tier App Architecture in the Virtualized World

Virtualization within a data center supports instantiation of any service on demand, which is a powerful concept. It fuels innovative designs customized for applications without redesigning the infrastructure. One of the most widely deployed application models is the three-tier web application wherein the client and database tiers are standardized and the application tier is where business services are created.

Note in Figure 7-1 the multiple attachment-points between the tiers; these are ideal candidates for security policies and standards. Depending on the protocol used or data exchanged between the tiers, protocol security or data security policies need to be implemented to protect the service. Besides security, the three-tier model also enables an independent capacity modeling for each tier to best cater to the service requirements.

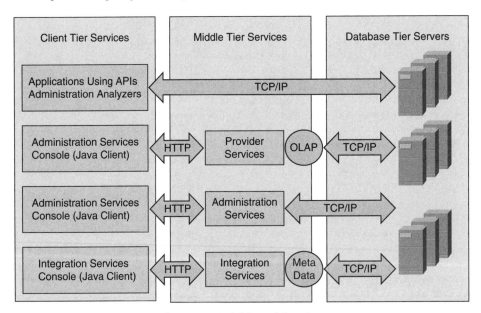

Figure 7-1   *Three-Tier Application Model Based Service*

You can simplify the three-tier application design shown in Figure 7-1 by using different network models depending on the scale and application design requirements. The application tier defines the network services required to be inserted in the path of the data flow, and this determines whether the network services are attached in a tree or chain at each tier, as shown in Figure 7-2.

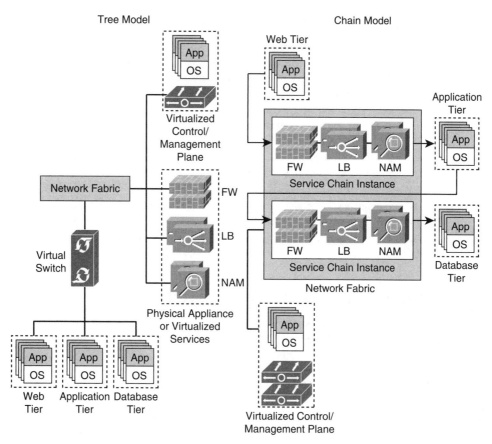

Figure 7-2 *Tree and Chain Models for Service Insertion*

The elements in both of the illustrated service insertion models in Figure 7-2 are the same and do not provide a cost benefit over each other. The major difference between each model is the flexibility in design and scale that can be engineered. In a tree model, the network fabric provides connectivity to the service instances (appliance or virtual), which does not require the services to coexist with the server instances (physical or virtual). The intelligence to route or switch the packet to service instances is enabled by a virtual switch (Cisco N1000v) using vPath, which provides a fast path for the flows generated by the application tiers. This model thus enables a scalable, ubiquitous, and elastic model that uses every resource available in the domain. In a chain model, the service chain is a pre-defined entity and is nailed down as the gateway for each of the tiers. This model enables a tight binding between the application tiers and the services, thus enabling a sin-gular, agile, and moveable entity.

Note *Fast path* refers to the data path taken by a packet without requiring CPU process-ing. Packets are processed outside the OS environment, thus avoiding the OS overheads and contributing to performance enhancement.

Provisioning and Management

As shown in Figure 7-2, there is a control and management plane that is not embedded in the data path. This enables offloading the non-data plane functions to a host that can be scaled and managed as a separate entity. Besides, this enables the control plane to be multitenant capable and customizable to drive the application tier requirements for each tenant. Therefore, the administrative and operational tasks can be separated out as separate instances without having to define complex policies. A port profile would effectively define the access and control scope for each management instance, allowing elasticity of the service. The control plane would also use a port profile concept to define the fast path in the virtual switch (Cisco N1000v) so that the flow does not follow a circuitous path via the services toward the destination. This implies that the virtual switch is service aware and can insert a service chain in the fast path. For example, if multiple tenants define a service chain that varies in order and number of service elements in the chain, the virtual switch can insert the services in the desired order and provide a service vector in the data path.

Application Performance in the Cloud

The multitude of applications supported by the IT group comes with its own set of challenges. Applications exhibit unique characteristics based on the software architecture used to build them. These characteristics can be categorized as follows:

- **Transport characteristics:** Bandwidth, congestion, latency, and packet loss deeply impact the application performance. A negative influence of either of these characteristics could lower the application throughput and result in a sluggish response and ultimately affect end-user productivity. This is especially true if the end user is located in a branch/remote office and is accessing applications hosted in the data center. Applications such as audio/video conferencing and real-time collaboration tools such as VNC and WebEx could drive the throughput requirements heavily.

  Throughput decreases as the distance or packet loss increases. Distance, along with the number of IP hops a packet traverses in its journey between a data center and the destination, affects the latency of a service hosted in the data center. For most traffic, a 1% packet loss in the transport could degrade the application performance by 50%. Similarly, as the distance between the application host and client increases, an exponential decrease in throughput occurs. Although some transport protocols are more resilient to these factors, it is important to understand how these attributes affect a particular application performance. So, there is a dependency on the type of transport used for a particular application. For example, a collaboration application could use HTTP/TCP to transport video-sharing and file-sharing or download capabilities. Packet loss and distance between source and destination could cause static video or slow downloads, thus affecting the overall performance of the collaboration application, as shown in Figure 7-3.

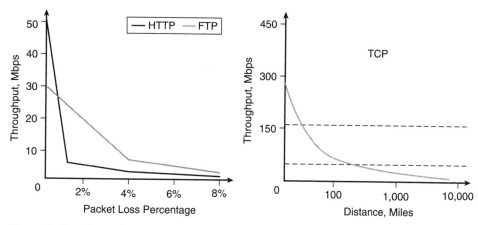

Figure 7-3   *Throughput, Distance, and Packet-Loss Correlation*

■ **Security and authentication:** Security and authentication is important not only to protect the application from attacks but also to sustain the quality of experience. An attack could be a hijack of resources, including network bandwidth or breaking the software stack that is used to host the application. A typical security strategy involves creating trusted and untrusted zones. In a trusted zone, the user device is controlled and managed by a predefined policy. In contrast, in an untrusted zone, the user device is an uncontrolled and unmanaged device. In an untrusted zone, maintaining the security and authentication state is an important security strategy and needs to be audited periodically. Lack of it could potentially create the effect of a security attack, such as *distributed denial of service* (DDoS), even though the user is legitimate.

Multilayered security design achieves the desired goals of minimizing and throttling the effects of an attack on the infrastructure and applications. A security architecture as shown in Figure 7-4 helps in defining a well-rounded security strategy for the data center.

■ **Client responsiveness:** Most applications are web based, but the media-rich clients such as audio, video, and collaboration accessing the back-end services (middleware and database) are predominantly transactions based and drive up the throughput and latency requirements. Applications such as a trading platform drive high-frequency content refresh cycles, which further adds stress to the application servers.

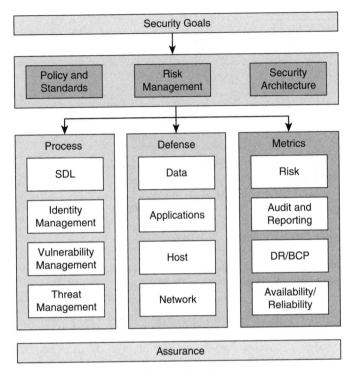

Figure 7-4 *Example of a Security Strategy*

- **Chatty applications and protocols:** Some applications, such as instant messaging, email, and conference tools, are chatty by nature, as illustrated in Figure 7-5. They need to exchange presence/state information at a high rate to just maintain steady state.

  A chatty application is characterized by the transactions a client or application uses to maintain steady state. The number of transactions an application requires has a direct impact on the amount of bandwidth required and on more stringent latency requirements.

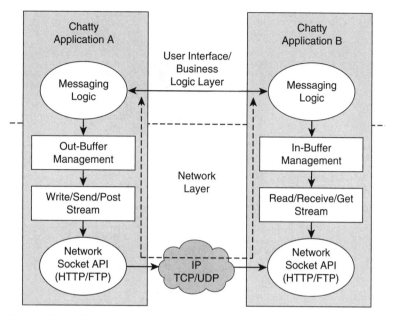

Figure 7-5 *Example of a Chatty Application*

■ **Remote/mobile clients:** Users are increasingly remote/mobile. This implies that they are constrained by bandwidth and latency limits available to a mobile device. Besides the constraints, the Internet introduces the hop-by-hop best-effort behavior, which adds to the latency and uncertainty of the *quality of service* (QoS) and security requirements of the application.

Figure 7-6 shows the elements responsible for the latency characteristics affecting the service/application performance. It illustrates the hop-by-hop best-effort behavior of the Internet. For example, a web page with multiple contents and objects may require as many transactions to load the web page. Depending on the content of an object, the throughput and latency requirements dictate the performance of the application or service.

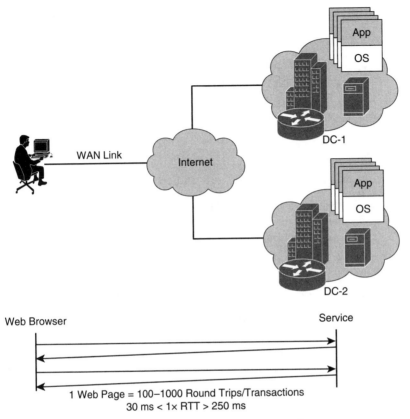

Figure 7-6   *Factors Affecting Application/Service Performance*

- **Regulation:** To maintain compliance with regional regulations posed by the state, the enterprise data centers might choose to consolidate their data center resources or move data centers between strategic locations. This could change the transport characteristics described previously or the resources available to do the same job. Federal and business regulations typically mandate security requirements that add to the overhead to processing and transport—significant factors affecting application and performance characteristics.

Although these characteristics are consistent between traditional and cloud deployments, their manifestation in each deployment varies. Whereas traditional data center deployments depend on distributed resources, cloud deployment is predominantly consolidated resources. This also means that bandwidth requirements in cloud deployments increase linearly with scale unless some optimizations are performed at each transport layer.

A cloud model leverages virtualization to enable an omnipresent service with proximity-based latency and throughput characteristics. The user experience with such a service could be consistent independent of the location or device.

Drivers for the Transition from Physical to Virtual Network Services

The decision-making process to plan for a transition from a physical to a virtualized network services model primarily depends on the cost savings, operational efficiencies, and resource optimizations achieved in a virtualized model. These benefits are realized via an agile, elastic, scalable, and multitenant-aware virtualized services model. The following sections elaborate on the critical factors that drive the transition from a physical model to a virtual model.

Virtualization Awareness

A cloud model predominantly assumes and builds on virtualized applications that have no dependency on the underlying hardware, but it does not advocate a forklift upgrade of infrastructure. It emphasizes virtualization awareness that enables reuse of an existing application-specific infrastructure to extend its services seamlessly to a virtualized environment. The following are some key tasks that must be considered when virtualizing applications and services:

- **Virtual interfaces:** The first change in transitioning from a physical to a virtualized environment is the presence of virtual interfaces. The challenge with virtual interfaces lies in using a segmentation strategy that enables separation of the forwarding paths equivalent to a physical interface. These segmentations could be Layer 2/ Layer 3 and need to be managed as a single entity via a simple management interface.

- **Fast-path capability:** One of the major benefits of the physical deployment model is its ability to perform optimizations and services in the path of the flow. In a virtualized environment, unless there are services inserted in a single pass, there will be oversubscription of interface bandwidth (clearly, at some point, a limiting factor to consolidate virtualized application tiers).

- **Policy-based provisioning:** Provisioning and managing virtual services could easily become a repetitive and tedious task considering the differing *command-line interfaces* (CLI) and troubleshooting logic followed by the different vendors. The success of transitioning into a virtualized model relies on simplifying the provisioning and management of these virtual services. A policy-based provisioning model that uses some form of an API could be the first step in simplifying the operations in a virtualized environment.

Agility, Elasticity

Applications are virtualized to consolidate the compute resources while enabling a dynamic environment where an application instance can scale and move across virtualized hardware. A network fabric enables the compute resources to scale seamlessly without impacting the service. In addition, network services such as load balancers, firewalls, and network analysis modules are integral to the application performance. Hence, to create a truly agile and elastic application, it is important to consider virtualizing or making the service layer virtualization aware. As shown in Figure 7-2, a tree or chain service model enables a virtualized service layer. This implies that the service layer when virtualized will be scalable, movable, and can be restarted just like an application.

Multitenancy

One major benefit of cloud-enabled data centers is their ability to enable multitenant environments. This means that one or more segmentation methods are used to group and bind together multiple tiers of an application. Network services such as load balancers, accelerators, and network analysis modules that contribute to the application performance need to be introduced in the fast path of the flow instead of using a hairpin model. This requires the network service appliances to be aware of the segmentation methods used. The segmentation used could be a combination of Layer 2 and Layer 3 isolation, and the network service appliance could be connected in a one-arm direct routing mode or as the gateway node. In addition, the service appliance needs to be able to provide a clear isolation of resources dedicated to a tenant. Zone-based and virtual context-based services are common methods used to partition service resources in a multitenant environment.

Virtualized Application Delivery Solutions

The journey to cloud enable the data center includes virtualizing the network services layer as well. This is a significant requirement because the network services are an integral part of the data center infrastructure that improves application performance. One of the key challenges involved in virtualizing the services layer is to enable a scalable and optimized model. The rest of this section examines these aspects of virtualizing WAN optimization and server load-balancing services.

WAN Acceleration

The WAN link used to connect data center services to the remote branch or telecommuter is typically an oversubscribed resource. It is imperative that this resource utilization is maximized by enabling multitenancy and that the transport protocol used is optimized to ensure application performance. WAN acceleration uses multiple methods to increase throughput, such as route optimization, compression, caching content, and tweaking the TCP/IP protocol. As shown in Figure 7-3, throughput is a significant contributor to the application performance. Another factor that affects application performance is the latency variation. Applications such as real-time collaboration and video sessions can usually tolerate a consistent latency and packet-loss characteristics of the transport, but a variable latency or packet-loss metric degrades the experience exponentially.

WAN optimization strategy includes route optimization and WAN acceleration methods. These techniques provide a predictable transport layer performance for the application to deliver a consistent experience to the end user. Following are some of the typical WAN optimization techniques:

- **Data de-duplication:** Data backup operations are significant consumers of WAN bandwidth. Data de-duplication is a technique used to minimize the bandwidth requirement for this operation. It is an algorithm that analyzes data blocks for changes and backs up only those blocks that are unique or have changed. This usually reduces the amount of data required to be backed-up substantially—almost up to 99% based on some analysis—which in turn reduces the bandwidth consumption on the WAN links. In a virtualized environment, the burst in the number of OS instances increases the number of system files required for each OS instance, even though there are common elements between all the instances. Using data de-duplication could reduce the number of system files required for each instance of the OS spawned. Another case could be that of an email message with a large attachment that is sent to multiple recipients. It could be stored as a single copy on the server and be made available for download by individual recipients.

- **Content and data caching:** User experience of a service depends on the proximity to the application and content. In a virtualized server environment, mobile workloads require mobile data so that the latency characteristics of the application remain consistent. Content and data caching techniques stage repetitively accessed data closer to the consumer such that the user experience is consistent independent of the user location. Similarly, when a virtual server is moved from one location to another, caching provides quick access to the data to be processed by the server. In a cloud environment, data caching itself is used as a service, which enables an enterprise to reduce *capital expenditure* (CapEx) on storage equipment. An enterprise can leverage cloud for data storage and cache constantly accessed data on premises.

- **Compression:** Storage, video, audio, and collaboration services rely heavily on transporting or streaming content to the end clients. These services would choke the WAN links easily and so are a CapEx nightmare, restricting the growth of the business. Compression algorithms such as *Lempel-Ziv* (LZ) methods reduce the size of the content to be transported or streamed. Coupled with *data redundancy elimination* (DRE), LZ compression methods greatly reduce the size of data to be transported without compromising quality.

- **Transport flow optimization (TFO):** Applications using TCP as the transport protocol are usually affected by the unpredictable characteristics of the Internet that affect the application performance. You can optimize TCP over the WAN link to offer a predictable transport layer for the applications. Refinements such as TCP window-size optimization, congestion-control methods, and selective acknowledgments, when coupled with optimization of application proximity to the end user, can greatly enhance the latency characteristics.

- **QoS:** Fair allocation of the WAN bandwidth to an application or service depends on the precedence set for the application. Because WAN links are typically oversubscribed resources, it is imperative to have a comprehensive QoS strategy, including rate-limiting, Layer 4 to Layer 7 session/connection limits, and priority queuing.

- **Spoofing:** Some applications or services that leverage spoofing include CIFS and print services. CIFS being a chatty application, the messages are cached and a local proxy service responds to requests, thus reducing the number of transaction messages traversing the WAN link. Printer drivers can also be cached locally to avoid usage of WAN bandwidth for repeated use.

- **Error correction:** When WAN links have reliability issues, a whole bunch of retransmissions are triggered by higher-layer protocols (Layer 4 to Layer 7) that drastically affect the latency and QoS. A simple method that you can implement to minimize the effect of flaky WAN links is to introduce an error-correction packet periodically within a stream. This would allow the receiving end to rebuild the content even in case of some corruption. Depending on the error-correction algorithm used, the stream could tolerate even a high level of corruption to the data stream.

Chapter 10 covers various WAN optimization use-cases, focusing on physical WAN optimization appliances and integrated routers. Subsequent sections delve deeper into the virtualization of WAN optimization application.

In a cloud environment, a service should be enabled on demand and also be sensitive to mobility of the *virtual machines* (VM). This requires the decoupling of the control plane from the forwarding plane and a simplified management plane. This requires a forwarding plane that is flexible enough to offload services into the fast path.

Figure 7-7 illustrates how each service policy provisioned by the control plane (virtual appliance) is offloaded to the forwarding path in the *virtual switch* (vSwitch).

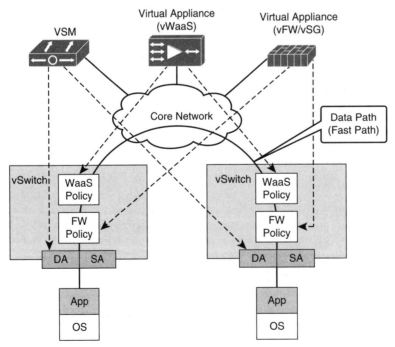

Figure 7-7   *Service Offload to the Fast Path*

For each flow, a service chain is offloaded to the Nexus1000V virtual switch, which makes forwarding decisions locally. The *virtual supervisor module* (VSM) provides the base data path to the vSwitch that is used to forward packets from source to destination. Each control plane, including the Virtual Supervisor Module (VSM), virtual Wide Area Application Services (vWaaS), and the virtual firewall (vFW)/virtual Security Gateway (VSG), is instantiated as a virtual appliance and is managed as a VM. Provisioning is controlled via a centralized management plane such as a policy manager or a more sophisticated orchestrator that is responsible for the end-to-end provisioning, such as Cisco Intelligent Automation for Cloud (CIAC) or BMC-Cloud Management Software (BMC-CLM).

Server Load Balancing

A well-designed cloud-enabled data center can add or delete scale on demand. This capability, along with the network fabric, enables an elastic cloud implementation. Therefore, you need to understand the server load-balancing service and its characteristics in a virtualized environment. As illustrated in Figure 7-2, you could implement various models of application tiers and the load-balancing service in either a tree model or a chain model. The tree model enables reuse of physical appliances to offload the service onto the vSwitch forwarding path. The chain model creates a tightly integrated service model that shadows the application tiers. Because the server load balancer also enables a resilient cloud model, the health of the server instances must be continuously monitored so that services are sustained even under failure scenarios. This implies that the compute resource or the VM is a dynamic resource and could be constantly increasing or decreasing based on scale requirements. Managing such a service could be an overwhelming task.

As illustrated in Figure 7-7, a virtual appliance could help to create a simple integrated management plane that controls the forwarding and the service insertion tasks and offloads all these services onto the forwarding path. This enables an integrated model and delivers greater control over available resources and the optimal utilization thereof.

Summary

The WAN link is an oversubscribed resource connecting the data center with the Internet or the remote branch. Techniques for WAN optimization discussed in this chapter enable a robust strategy to maximize investments in the WAN to suit business priorities. Cloud models enable these techniques to be offered as a service, thus allowing enterprises to keep operations simple yet effective.

Virtualization of a workload assumes that the application is an individual entity that can be moved between locations. For an application to guarantee performance, the network protocol stack must be optimized and enhanced to deliver seamless user experience independent of the mode of access. When application optimization, a core component of WaaS, is virtualized, it ties together the mobility aspect with the performance characteristics of a virtualized workload. This ensures business agility without sacrificing application performance.

Review Questions

1. What can be considered a typical service deployment model?

   a. Two-tier model
   b. Three-tier model
   c. Four-tier model
   d. Five-tier model

2. Which services are key to improve application performance?

   a. Security
   b. Server load balancing
   c. Network analysis
   d. WaaS

3. What factors influence the performance of an application?

   a. Latency
   b. Bandwidth
   c. Packet loss
   d. IP
   e. L2

4. Which of the following are techniques used in WAN optimization?

   a. Compression
   b. TFO
   c. De-duplication
   d. Rate-limiting
   e. ACLs

5. How does vSwitch enhance the service insertion?

   a. Minimizes latency of the application
   b. Reduces the bandwidth consumption by an application
   c. Eliminates packet loss
   d. Inserts the services into the fast path

Chapter 8

IP NGN Infrastructure That Supports Cloud Services

In this chapter, you learn about the following:

- Adoption of the cloud and the impact it has on NGN traffic patterns
- Role of the DCI technologies in delivering cloud services
- Workload mobility enabled by the DCI framework
- DCI requirements, framework, and solutions
- Route and path optimization with advance routing technologies like LISP

The cloud and the services it offers have garnered significant interest worldwide. The cloud offers an elastic model that allows infrastructure capacity to be increased and decreased on demand. The cloud's usage-based model helps enterprises increase business agility and reduce costs by moving applications and consuming infrastructure resources from the cloud.

Despite all the benefits, enterprises have been cautious about adopting the cloud because of concerns about availability, security, and application performance. Cloud providers with network assets looking to tap in to cloud-generated revenue streams can effectively monetize and increase profitability if they overcome these challenges in their IP next-generation networks (NGN). By ensuring that the cloud data centers, networks, applications, and services are tightly integrated, cloud providers can further differentiate their services from other providers.

To facilitate revenue growth by capturing this new market and reduce costs through operational efficiency, cloud providers' existing IP NGN infrastructure must evolve in line with the needs of the enterprises.

This part of the book breaks down the cloud adoption challenges in IP NGNs and how they are addressed as follows:

- **High availability, workload mobility, route optimization:** This chapter discusses these topics in detail.

- **Secure access to the cloud and securing of the cloud edge:** Chapter 9, "Securing Cloud Transport and Edge Using NGN Technologies," discusses these in detail.

- **Enhancing the performance of cloud services:** Chapter 10, "Optimizing and Accelerating Cloud Services," discusses this in detail.

IP NGNs Evolve in Line with the Cloud

Part II of this book discussed the virtualized data center and the role of the network fabric in supporting the scale and mobility of cloud resources cost effectively within the data center. These cloud resources could be concentrated in a single location that contains several cloud data centers or spread across various locations to enable the flexibility and availability required by the cloud

Cloud providers are grouped as follows:

- **Enterprises:** Offering cloud services to its users; these services can be offered in a private or a hybrid cloud.

- **Service providers:** Incumbents who want to claim their stake in the cloud offer cloud services to enterprise and subscribers.

- **Over-the-top providers:** Offer cloud services to enterprises and subscribers.

The IP NGN, which provides the access from enterprises to one or more data centers of these cloud providers, can also enable the cloud resource pools to be flexibly extended across multiple geographically distributed data centers through data center interconnect (DCI) technologies.

Figure 8-1 shows a consolidated view of various DCI models to achieve high availability, workload mobility, disaster avoidance, and so on in cloud provider networks.

These data center interconnect models can be summarized as follows:

- Enterprise to Enterprise (E2E)

- Enterprise to the Cloud Provider (E2CP)

- Cloud Provider to Cloud Provider (CP2CP)

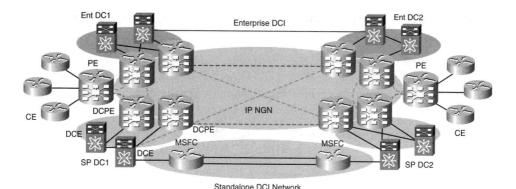

Figure 8-1 *Cloud Provider DCI Models*

Before the advent of the cloud, traffic that flowed in the IP NGNs was unidirectional—it flowed from the subscriber to the network (for example, any client/server application) and from the server to the subscriber (for example, video streaming). With cloud and virtualization, the network traffic has become multidirectional; the traffic moves from the subscriber to the server and between the network servers (for example, virtualized workloads). This network traffic between servers can flow either Intracloud (within the local or geographically dispersed data centers) or Intercloud (across two cloud providers).

Clustering applications such as *Microsoft Cluster Service* (MSCS) that are enabled using active/standby scenarios across geographically dispersed cloud data centers have also contributed to this multidirectional traffic.

Virtualization has acted as a strong catalyst for the proliferation of the cloud where compute capacity has been optimized through server consolidations. Once virtualized, the live workload can move from a server in one geographical location to a server in another geographical location as long as both locations are connected using a Layer 2 connection. A prime example of this is the VMware *virtual machine motion* (vMotion) that allows the movement of workloads across geographically dispersed data centers (from one server to the other server), resulting in effective use of infrastructure resources in normal times and disaster avoidance during natural calamities.

Cloud consumers require the same great experience they enjoyed before moving to the cloud. Cloud providers must provide high availability of services and applications and efficiently move data throughout the entire cloud infrastructure.

These drivers, and the changing traffic patterns brought about by the cloud, are driving the evolution of the IP NGNs, which need to fully integrate the network, data centers, and cloud applications and services in a cohesive manner.

Role of DCI Technologies in Delivering Cloud Services

Data Center Interconnect (DCI) Technologies is expected to play a key role in the evolution of IP NGNs to deliver business-grade cloud services. DCI technologies meet the requirement of high availability of cloud services and applications and efficiently move data throughout the entire cloud infrastructure.

Key Use Cases Enabled by DCI in the Cloud

Figure 8-2 summarizes key use cases enabled by the DCI technologies in the cloud as described further in the list that follows.

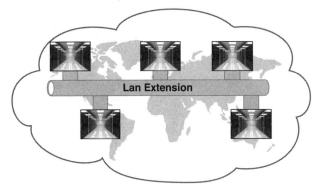

Key Use Cases of DCI Technologies in
Cloud-Ready IP NGNs and Data Centers

- Allow Distributed Applications
- Offer Legacy Applications
- Disaster Management
- Data Center Maintenance/Migration
- High-Availability Clusters
- Data-Center Consolidation

Figure 8-2   *Use Cases Enabled by Data Center Interconnect Technologies*

- **Allows distributed applications:** DCI allows the extension of operating systems, file system clusters, and database clusters across geographically dispersed data centers and enables the cloud providers to realize service efficiencies (service the customer from the closest touch point).

- **Offers legacy applications:** These applications require Layer 2 connectivity. DCI technologies allow for this Layer 2 extension across geographic boundaries and enable these applications to be consumed from the cloud.

■ **High availability:** Clustering applications, such as Microsoft MSCS, Solaris Sun Cluster Enterprise, and Oracle *Real Application Clusters* (RAC), are offered in active/standby scenarios across geographically dispersed cloud data centers. Interserver heartbeats, status, and database replications are synchronized through private networks while public communication is carried out via the virtual IP (VIP) of the cluster. These applications require a Layer 2 path/extension between servers, as illustrated in Figure 8-3.

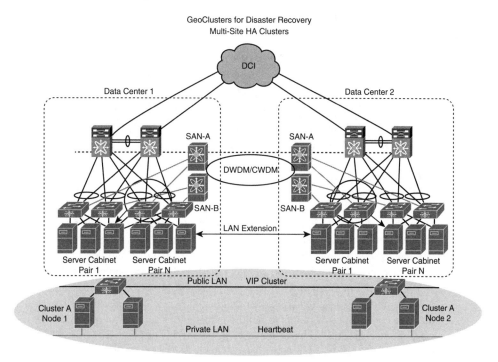

Figure 8-3 *High Availability Clusters Show LAN Extensions Across Geographically Dispersed Data Centers*

■ **Disaster management:** Business continuity is the key driver for disaster management. The goal is to anticipate and move mission-critical applications from data centers that are in the path of natural calamities (hurricanes, tsunamis, and so on) to data centers that are not affected by such calamities. Once the natural calamity subsides, affected data centers are operationalized again, and workloads are moved back to their original data centers. This scenario is applicable to geoclusters. This use case requires workload mobility.

■ **Data center maintenance/migration:** Data center infrastructure maintenance (software/hardware upgrades, storage upgrades, patches, and so on) can be performed, without downtime, after moving the workloads to another data center. This is considered proactive workload mobility. Figure 8-4 shows workload within and across data centers.

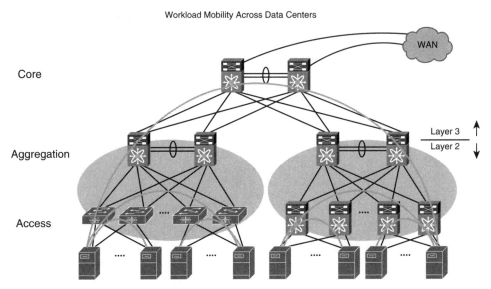

Figure 8-4 *Workload Mobility from Data Center Going Under Maintenance to an Operational Data Center*

■ **Data center consolidation:** Providers are under huge pressure to reduce energy costs to remain competitive and reduce emissions to establish themselves as responsible companies. Take General Electric, for example. It built a platinum-level LEED certified data center in Kentucky.[1] So what is LEED, and why are companies like GE striving for it? LEED stands for *Leadership in Energy and Environmental Design*, a program managed by the U.S Green Building Council. With platinum as its highest feat, the council awards points to buildings that adopt various energy- and water-efficient mechanisms. So what does GE gain from this LEED certification? The most tangible benefits are reduced energy costs (lower power and cooling costs) and an accredited certification to establish itself as a company that cares about the environment. This push to reduce energy costs by lowering power and cooling costs is not confined to GE only; it is an industry-wide phenomenon that is in line with Pike Research's recent report, according to which the adoption of the cloud "has the potential to chop data center energy consumption by 31 percent from 2010 to 2020."[2]

To achieve higher output per unit of infrastructure equipment, providers are also looking at ways to effectively use underutilized servers that are available in data centers spread across geographic boundaries. This phenomenon, dubbed *server consolidation*, is improving server utilization "rates from 5–15% to 60–80%."[3] This improved server utilization is being achieved by first virtualizing services and then moving these VMs within or across data centers depending on the server loads. If the VM is moved within the data center, it is called intra-DC vMotion. If the VM is moved across data centers, it is called inter-DC vMotion. Moving virtual workloads to data centers that are in areas where the power tariffs are cheap is the most compelling trend driving data center consolidation. VMware estimates that providers are saving 7000 kWh of electricity, which translates to about $700 in energy costs per server per year.[3] This has a direct impact on reducing the carbon dioxide emission footprint and propels the providers nicely toward being known as green providers.

Workload Mobility in the Cloud

Workload mobility in the cloud is enabled by VMware ESXi and other hypervisors, such as KVM for LINUX, Hyper-V from Microsoft, and Xen from Citrix.

Workload mobility is discussed here as it relates to two important cloud use cases:

- **Intercloud:** Live workload mobility within data centers managed by different cloud providers

- **Intracloud:** Live workload mobility within data centers managed by the same cloud provider

According to VMware, "VMware VMotion enables the live migration of running virtual machines from one physical server to another with zero downtime, continuous service availability, and complete transaction integrity. VMotion is a key enabling technology for creating the dynamic, automated, and self-optimizing data center."[4]

DCI provides the necessary transport that enables long-distance vMotion. Each VM emulates a physical computer by creating a separate operating system environment. With long-distance vMotion, you can move the live VM across geographically dispersed data centers. Data Center Interconnect is crucial to the enablement of long-distance vMotion.

Figure 8-5 shows long-distance VMotion that is enabled by the Cisco ASR1000 series of routers and VMware vCenter. In this figure, a VM is moved between two geographically dispersed data centers.

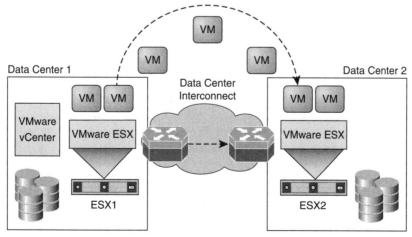

Figure 8-5 *Long-Distance vMotion-enabled by Components from VMware and Cisco*

Data Center Interconnect Requirements for the Cloud

The following key DCI requirements will drive the transformation of IP NGN so that it can support the high availability and resiliency required by the cloud:

■ **Layer 1 network connectivity:** This typically refers to dark fiber that is used to transport various types of network and *storage-area network* (SAN) traffic.

■ **Layer 2 network connectivity:** Extends Layer 2 connectivity across data centers over various Layer 3 mechanisms (IP/MPLS) using Ethernet as transport.

■ **Layer 3 network connectivity:** Provides IP or MPLS *virtual private network* (VPN) connectivity between data centers with optimal routing, granular *quality of service* (QoS) controls, and load balancing.

■ **Topology:** Loop-free and spanning-tree-free topology that ensures that the broadcast traffic is significantly limited at the data center edge devices. The multicast traffic, on the other hand, should be optimized as much as possible.

■ **Convergence:** Support faster convergence algorithms to ensure minimal service disruption.

■ **Security:** DCI links must be secured to provide data integrity and confidentiality.

■ **Virtual Machine Mobility:** Must support workload mobility across geographically dispersed data centers.

■ **Shared Storage:** DCI needs to provide access to the shared storage across data centers that are separated by only a short distance. Data is located and updated at one location only. After the migration, virtual machines continue to access the data from its original location.

■ **Active-Passive storage:** DCI needs to allow active-passive storage configuration that assumes that the storage is provisioned identically at both data centers. In this scenario, the storage is migrated before the VM is moved from one data center to the other. Because of complexities that are required to explicitly control operations to make the storage replica accessible to the server in the secondary data center, it is not considered a viable option for virtual machine mobility.

■ **Active-Active storage:** DCI needs to support active-active storage to ensure that data is replicated and available at both data centers at all times. This is the preferred approach, because in this mode the VM is the only thing that needs to be moved from one data center to the other. Data is available at the new data center where the VM is moved to.

■ **Latency and distance:** Supports latency no greater than 5 ms across geographically dispersed data centers (that is, latency between VMware Vsphere servers *cannot* exceed 5ms).

■ **Data replication:** Supports both synchronous and asynchronous data replication techniques. Synchronous replication ensures that each write is replicated to both primary and backup storage volumes. Synchronous replication offers zero packet loss at the cost of reduced performance. Asynchronous replication replicates data on primary and backup storage volumes in a serial fashion. Asynchronous offers better performance without any guarantee of making recent data available in case of a failure in which the primary storage volume fails.

■ **Disaster avoidance/recovery:** Supports minimum *recovery time objective* (RTO) (measured in minutes) and zero *recovery point object* (RPO).

■ **Path optimization:** Supports optimal traffic routes and low-latency responses from internal servers to external clients. There are two types of path optimizations:

  ■ **Ingress path optimizations:** Ingress path optimizations are realized with LISP and DNS based resolution with Cisco Global Site Selector (GSS)/Application Control Engine integrated with VMware vCenter.

  ■ **Egress path optimizations:** Achieved through First Hop Redundancy Protocol (FHRP) with Host Standby Router Protocol (HSRP) localization.

DCI Solutions to Build Virtualized and Distributed Cloud Data Centers

This section focuses on various DCI solutions that will meet the need of applications that require Layer 2 connectivity using different types of transports connecting geographically dispersed data centers (see Figure 8-6).

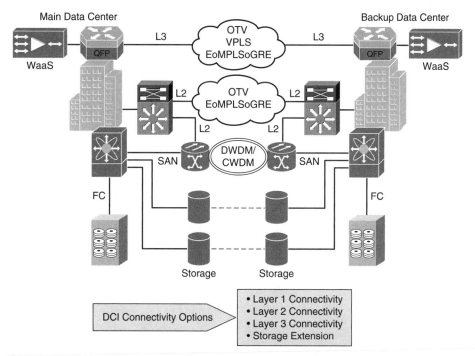

Figure 8-6 *Network Diagram Showing Various DCI Solutions*

Transport Option 1: Layer 2 over Dark Fiber

Layer 2 over dark fiber transport is also called native mode and helps achieve Layer 2 extension for the following two solutions:

- *Virtual Switching System* (VSS), which is Catalyst 6500 based

- *Virtual Port Channel* (vPC), which is Nexus 7000 based

VSS is a technology that allows two Catalysts 6500 switches to be connected together and form a single logical switch. VSS is executed in hardware (custom ASIC) and has no degrading effect on performance. Data plane switching capacity is doubled with VSS because two physical switches are acting as a single logical switch with pooled switching resources. Both 720 and 2T Catalyst 6500 Supervisor engines support VSS. Figure 8-7 shows two Catalyst 6500s configured with a Supervisor 720 engine. Each Supervisor 720 engine is capable of delivering 720 Gbps of throughput; since both data planes (in two switches) are active concurrently, the combined forwarding data plane capacity results from VSS 1440 Gbps (2 × 720 Gbps).

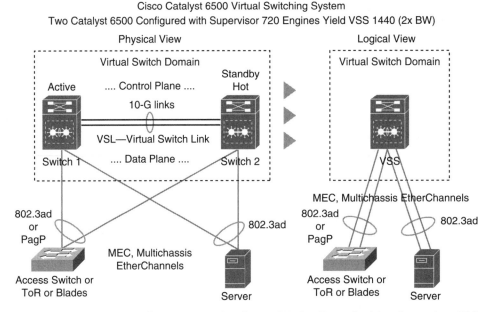

Figure 8-7 *VSS 1440 Gbps Has Two Catalyst 6500 Configured with a Supervisor 720 Gbps–Capable Data Plane on Each Switch*

In VSS, the control plane is active on only one of the virtual switch members. Both chassis are kept in sync to achieve an interchassis *stateful switchover* (SSO) mechanism along with *nonstop forwarding* (NSF) to provide nonstop communication in the event of failure of one of the member Supervisor engines or chassis. VSS with a single control plane simplifies management and operations (configurations are replicated across the two switches automatically). VSS offers non-STP and no-loop design without the need of First Hop Routing Protocol (FHRP).

VSS enables you to run multiple uplinks from either of the two physical Catalyst 6500 switches to form a single logical port channel split known as *multichassis EtherChannel* (MEC) between physical switches. As illustrated in Figure 8-8, MEC is an advanced Etherchannel technology that extends link aggregation across two physical switches.

Multichassis EtherChannel with VSS
Multichassis EtherChannel Prefers to Route Traffic Over Locally Attached Interfaces

Blue Traffic destined for the server will result in **Link 1** in the MEC link bundle being chosen as the destination path.

Orange Traffic destined for the server will result in **Link 2** in the MEC link bundle being chosen as the destination path.

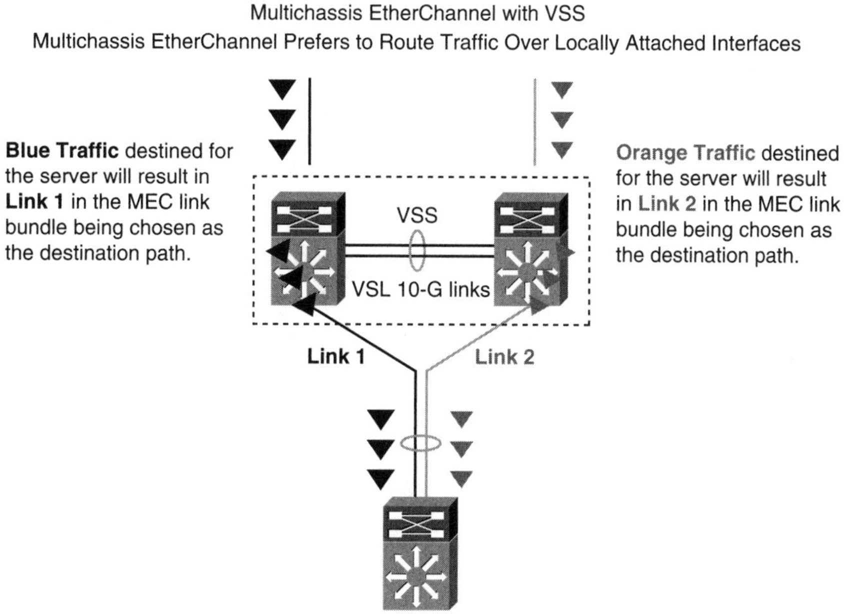

Figure 8-8 *Multi-chassis EtherChannel (MEC) Diagram*

VSS is used to build simplified and scalable network topologies by connecting geographically dispersed data centers over dark fiber links. Figure 8-9 shows two remote data centers connected using *dense wavelength-division multiplexing* (DWDM) or *coarse wavelength-division multiplexing* (CWDM) techniques to achieve high availability across two physical switches located in two different data centers but belonging to the same VSS.

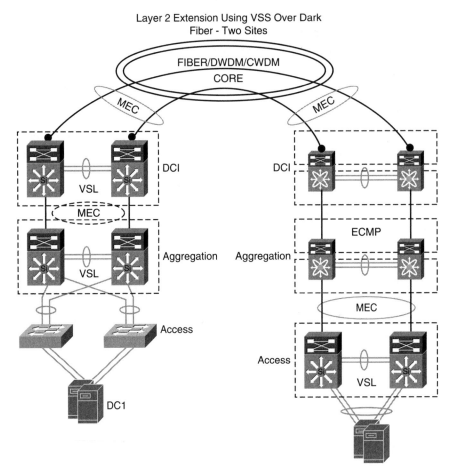

Figure 8-9   *High Availability with Two Physical Switches at Two Remotes Sites Belonging to the Same VSS*

vPC is based on Nexus OS, and it allows grouping of two physical switches (for example, Nexus 7000) to form a single logical switch to any downstream device such as a switch or a server. vPC combines the benefits of hardware redundancy (two physical switches running their own control) and port channel loop management. Figure 8-10 shows how vPC extends link aggregation to two separate physical switches.

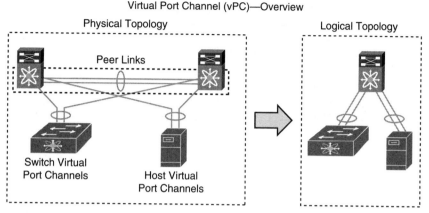

Figure 8-10 *Key Benefits of vPC*

vPC offers the following benefits:

■ vPC-based single virtual switch to use a port channel across two downstream switches

■ Creates resilient Layer 2 topologies with link aggregation and eliminates the need for spanning tree protocol (STP) between access and distribution layers

■ Increases bandwidth by putting all the links in the forwarding state

■ Maintains independent control planes across the two switches

■ Faster convergence with link/device failure

vPC and VSS are similar technologies but with subtle differences. For example, in VSS, only one of the Catalyst 6500 chassis (control plane) needs to be configured, and the configuration is then replicated to the other chassis, which reduces management and provisioning overhead by 50%; whereas in vPC, both Nexus 7000 switches (for example) need to be configured separately.

vPC has one key advantage over VSS: because vPC has dual control planes, it offers *In Service Software Upgrade* (ISSU), which allows upgrading one of the two switches to the latest code without causing service interruption.

Figure 8-11 shows both VSS and vPC deployed across geographically dispersed data centers that are interconnected with dark fiber.

Despite all its benefits, vPC does fall back to *Spanning Tree Protocol* (STP). With STP in place, less bandwidth (East-West) is available and workload mobility is restricted to small bridge domains. Reliance on STP can be fully circumvented by a new breed of solutions that are based on TRILL and Cisco FabricPath. With TRILL and FabricPath, more bandwidth is available for the East-West traffic, and workload can move across a very large network domain.

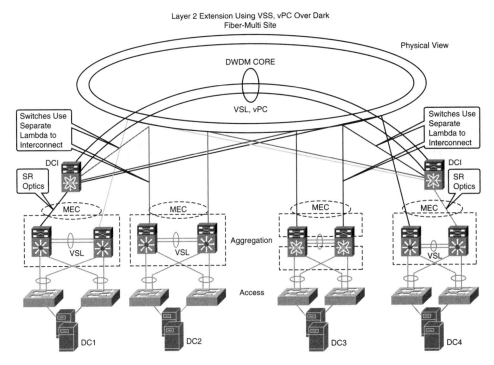

Figure 8-11 *Multisite vPC Solution*

Both TRILL and FabricPath are discussed briefly in the following paragraphs to show how they solve the spanning-tree problems within a data center and how these two technologies compare to *Overlay Transport Virtualization* (OTV) that solve the same spanning-tree-elimination problem across the DCI link.

Transparent Interconnect of Lots of Links (TRILL) is underway at IETF; TRILL combines the best of both bridges and routers in devices called *router bridges* or *RBridges*. TRILL advocates a significant departure from spanning-tree architecture and offers multiple paths of data flows. (Spanning tree promulgates that there is only a single tree in the switching fabric, and there is only one path irrespective of how inefficient it is from a source to a destination.) TRILL is considered important for building clouds and helps with the following:

- Better migration of VMs

- Efficient use of switching infrastructure through multiple paths

- Elimination of STPs

- Efficient use of switching capacity (bandwidth)

- Minimal or no configuration for the RBridges to be operational

- Routing loop avoidance

- Faster convergence in failure scenarios

- Load sharing across multiple links

Cisco FabricPath is yet another useful solution for building cloud data centers. Cisco FabricPath introduces *Layer 2 multipathing* (L2MP). Cisco L2MP is based on TRILL and offers additional cloud-useful enhancements, such as the following:

- Conversational learning, which can overcome limitations of MAC address table sizes

- vPC+, which allows connecting classic Ethernet devices to FabricPath in an active/active way and without resorting to STP. This would allow non-FabricPath switches to connect to FabricPath switches using vPC.

- Multiple topologies, which helps create several Layer 2 domains that will separate one set of VLANs from another set of VLANs. This could prove useful in a multi-tenant environment where a certain set of VLANs that are assigned to a tenant need to be isolated from other tenants to achieve an increased level of security.

Transport Option 2: Layer 2 over MPLS

For the Layer 2 over MPLS DCI solution, four solutions are available:

- **Ethernet over MPLS (EoMPLS):** Enabled by Cisco Catalyst 6500 and ASR1000, EoMPLS is a point-to-point solution to allow transport of Ethernet frames over an MPLS network. EoMPLS simply extends LAN connectivity across two different customer sites that are connected by a service provider MPLS network. EoMPLS emulates the LAN and uses pseudowires (or virtual circuits) to transport Ethernet frames over the MPLS backbone

- **Advanced VPLS (A-VPLS):** Enabled by Catalyst 6500 series switches and offers the following key benefits:

  - Ease of configuration, with A-VPLS offering simplified configuration

  - Fast subsecond convergence

  - Layer 2, Layer 3, Layer 4 flow-based load balancing

  - Optimal bandwidth utilization enabled by VSS

- **Virtual Private LAN Service (VPLS):** Offers multipoint Ethernet-based LAN services over IP/MPLS networks (see Figure 8-12). VPLS are also referred to as *transparent LAN services*. VPLS employs traditional data plane MAC learning, split horizon (helps avoid routing loops in distance-vector protocols like *Interior Gateway Routing Protocol* [IGRP] by disallowing a router from advertising a route back to the interface from which the route was learned), and a full mesh of pseudo-wires for loop avoidance. VPLS does not use STP. VPLS allows two methods for control plane communication that are discussed in RFC 4761 (*BGP-based VPLS Auto-Discovery and Signaling*) and RFC 4762 (*LDP-Based VPLS Signaling*). The control plane communication is composed of finding all the *provider edge* (PE) routers using autodiscovery to establish and tear down pseudowires using signaling. A *Border Gateway Protocol* (BGP)-based control plane mechanism in VPLS (RFC 4761) offers an advantage in that it offers autodiscovery of PE routers in the same VPLS instance. An LDP-based VPLS control plane mechanism only offers signaling and no autodiscovery. (All the PE peers participating in a VPLS instance are configured manually on each PE router.) In Figure 8-12, VPLS defines an architecture to provide connectivity between geographically dispersed sites in the cloud as if they were connected using a LAN.

Additionally, pseudowires are established among all the devices participating in the VPLS network. The top portion of Figure 8-12 shows split horizon in action where a route is not advertised on the same port from where it was learned.

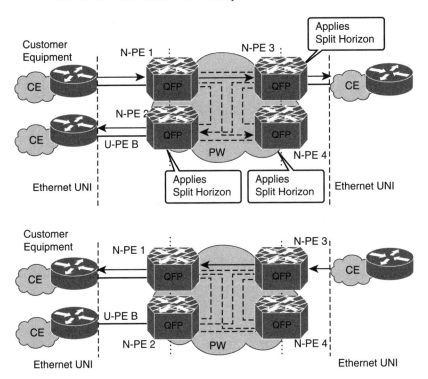

Figure 8-12 *Virtual Private LAN Services solution overview*

VPLS-based DCI solutions are attractive for cloud deployments because they offer any-to-any connectivity. Cloud providers can use VPLS to offer transparent private peering between multiple cloud providers across their MPLS infrastructure. With VPLS, cloud providers can support geographically dispersed applications (high-availability server clusters and so on).

VPLS comes in two flavors: *nonhierarchical VPLS* (VPLS) and *hierarchical-VPLS* (H-VPLS). VPLS is suitable for small-scale deployments where MPLS-capable edge devices are burdened with the following:

- Routing protocols and holding of forwarding information

- Label Distribution Protocol

- Replicate multicast and handle broadcast traffic

These responsibilities burden the edge devices, which reduces overall network efficiency, to meet the needs of small-scale deployments.

In contrast to nonhierarchical VPLS, H-VPLS builds a hierarchical framework by partitioning the network into several edge domains that are connected via MPLS. With H-VPLS, the edge devices only need to establish relationship with their neighboring n-PE devices and are not burdened with large routing table. H-VPLS participating edge devices can use IEEE 802.1ad technology to offer q-in-q (also known as VLAN tag stacking) to achieve higher VLAN scaling.

VPLS is a useful technology, but when applied to DCI, it is not without challenge, especially when configured in mulithoming scenarios. VPLS challenges are solved by the following:

- **Loop avoidance:** The remedy is achieved by using a technology called *Multi-Chassis Link Aggregation Protocol* (MC-LAG). MC-LAG is a combination of two protocols: LACP (802.1ax, *Link Aggregation Control Protocol*) and ICCP (*Inter-Chassis Control Protocol*). MC-LAG helps ensure that an enterprise *customer edge* (CE) router that connects to two SP PEs for resiliency is communicating with a single PE router at any given time using an active connection while the connection to the other PE is standby.

- **Load balancing:** The challenge is to support multiple points of failure and effective use of resources. Per-VLAN-based load balancing is achieved by using pseudo MC-LAG (802.3ad). By using pseudo mLACP, for example, VLANs 1 through 10 can be routed over one link to PE1 (SP1), and VLANs 11 through 20 can be routed over the second link to PE2 (SP2). This can also be referred to as an *active-active configuration*.

- **Scaling:** MAC address scaling is a significant challenge for any cloud provider looking to build scalable Layer 2 bridged networks. For example, a cloud provider looking to build 20 data centers where each data center is expected to host 500K MAC addresses is going to look for a PE solution that can scale at a size of one million MAC addresses. A viable alternative to building a device that can scale that high is to use the MAC-in-MAC (also known as PBB or *provider backbone bridges*) technique discussed in IEEE 802.1ah.

■ *Ethernet Virtual Private Network* (EVPN) relies on BGP to distribute *client/customer MAC* (C-MAC) reachability and client-multicast group information between the edge devices. EVPN, like VPLS, uses traditional data plane learning mechanisms to learn the MAC addresses of locally attached clients. Remote MAC address learning, however, differs from VPLS; that is, EVPN uses the BGP control plane to learn the MAC addresses advertised by other PEs.

EVPN offers some potential benefits over VPLS, such as the following:

■ Natively supports georedundancy

■ Simplified provisioning and operations

■ Seamless integration with TRILL and 802.1Qbp

EVPN, like VPLS, requires PBB to scale and meet the needs of large-scale cloud provider networks.

Provider Based Bridging-Ethernet Virtual Private Network (PBB-EVPN) is an emerging standard[5] that combines IEEE802.1ah (PBB) with EVPN to achieve reduction in the BGP MAC advertisement routes and a very high scale of MAC addresses.

Transport Option 3: Layer 2 over IP

This section discusses various solutions that will enable Layer 2 extension over IP networks, including the following:

■ Ethernet over generic routing encapsulation (EoMPLSoGRE) enabled by Cisco Catalyst 6500 series or Cisco Aggregation Services Routers 1000 Series (Cisco ASR1000 Series)

■ Layer 2 Tunneling Protocol v3 (L2TPv3) enabled by Cisco ASR1000 Series

■ A-VPLS over GRE enabled by Cisco Catalyst 6500 series routers

■ OTV supported by ASR1000, Catalyst 6500, and Nexus 7000

■ Virtual extensible local-area network (VXLAN) supported by Nexus1000v

EoMPLSoGRE is a viable option to extend Layer 2 domains in a point-to-point fashion over an IP network. EoMPLSoGRE is useful when the enterprise edge is peering with an IP-only PE device and creating an overlay is the only option to extend the Layer 2 domain. Moreover, EoMPLSoGRE also offers enhanced security by allowing IPsec-based traffic encryption (required by financial institutes and federal government). The benefit to this approach is that all the traffic can be encrypted using IPsec and a higher level of security is attained.

VPLSoGRE and A-VPLSoGRE are the two scalable multipoint solutions that also extend Layer 2 domains over IP networks and avoid having to build either an MPLS network or interface with a provider that only offers MPLS. Enterprises can use the existing IP core or interface with a provider that offers IP-based connectivity. This solution can also be referred to as *any transport of MPLS over GRE* (AToMoGRE) or Layer 2 VPN over GRE. In a nutshell, it works like this: A GRE tunnel is created, and the AToM frames are hardwired-switched on top of this tunnel with a high scale and performance.

Layer 2 over IP-based data center design offers similar capabilities as were discussed previously for Layer 2 over MPLS. To summarize, EoMPLSoGRE offers point-to-point connection, while VPLSoGRE and A-VPLSoGRE offer scalable multisite data center design.

Layer 2 Tunneling Protocol version 3 (L2TPv3) allows for a high-speed Layer 2 extension between the enterprises and the cloud providers. L2TPv3 benefits from the flexibility and scalability of IP and allows for the delivery of cloud services that require a Layer 2 extension. L2TPv3 offers considerable cost advantages to small and medium-sized businesses. Instead of the enterprise setting up and managing point-to-point connections between each office, the enterprise connects from its main location to a cloud provider. The cloud provider then takes care of setting up customized Layer 2 Virtual Private Network (L2VPN) services for the enterprise offices to be connected using L2TPv3. The cloud provider benefits from generating additional revenue opportunities from L2TPv3-based VPNs and cloud-based services.

Apart from these Layer 2 extensions over IP technologies is a new and innovative Cisco technology called *Overlay Transport Virtualization* (OTV). As illustrated in Figure 8-13, OTV offers an overlay that extends Layer 2 connectivity between separate Layer 2 domains while keeping these domains independent and thus preserving the fault isolation (*bidirectional forwarding detection* [BFD]), resiliency (fast reroute), and load-balancing benefits of an IP-based interconnection. Cisco ASR1000 and Nexus 7000 both offer OTV solutions.

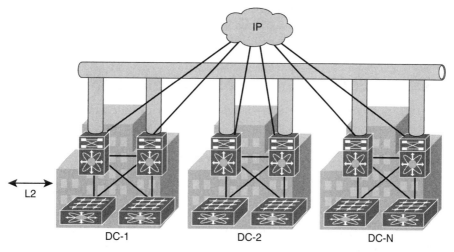

Figure 8-13   *Overlay Transport Virtualization*

OTV has built-in loop prevention and does not rely on IS-IS for MAC learning across geographically dispersed data centers.

Compared to other Layer 2 extension over IP technologies, such as EoMPLSoGRE, VPLSoGRE, and A-VPLSoGRE, OTV is more suitable for cloud-oriented deployments because it offers the following benefits:

- Works on any transport (IP/MPLS)

- Natively supports multihoming

- Supports efficient multicast replication

- Offers MAC in IP routing to benefit from scalable nature of IP networks

Data center links that are based on OTV can be secured with scalable technologies such as *Group Encrypted Transport Virtual Private Network* (GETVPN) and MACsec (IEEE MAC Security Standard ratified as 802.1AE) security technology. GETVN is tunnelless and provides IPsec-based Layer 3 encryption. MACsec provides bulk encryption at Layer 2 and encrypts all Ethernet frames irrespective of the upper-layer protocol.

Virtualization of compute, storage, and network resources has acted as a big catalyst to cloud adoption. Virtualization adds the agility and flexibility that helps pooled resources to grow on demand, allowing workloads to migrate from one data center to another. Each VM requires a unique MAC address to communicate, and each tenant needs at least one VLAN to segment its traffic. The virtual-to-physical ratio is increasing exponentially as the demand for virtual compute and storage grows, giving rise to the exponential demand of MAC addresses needed for that many VMs. The existing VLAN scale of 4K (12 bits of VLAN identifier) is not able to meet this demand. *Virtual Extensible LAN* (VXLAN) offers a 24-bit unique identifier that offers 16M VLANs and uses a well-known method of transport: UDP/IP. VXLAN is supported by Nexus 1000V, and solves the VLAN scalability problem and acts as a complementary technology to OTV and LISP.

Ingress and Egress Route Path Optimization

Locator ID Separation Protocol (LISP) is a network routing architecture and a set of protocols that separate the endpoint identity from the location of the endpoint. LISP, unlike the legacy IP addressing scheme, introduces two naming spaces and uses a new semantic for IP addressing. (The existing IP addressing scheme uses only a single naming space.) LISP introduces several new terminologies: *endpoint identifiers* (EID), which represent the end hosts; and *routing locators* (RLOC), which are assigned to devices (primarily routers).

LISP was introduced to manage the growth of the Internet routing table that was based on the legacy IP addressing scheme that uses a single naming space—IP address represented both the identity and the location of the network to which the endpoint attached. The IP addressing scheme that is based on the single naming space has manifested in the rapid growth of the Internet's *default-free zone* (DFZ), mainly resulting from sites using multihoming, traffic engineering, nonaggregatable address allocations, and business events such as mergers and acquisitions.

The problem of exponential and undesired growth of the Internet routing table has been further exacerbated by the following conditions:

- Depletion of IPv4 addresses, which has resulted in a finer break up with less potential of aggregation, especially in the case of provider independent addressing.

- Dual-stack routers supporting both IPv4 and IPv6. IPv6 did solve the problem of address depletion through a longer address but did not do anything different to separate the identity and location of the endpoint.

- Increased demand in dual-homed routers at the customer edge to efficiently use network bandwidth and achieve resiliency. BGP can achieve this, but it requires a network staff that is extremely competent in BGP.

- Ability to switch cloud providers to realize lower-cost Internet connections. The complexities that are associated with IP renumbering when changing CPs are quite formidable for the small and medium enterprises to handle.

LISP overcomes these issues by separating the identity of the endpoint from the network location it is deployed in. This results in the following benefits:

- Reduced Internet routing table size through topologically aggregated routing locators (RLOC)

- IP portability (like number portability in telecommunications) through provider-independent addresses

Figure 8-14 illustrates the application of LISP in use cases such as efficient multi-homing, IPv6 transition, high-scale VPNs, and virtual machine mobility. Looking at the VM Mobility use case, which is one of the focus areas of this chapter, we know that workloads are moved across geographically dispersed data centers in one of two ways: Live moves requiring state preservation, or cold moves that allow for a shutdown of the host VMs in one data center and a restart in the other data center. This physical move of host/workload has implications for the IP addresses in the following two cases:

- **Case A:** Host X moves from East data center to West data center, and the subnet is *extended*. This means that subnet does not retain its location semantic and that routing to this host may take a suboptimal path: Packets will continue to be routed to its original location (East data center) and then forwarded to the new location (West data center).

- **Case B:** Host Y moves from West data center to East data center, and the subnet is *not extended*. This means that all of the existing connections (TCP and so on) to this host have to be reestablished, causing unnecessary delays in re-sorting service and inefficient utilization of infrastructure resources.

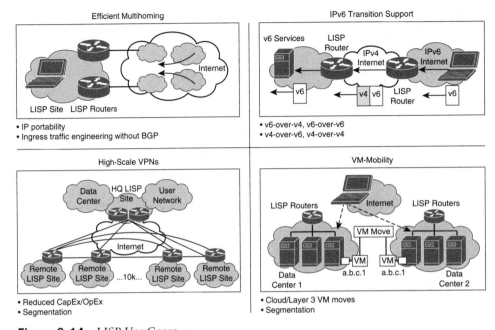

Figure 8-14 *LISP Use Cases*

Figure 8-15 describes the challenges of Case A and how LISP can help overcome that.

The suboptimal routing problem of Case A can easily be resolved by LISP because it separates the endpoint ID (host ID) from the location. As the host X moves to the new data center, the LISP mapping database (database that maps EIDs) to RLOCs is automatically updated. All traffic routed to this host X will automatically be routed to its new location (West data center).

The connection reset problem of Case B is overcome by the LISP as well, because it allows the endpoint to retain its IP address even after moving to the new location (East data center). All of the existing connections (TCP and so on) will remain up.

LISP does not burden the network administrator to change the firewall policies as the hosts or workloads move from one data center to the other data center.

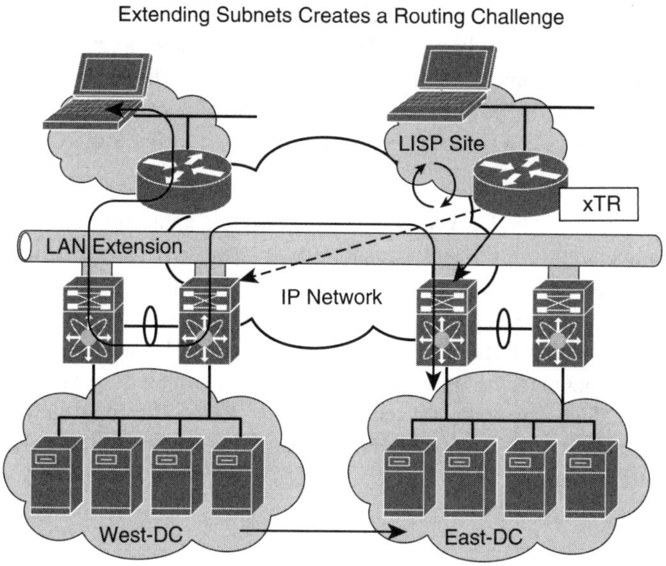

Extending Subnets Creates a Routing Challenge

Figure 8-15 *Routing Challenges in the DCI*

Figure 8-16 shows clustering applications such as MSCS that are enabled using active/standby scenarios across geographically dispersed cloud data centers. By combining OTV and LISP, the following benefits can be achieved:

- Applications running in the VMs use nonroutable traffic; for example, node discovery and heartbeats in clustered applications

- With virtualization, application members can be distributed across PODs/data centers

- Moving and distributing application members across locations should not break the application

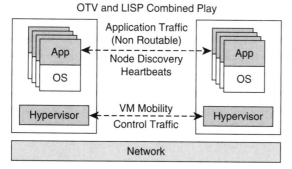

Figure 8-16 *LISP and Optimized Routing*

Cluster applications often use non-IP link-local multicast signaling between the application clustering server members. This signaling includes peer discovery and heartbeat mechanisms. All other communications to these clustered applications consist of normal IP routable traffic. The non-IP link or the secure extension of Layer 2 connectivity across geographically dispersed locations can be achieved through any DCI technology: OTV, VPLS, and so on.

For the case of workload mobility where a VM is migrated from one data center to another, extending the subnet can result in suboptimal routing because of a hairpinning effect. All the packets that are destined to this VM will go to the original data center, from where they will be routed to the new data center where the workload has migrated. The same would be true for any return traffic. LISP solves this problem by separating the EID from the RLOC. The virtual machine IP addressed (EID in this case) will move from the original data center (RLOC) to the new data center with new RLOC information while preserving its original IP addresses. LISP mapping databases can keep track of the workload moves with immediate updates.

Summary

Despite all the benefits, enterprises have been cautious to adopt the cloud because of concerns about availability, security, and application performance. Cloud providers looking to tap into cloud-generated revenue streams can effectively monetize and increase profitability if they overcome these challenges in their IP *next generation networks (NGNs)*. By further ensuring that the cloud datacenters, networks, applications and services *are tightly integrated,* cloud providers can differentiate their services from other providers.

Cloud consumers require the same great experience they enjoyed before moving to the cloud. The IP NGN, which provides the access from enterprises to the multiple data centers of these cloud providers, can also enable the cloud resource pools to be flexibly extended across multiple geographically distributed data centers through data center interconnect (DCI) technologies.

To facilitate revenue growth by capturing this new market and reduce costs through operational efficiency, cloud providers' existing IP NGN infrastructures must evolve in line with the needs of the enterprises. DCI technologies are expected to play a key role in the evolution of IP NGNs to deliver business-grade cloud services through the tight integration of cloud services, applications, and IP NGNs.

Many DCI solutions are available, and the selection of a given solution depends on the needs of the enterprise. For example, with IP-based enterprise networks, a cloud provider can offer OTV as a preferred DCI solution. DCI links can be encrypted using layer 3 GETVPN encryption or layer 2–based MACsec encryption.

Live workload mobility can result in suboptimal routing (ingress traffic is routed through the data center from which the workload was moved) if the subnet is extended across geographically dispersed data centers. If the subnet is not extended across geographically dispersed data centers, all the TCP connections to moved hosts must be reset. Suboptimal routing and connection reset problem can be addressed by *Locator ID Separation Protocol* (LISP), which provides a network routing architecture and a set of protocols that separate the endpoint identity from the location of the endpoint.

Review Questions

You can find answers to these questions in Appendix A, "Answers to Review Questions."

1. Name the two leading trends that are transforming data centers.

    a. Reduce energy costs

    b. Server virtualization

    c. Storage virtualization

    d. Server consolidations

2. Which DCI technology solution offers only site-to-site connectivity?

    a. EoMPLS

    b. VPLS

    c. Layer 2 over Fiber

    d. A-VPLS

3. What is required to move workloads from one data center to another data center?

    a. VMware vMotion

    b. DCI

    c. Dark fiber

    d. All of the above

4. What is the maximum possible latency allowed between two graphically dispersed data centers?

    a. 1 ms

    b. 2 ms

    c. 5 ms

    d. All of the above

5. A-VPLS is supported on which of the following?

    a. Catalyst 6500

    b. Nexus 7000

    c. ASR1000

    d. A and B

References

1 GE Achieve Platinum LEED certified Data Center: http://greenbuildingelements.com/2011/08/22/ge-achieve-platinum-leed-certified-data-centre/

2 Cloud Services Axe Data Center Energy Consumption, Power Costs: http://www.crn.com/news/cloud/231601736/cloud-services-axe-data-center-energy-consumption-power-costs.htm?itc=refresh

3 See how VMware customers are cutting energy costs: http://info.vmware.com/content/GreenIT_LP/?src=WWW_08Q3_VMW_CSGN_ENERGY_EFFICIENCY_SOLUTIONS_PAGE

4 VMware VMotion, Live Migration for Virtual Machines Without Service Interruption: http://www.vmware.com/files/pdf/VMware-VMotion-DS-EN.pdf

5 Provider Backbone Bridging-EVPN: http://tools.ietf.org/html/draft-ietf-l2vpn-pbb-evpn-03

- See how VMware customers are cutting energy costs: http://info.vmware.com/content/GreenIT_LP/?src=WWW_08Q3_VMW_CSGN_ENERGY_EFFICIENCY_SOLUTIONS_PAGE

- Virtual Machine Mobility with VMware VMotion and Cisco Data Center Interconnect Technologies: http://www.cisco.com/en/US/solutions/collateral/ns340/ns517/ns224/ns836/white_paper_c11-557822.pdf

- Cisco Data Center Interconnect: http://www.cisco.com/en/US/solutions/collateral/ns340/ns517/ns224/ns949/ns304/ns975/at_a_glance_c45-493703.pdf

- Data Center Interconnect; Design Considerations for Virtualized Workload Mobility with Cisco, NetApp, and VMware: http://iwe.cisco.com/c/document_library/get_file?folderId=104401754&name=DLFE-81718394.pdf

- Buddy.com Launches Cross-Platform cloud Services for Mobile Developers: http://www.prweb.com/releases/2011/9/prweb8819476.htm

- 6fusion and Cloud Service Depot Team Up to Enable Partners in the Cloud: http://www.channelprosmb.com/article/25902/6fusion-and-cloud-Service-Depot-Team-Up-to-Enable-Partners-in-the-cloud/

- Verizon's 2011 Cloud Services Investment: 'Well Over $2 Billion': http://www.crn.com/news/cloud/231602081/verizons-2011-cloud-services-investment-well-over-2-billion.htm?itc=refresh

- Cloud Services Axe Data Center Energy Consumption, Power Costs: http://www.crn.com/news/cloud/231601736/cloud-services-axe-data-center-energy-consumption-power-costs.htm?itc=refresh

- Cisco NX-OS Virtual PortChannel: Fundamental Design Concepts with NXOS 5.0: http://www.cisco.com/en/US/prod/collateral/switches/ps9441/ps9670/design_guide_c07-625857.pdf

- Gartner Top Predictions for 2011: IT's Growing Transparency and Consumerization, Gartner, Inc.

- Gartner Security and Risk Management Summit 2011, Gartner, Inc.

- Cisco Global Cloud Index: Forecast and Methodology, 2010-2015

- Forecast: Hosted Virtual Desktops, Worldwide, 2010-2014 (2010 Update), Gartner, Inc.

- Cisco Visual Networking Index: Forecast and Methodology, 2010-2015

- Cisco Virtualized Workload Mobility Introduction: http://www.cisco.com/en/US/ docs/solutions/Enterprise/Data_Center/DCI/4.0/EMC/EMC_1.html

- Distributed Virtual Data Center for Enterprise and Service Provider Cloud: http://www.cisco.com/en/US/prod/collateral/routers/ps9853/white_paper_ c11-694882_ns975_Networking_Solutions_White_Paper.html

- Provider Backbone Bridging-EVPN: http://tools.ietf.org/html/ draft-ietf-l2vpn-pbb-evpn-03

- Google Music vs. Amazon vs. Apple's iCloud vs. Spotify vs. Rdio vs...: http://www.networkworld.com/community/node/77393

- HostingCon 2011: Four Trends for Cloud Service Providers: http://www. talkincloud.com/hostingcon-2011-four-trends-for-cloud-services-providers/

- Scoop: Sprint to launch cloud services in 4th quarter, August 10, 2011: http://news.cnet.com/8301-1035_3-20090584-94/ scoop-sprint-to-launch-cloud-services-in-4th-quarter/

Chapter 9

Securing Cloud Transport and Edge Using NGN Technologies

In this chapter, you learn the following:

- Key security challenges that are impeding the adoption of the cloud

- Key requirements to overcome these key security challenges

- Technologies that provide secure access to the cloud

- Technologies that protect the cloud edge/infrastructure from various attacks

Security Challenges in the Cloud

Moving to the cloud brings many operational benefits and economic advantages. The cloud offers the flexibility to increase and decrease infrastructure capacity (compute, storage, and network) on demand. Savings result from the usage-based model; you pay for use and release resources when you do not need them.

Cloud computing is poised for growth across different segments (finance, education, healthcare, manufacturing, public sector, and so on); however, concerns about security, privacy, confidentiality, and lack of regulatory compliance has impeded the adoption of cloud computing.

In 2012, Cisco Systems Inc. conducted a survey where more than 1300 information technology experts were interviewed to understand their topmost priorities and network challenges. The survey revealed that "during the cloud migration process, data protection security (72 percent) was cited as the top obstacle to a successful implementation of cloud services...."[1]

This can be traced to the following challenges inhibiting the adoption of the cloud:

- Access to the cloud is not inherently secure.

- The cloud edge and infrastructure behind it are prone to attacks.

- The cloud does not mandate regulatory compliance.

- Data can be leaked and stolen from the cloud.

- Fault tolerance is not an intrinsic component of every cloud.

- The cloud does not provide ubiquitous and device agnostic access inherently.

- Multitenant traffic (across shared resources of the cloud) may not be adequately segmented and isolated.

- Next Generation Network (NGN) devices that are expected to be part of the cloud are not inherently cloud ready.

Meeting these key security challenges is critical to accelerate the enterprise adoption of the cloud.

Key Requirements to Secure the Cloud

An NGN remains the most strategic component to the cloud because it is the network that provides the framework to transparently interconnect various networks and resources together to form the cloud. Chapter 8, "IP NGN Infrastructure That Supports Cloud Services," discusses in detail how this NGN needs to evolve to support fault tolerance (high availability) across geographically dispersed data centers, allow disaster avoidance, enable data center upgrades, and provide load bursting via workload mobility while maintaining optimal routing.

Security is yet another critical dimension that places new demands on the NGNs to make them cloud ready. Security strategy in the cloud needs to be comprehensive and implemented across different layers of the network—access, distribution, and core layers. This multilayer frame is well established and has been in use for quite a long time. Security in a data center is discussed in Chapter 6, "Securing and Optimizing Cloud Services."

To achieve cloud security, NGNs need to do the following:

- **Provide secure access to the cloud:** Securing the network transport is the key to achieve security and compliance. Cloud-ready NGNs need to provide data integrity, authentication, and confidentiality (encryption).

- **Prevent cloud infrastructure attacks:** The cloud infrastructure needs to be protected from all types of attacks.

- **Comply with regulatory requirements:** Provide one or more of these regulatory compliances: Payment Card Industry Data Security Standard (PCI-DSS), Health Insurance Portability and Accountability Act (HIPAA), Sarbanes-Oxley Act (SOX), Gramm Leach Bliley Act (GLBA), Federal Information Processing Standard (FIPS 140-3), Common Criteria Evaluation Assurance Level 4 (CC EAL4).

- **Ensure data leak prevention (DLP):** Protect sensitive data leakage prevention, content categorization, filtering, and monitoring.

- **Allow ubiquitous access:** Allow secure access anytime, anywhere and at any device.

- **Ensure service continuation:** Ensure business continuity through fault tolerance.

- **Scalability:** Offer a security solution that can scale-in and scale-out on demand.

- **Store data securely:** Data stored in the cloud must be protected from theft and breach of privacy. Mechanisms are required to encrypt and decrypt data stored in the cloud.

- **Separate tenant traffic:** Multitenant cloud traffic needs to be segmented and isolated from each other.

- **Make it easy to manage:** NGN devices that need to provide secure access and protect the cloud edge need to support ease of management; these devices should support *application programming interfaces* (API) to integrate with cloud orchestration, management, monitoring, and billing infrastructure.

Successfully implementing these requirements in the cloud will help achieve security and regulatory compliance and thus encourage enterprises to migrate to the cloud.

NGN Solutions to Secure the Cloud

Securing the cloud requires a comprehensive approach to security, where multiple points of the cloud are secured using a diverse set of technologies deployed in the NGN and in the data center. The need to offer services (infrastructure-as-a-service [IaaS], platform-as-a-service [PaaS], software-as-a-service [SaaS]) with the required security remains fundamental to the further proliferation of the cloud.

Securing virtualized infrastructure resources and data in rest and in flight are discussed in detail in Chapter 6.

This chapter complements the security discussion for the data center and primarily focuses on the following:

- Securing the access and transport to the cloud

- Securing the edge of the cloud

- Separating and segmenting multitenant traffic

Providing Secure Access to the Cloud

Secure access to the cloud is achieved by securing the IP NGN transport to the cloud. The cloud transport is either Layer 2 (*Multiprotocol Label Switching* [MPLS], virtual private LAN services, and so on) or Layer 3 (IP *virtual private networks* [VPNs]). These transport VPNs are secured using the following technologies and are then characterized as secure VPNs:

- *IP Security* (IPsec)

- *Secure Sockets Layer/Transport Layer Security* (SSL/TLS)

- *Datagram Transport Layer Security* (DTLS)

Knowing that you have secure access to the cloud is equally important for the consumers (enterprises) and the providers of the cloud. Enterprises are assured that access to the cloud guarantees privacy, confidentiality, and prevention of man-in-the-middle and fingerprint attacks. These attacks attempt to steal the identity of a cloud consumer and illegitimately consume cloud services.

Providing secure access to the cloud covers all types of cloud implementations—private, hybrid, or public clouds.

Many secure VPN solutions are available for the cloud. Not all of them are as diverse, feature rich, robust, flexible, and scalable as the Cisco VPN solutions are in meeting the unique needs of cloud deployments.

Secure VPN offers the following three main services:

- Data integrity

- Authentication

- Data confidentiality

Secure VPNs are grouped as follows:

- **Site-to-site VPNs:** Secure tunnels are established between networking infrastructure equipment (usually routers). Enterprises connecting to the cloud will have their networking infrastructure establish tunnels with the cloud provider equipment.

- **Remote-access VPNs:** Secure tunnels are established from remote location/user devices (routers, computers, smart devices, and so on) to the networking infrastructure equipment (usually routers). Enterprise users can connect to cloud resources from remote locations using remote access VPN devices.

Cisco Systems, a leading vendor in networking, offers industry-proven, diverse end-to-end solutions that are cloud ready and offer elastic scale, multitenancy, and ease of management.

Depending on the underlying transport (IP or MPLS), Cisco secure IPsec VPN solutions can offer the following:

- IPsec-based encryption (site-to-site VPN)

- Group Encrypted Transport Virtual Private Network (GETVPN)

- Dynamic Multipoint Virtual Private Network (DMVPN)

- Flex Virtual Private Network (FlexVPN)

Figure 9-1 provides a consolidated view of the secure VPN solutions based on the following:

- Cisco ASR1000 family of routers

- Cisco ISR G2 family of routers

- Cisco Cloud Services Router (CSR) 1000V series

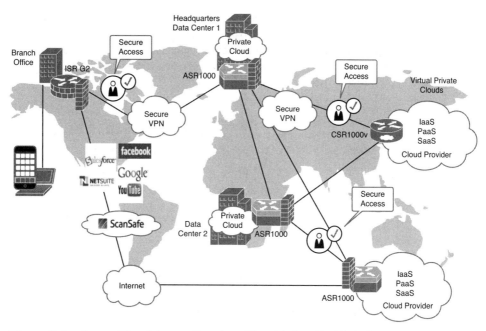

Figure 9-1   *Secure Cloud Access Based on Cisco End-to-End Solutions*

The Cisco CSR 1000V series router runs as a single tenant software service in a virtualized environment and offers integrated routing and secure connectivity capabilities.

You can deploy secure VPN solutions as follows:

■ **Managed service:** The cloud provider may own and manage the transport and access to the cloud to ensure that enterprise data privacy is guaranteed and customers are protected from man-in-the-middle and fingerprint attacks. The cloud provider equipment and software is collocated at the customer facility (for example, the Cisco ISR G2 and ASR1000 family of routers) and in the cloud (for example, Cisco Cloud Services Router 1000V). Selection of these routers is scale- and use-case–dependent.

■ **Self-managed:** Enterprises own and manage end-to-end secure access to the cloud. The secure access is initiated from the enterprise premise equipment (for example, the Cisco ISR G2 and ASR1000 family of routers) to terminate in the cloud provider equipment (for example, CSR1000v running as a virtualized service).

Before exploring the applicability of various VPN technologies to provide secure access to the cloud, the following section takes a quick look at the IPsec suite of protocols.

Internet Protocol Security

Internet Protocol Security (IPsec) is a protocol suite designed to provide secure connectivity for IPv4 and IPv6 endpoints. IPsec-based security offers connectionless integrity, data-origin authentication, and integrity and confidentiality of data packets that match a user-defined selection criterion, such as source and destination. IPsec is used to secure other Layer 3 protocols, too, including the IP itself.

IPsec has two modes of operation:

■ **Transport mode:** Ideal for host-to-host communication (for example, client accessing a server), it offers encryption of the payload and leaves the IP header intact.

■ **Tunnel mode:** Ideal for site-to-site VPNs and remote access, it offers entire IP packet encryption and encapsulation into another IP packet (IP in IP).

For additional information about IPsec and operational details, see RFC 4301.

IPsec VPNs

IPsec VPNs are also known as site-to-site VPNs that use crypto maps and security keys. These crypto maps and security keys are configured manually on all the devices that enable end-to-end IPsec VPN. Security keys are essential to IPsec VPN functionality and, therefore, require mechanisms for their distribution. For managed cloud IPsec VPN deployments, the cloud provider manages the distribution of security keys across all of its secure connectivity equipment.

For self-managed deployments, the enterprises need to either agree with the cloud provider on a set of pre-shared keys or collocate the secure VPN connectivity equipment at the cloud provider facility and manage the keys.

More advanced next-generation encryption mechanisms, such as Suite-B, are also available. Suite-B offers stronger authentication, key exchange, digital certificates, and entropy.

Suite-B supports the following cryptographic algorithms:

- Suite-B-GCM-128/256 comes in two flavors: 128 bits and 256 bits Advanced Encryption Standard using Galois and Counter Mode (AES-GCM). This algorithm is used when both ESP integrity protection and encryption are needed. These cryptographic algorithms are described in RFC 4106.

- Suite-B-GMAC-18/256 comes in two flavors: 128 bits and 256 bits Advanced Encryption Standard Galois Message Authentication Code (GMAC). This algorithm is described in RFC-4543 and is used when ESP integrity protection is required without encryption.

Internet Key Exchange (IKE) uses Advanced Encryption Standard Cipher Block Chaining (CBC) mode to provide encryption and Secure Hash Algorithm (SHA)-2 supports. This secure hashing algorithm is available as SHA-256 and SHA-384 and is described in RFC 4634.

Entropy (a better method for key generation) is discussed in the NIST's special draft publication named 800-90B. Additional details are available at NIST and online.

IPsec VPNs have been in use for a long time and have matured over the years. IPsec VPNs are deployed using hub-and-spoke topologies. That is, a site-to-site tunnel is established between every spoke to the hub, and communication between spokes is carried out via the hub. An IPsec VPN requires symmetrical configuration between each spoke and a hub router. For every spoke, the crypto map characteristics, the access list, and the *generic routing encapsulation* (GRE) tunnel information need to be mirrored on the aggregating hub router; otherwise, the encrypted traffic will be dropped at the hub router.

For a large-scale deployment like the cloud, an IPsec VPN solution might not scale very well. Consider a managed cloud deployment that involves 4000 spokes (customer sites) connecting to a cloud provider hub. To establish this topology, 4000 configuration profiles that match 4000 spokes need to be configured on the cloud provider hub router. Establishing such a complex configuration is not only time-consuming and error-prone but also difficult to troubleshoot if an issue arises with a spoke not coming up.

IPsec VPN might not be an ideal solution for a cloud deployment that mandates an instant turning on and off of a service and easy troubleshooting.

Dynamic Multipoint VPN

Cisco *Dynamic Multipoint VPN* (DMVPN) overcomes the limitations of the IPsec VPN and enables you to group many spokes into a single profile enabled by a multipoint GRE interface. This greatly simplifies the size of the VPN configuration because it removes the constraint of having a distinct physical or logical interface for each spoke on the hub. Using the previous example of connecting 4000 sites (customers) to a hub, DMVPN is preferred over site-to-site VPN because a managed cloud provider can group multiple spokes (customer sites) sharing similar characteristics in a single mGRE interface. By using an mGRE interface per tenant, the cloud provider can allow tenant-level separation. DMVPN allows spoke routers to get dynamically assigned IP addresses (through DHCP server), saving the cloud provider the burden of configuring all the customer-deployed routers with manually configured IP addresses. A cloud provider brings up a new spoke, lets it attain an IP address dynamically using a *Dynamic Host Configuration Protocol* (DHCP) server, and lets the spoke register with the *Next Hop Resolution Protocol* (NHRP) server running on the hub router. DMVPN offers site-to-site, hub-and-spoke, and spoke-to-spoke communications (not possible in site-to-site IPsec VPN deployments where all the communications have to go through the VPN hub router).

For self-managed enterprises, the cloud provider data center where the enterprise is connecting to consume the cloud service is considered just another VPN site (spoke) that registers with the enterprise headend and allows communication with any other enterprise site.

DMVPN is also known as an overlay network that operates on an IP network, including the Internet. This would allow the cloud providers to use private addresses for the *customer premise equipment* (CPE) and conserve scarce IPv4 addresses.

Because of its configuration simplicity, DMVPN is preferred over IPsec VPN as a solution for cloud providers offering managed cloud services. Because DMVPN enables site-to-site connectivity, the headend router of an enterprise can communicate with a spoke router of the cloud, as can any of the branches directly communicate with the cloud router (spoke-to-spoke communication). DMVPN also allows cloud-to-cloud communication; the two DMVPN routers deployed in the cloud can act as two spokes communicating with each other. It also enables the cloud providers to burst work load from its data centers to another cloud provider (intercloud).

In the managed service case, the provider manages key distribution. For self-managed enterprises, either the secure connectivity equipment is collocated at the cloud provider environment (a physical router like ASR1000) or initiated as virtual instance (a virtual router like CSR1000v), and the enterprise manages the key distribution.

DMVPN can use either IKEv1 or IKE v2 for key exchange.

Figure 9-2 provides a quick overview of DMVPN solution in action.

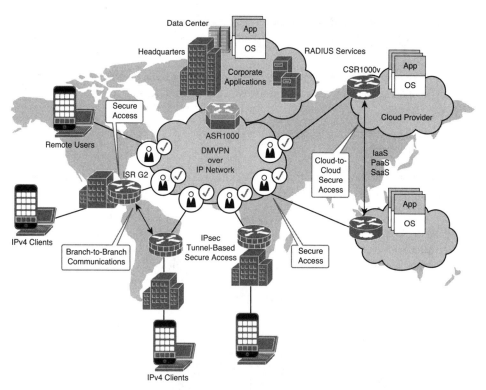

Figure 9-2 *DMVPN-Based Secure Access to the Cloud*

FlexVPN

Cisco FlexVPN uses the next-generation IKEv2 (*Internet Key Exchange*) key management protocol (RFC 4306) as a default on the Cisco ASR1000 and ISR G2 family of routers. Cisco FlexVPN is a two-in-one VPN that offers remote-access and site-to-site (hub-and-spoke, spoke-to-spoke) topologies. FlexVPN is similar to DMVPN in that they both support site-to-site (hub-spoke and spoke-spoke) communication.

Cisco FlexVPN is different from DMVPN because it offers remote-access VPN solution.

IKEv2 offers the following advantages over IKEv1:

- **Dead peer detection:** IKEv2 has built-in support for dead peer detection.

- **Network Address Translation - Traversal (NAT-T):** Allows cloud providers to assign RFC-1918 IPv4 addresses to multiple customers sharing the same address space and NAT the customer traffic to save on the scarce public IPv4 addresses. IKEv2 performs this automatically, whereas IKEv1 uses NAT-T as an add-on function.

- **Certificate URLs:** The certificates can be referenced via URLs and hash instead of via IKEv2 packets; this helps avoid fragmentation.

- **Denial of service (DoS) attack resilience:** IKEv2 performs better than IKEv1 in avoiding spoofing attacks; IKEv2 does not process a request until it determines the requester.

- **EAP support:** IKEv2 supports Extensible Authentication Protocol (EAP). This enables mobile devices to get properly authenticated before accessing cloud resources.

- **Multiple crypto engines:** Crypto engines can be allocated to handle IPv4 and IPv6 traffic separately.

Based on these unique characteristics, FlexVPN is a flexible solution for secure remote-access (for example, Windows clients) and site-to-site deployments.

Figure 9-3 shows FlexVPN-based managed secure-access deployment for the cloud. The same deployment is used for self-managed enterprises except the key distribution part. In the managed service case, the provider manages key distribution. For self-managed enterprises, either the secure connectivity equipment is collocated at the cloud provider environment (a physical router, such as ASR1000) or initiated as a virtual instance (a virtual router, such as CSR1000v), and the enterprise manages the key distribution.

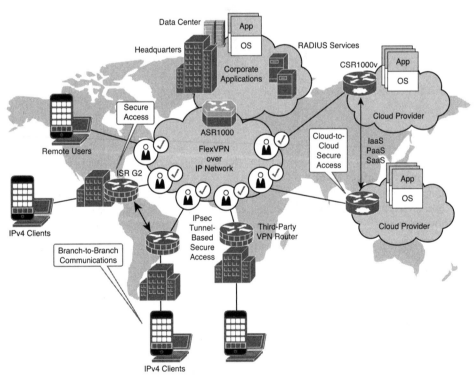

Figure 9-3   *FlexVPN Secure Access to the Cloud*

Group Encrypted Transport Virtual Private Networks

Group Encrypted Transport (GET) refers to the ability to encrypt traffic without the knowledge of the peer. The GETVPN solution offers a substantial paradigm shift from traditional IPsec. That is, when using GETVPN, a receiver of an encrypted unicast packet can decrypt the packet without knowing its source. This is in contrast to traditional IPsec, which relies on peer-to-peer communication for key exchange and security association. Handling multicast and broadcast data flows is one of the challenges that the traditional IPsec peer-to-peer model cannot address adequately and efficiently because it requires replicating the same content to each secure session established between peers.

GETVPN preserves all the original IP address and header information while encrypting the data portion, commonly known as IP address preservation. GETVPN is also considered a tunnel-less encryption technology because it does not require any advance secure tunnel setup between the devices that want to communicate with each other. Each device is already authenticated and has received an agreed upon key from a key server using the *Group Domain of Interpretation* (GDOI) protocol.

GETVPN has three main components:

- **Key server:** The key server distributes the keys used for all communication, thus enabling all group members to communicate without having to set up direct connections to each other and exchange keys.

- **Group member:** Responsible for encrypting and decrypting traffic exchanged with other group members.

- **GDOI protocol:** Group members register with the key server using GDOI to authenticate and authorize the device for communication. GDOI informs the group member of the IPsec policy and the keys being used. After the group member is registered and has received the traffic encryption key, it can then communicate with any other group member without having to go through the key server.

Preserving the IP address allows the encrypted packets to carry the original source and destination IP addresses instead of replacing them with tunnel endpoint addresses. Some IP header parameters are also preserved. The exposure of the original IP addresses on the outside header enables the contiguous routing plane without building a routing overlay and allows multicast to follow the optimal multicast distribution tree through the network core.

Many network features, such as routing, basic firewall, *quality of service* (QoS), traffic management, and so on, work based on the information contained in the IP header. Because the IP header is preserved, all the network features continue to work as before. This eliminates many issues associated with deploying point-to-point encryption in a core network. MPLS VPNs provide the enterprise with scalable WAN network architecture with any-to-any connectivity, hierarchical routing, and efficient multicast forwarding.

As illustrated in Figure 9-4, GETVPN provides a way to secure any-to-any traffic. It is enabled by MPLS VPNs. GETVPN allows replication of the packets after encryption. This allows the multicast traffic to be replicated at the core, thereby reducing the load and bandwidth requirement on the *customer edge* (CE) equipment.

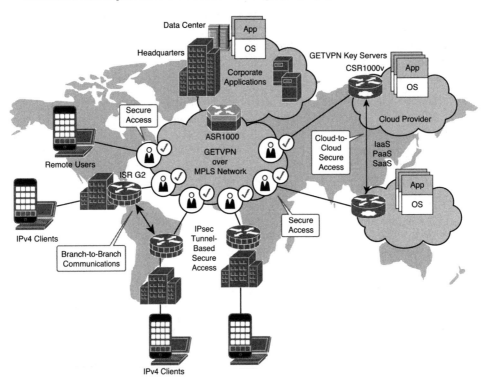

Figure 9-4 *GETVPN-Based Managed Cloud Access*

Key Distribution and Management in the Cloud

IPsec VPNs rely on unique keys to encrypt and decrypt data between devices providing secure access to the cloud (usually routers). These routers are either dedicated devices (Cisco ASR1000 and ISR G2 family of routers) providing secure access or running as a service in a virtualized environment (for example, Cisco CSR 1000V). Distribution and management of keys is an essential aspect of IPsec VPNs. For managed service deployments, the cloud provider manages the key distribution.

Before discussing the use case where a self-managed enterprise connects to the cloud, it is worth noting that a self-managed enterprise connects to a partner today using pre-shared keys that are exchanged in advance of establishing a secure tunnel between the two sites. You can use the same approach to connect with the cloud provider.

The same key distribution and management mechanisms apply to IPsec VPN, DMVPN, and FlexVPN deployments.

To solve the key management problem for GETVPN technology, enterprises have two options. The first option is to collocate the GETVPN key server at the cloud provider environment and register all the secure access routers (usually run as a service on a Cisco ASR1000 or ISR G2 router) to this GETVPN key server. The second option is to use the cloud provider key server (consume as a service) and register all the enterprise secure access routers with it.

Cloud providers can either dedicate key server equipment to a specific customer or use *virtual routing and forwarding* (VRF) to segment the customers.

Cloud providers can use IPsec VPN or GETVPN technologies to secure the *data center interconnect* (DCI) links across geographically dispersed cloud-ready data centers.

Secure key distribution remains as a challenge and is prone to man-in-the-middle attacks. One way to overcome this challenge is for the cloud provider (managed service case) or the enterprise (self-managed case) to physically load certificates or manually configure keys on the routers before making them operational.

IPsec VPN Summary

This wraps our discussion on IPsec VPN technologies. At this point, you might be wondering what the preferred VPN architecture for cloud access is. The answer really depends on the needs of a deployment scenario. For small-scale cloud deployments, IPsec VPN can be a preferred choice. For medium to large-size deployments, DMVPN or FlexVPN are often selected because they both offer ease and flexibility of configuration. GETVPN can also be selected as long as the enterprise is willing to expose its routing topology and select a provider that has an MPLS backbone to carry the enterprise traffic.

DMVPN is designed to work with a homogenous set of nodes (that is, sharing similar ACLs and routing policy and having nodes that are treated mostly the same). FlexVPN has the capability to work with a more heterogeneous set of nodes where each node can be treated differently (that is, different ACLs, routing policy, and so on.).

Very large cloud deployments require a selection of either DMVPN or FlexVPN or can run both concurrently. That is, DMVPN nodes can participate in FlexVPN networks, and FlexVPN (site-to-site) nodes can participate in DMVPN networks. For example, a cloud provider might want to deploy DMVPN to group a set of customers (more than one tenant) using one mGRE tunnel and provide site-to-site connectivity across the entire network. The cloud provider can also employ FlexVPN for another set of customers to provide remote access and per-tenant separation using one GRE tunnel per customer (this feature is inherent to FlexVPN).

FlexVPN also offers n+2 clustering support (for example, for a cluster of 10 head ends, 8 could be active and 2 as standby providing fault tolerance) to achieve a very highly scalable VPN architecture. With DMVPN, you can provide the same functionality by putting a server load balancer (SLB) in front of the DMVPN hub. Inherent to FlexVPN or DMVPN is the fact that they are both overlay VPN technologies that enable an enterprise to hide its routing topology from the cloud provider.

IPsec-based VPNs are not the only security solutions available to provide secure access to the cloud. *Secure Sockets Layer* (SSL) and *Transport Layer Security* (TLS) VPNs are just as robust and scalable as the IPsec-based VPNs are in providing secure access to the cloud.

The SSL VPNs have been in use on the Internet for a long time and have proven to secure web-based commerce and communications (browsing, email, faxing, VoIP, and so on).

The next sections focus on the technologies that allow secure access to the cloud based on SSL VPNs technologies.

Transport Layer Security Protocol

TLS is a standard-based protocol (RFC 5246) and incorporates protocol specifications of SSL 3.0 published by Netscape. TLS provides secure access to the cloud applications using asymmetric cryptography for secure key exchange, symmetric keys to achieve data confidentiality, and *message authentic code* (MAC) for message integrity. TLS ensures that access to the cloud is secured from eavesdropping, phishing, and tampering attacks. TLS consists of two layered protocols:

- Handshake protocol

- Record protocol

TLS relies on its handshake protocol to have the client and server authenticate each other, negotiate encryption algorithm/keys, and then start communicating with each other.

The handshake protocol offers the following basic services:

- Peers can authenticate each other using asymmetric or public keys.

- A shared secret is exchanged securely, which prevents man-in-the-middle attacks.

- Reliability that does not permit hackers to modify the connection between communicating parties without being detected.

The record protocol ensures the following:

- **Privacy and confidentiality:** Unique keys for each connection (shared secret exchanged during TLS handshake) and symmetric encryption based on AES, 3DES, RC4, IDEA, Camellia, and so on.

- **Integrity:** Ensures connection reliability based on integrity checks based on keyed MAC (for example, *Secure Hash 1* [SHA-1] is used for MAC computations).

TLS always uses TCP as a transport protocol and offers secure access from clients to servers. TLS relies on certificates to establish authentication and secure communications. These certificates issued by *certificate authorities* (CA) are of two types:

- **Single root:** The CA owns the root certificate that most popular browsers trust and have embedded in them.

- **Chained root:** The CA does not own the root certificate that is embedded and trusted in popular browsers. The CA needs to chain its root certificate to another third-party CA that is trusted by the most popular browsers

Datagram Transport Layer Security Protocol

TLS is a connection-oriented protocol that must use a reliable transport like TCP and therefore is not ideal for the (*Real Time Protocol* [RTP]) stream-oriented applications like voice and video that cannot tolerate the delays caused by TCP connection setup, teardown, and any resulting retransmission. (Signaling and exchange of control information of these applications is fine using TCP-based TLS.) To overcome this, an equivalent protocol using UDP datagrams is desired to transmit RTP streams securely. DTLS offers similar security as TLS but avoids transmission delays by employing connectionless UDP as a transport (in contrast to TCP, which is connection oriented).

Note   You can find additional information about DTLS at http://www.rfc-editor.org/rfc/rfc4347.txt.

Cloud providers can use TLS and DTLS together to offer secure access to unified communications and web-based applications from the cloud. TLS is an application-independent protocol and allows other protocols to ride on top of it. For example, *Session Initiation Protocol* (SIP) signaling can be exchanged between endpoints securely using TLS. Exchange of signaling communication (call setup) between peers can be based on authentication (based on strong RSA), encryption (based on AES), and integrity checking (based on SHA-1), providing a secure and robust connection of SIP over TLS. RTP streams, however, can take place on DTLS.

Clientless Versus Full Tunnel

The previous sections explored the TLS and DTLS protocols, which enable secure remote-access via SSL VPNs. This section examines the two deployment options for SSL VPNs: clientless and full tunnel.

Clientless denotes that the remote endpoint (laptop, smart device, and so on) does not have any specific client software installed on it. Remote access to the cloud is achieved using a TLS-enabled web browser to establish secure communication to the cloud.

This is a lightweight solution wherein a cloud consumer user does not need a dedicated tunnel to consume a service from the cloud. Clientless provides access to a limited set of applications that are accessible via a web browser.

Full-tunnel TLS solutions come in the form of custom-built applications designed for various mobile operating systems like iOS, Android, webOS, and BlackBerryOS. The cloud provider can use a custom built application that fully maintains stringent standards and allows secure access to the cloud resources. An example of a custom-built application would be a Salesforce.com application running on a smart mobile device that allows access to Salesforce.com running in the cloud.

Full-tunnel secure access can also be made available at the device level (as opposed to having a specific custom application). An example of that is Cisco AnyConnect client that uses SSL VPN to provide secure access to the cloud from all types of devices, including PCs, laptops, and smart devices that support mainstream operating systems (iOS, Android, Windows, OS X, and so on). The way AnyConnect works is that the device initiates an SSL connection from itself to the cloud; this secure connection is terminated on a security appliance like the Cisco *Adaptive Security Appliance* [ASA], and the device has access to all the cloud resources defined by the security policy.

Cisco ASA (running as an appliance or a virtualized service) allows an AnyConnect client to establish an SSL VPN connection to use two simultaneous tunnels: an SSL tunnel and a DTLS tunnel. Using DTLS avoids latency and bandwidth problems associated with SSL connections and improves the performance of real-time applications consumed from the cloud.

Before concluding the discussion on secure access to the cloud, it is imperative to highlight the importance of provisioning, automating, monitoring, and billing. To be considered cloud ready, the NGN devices that provide secure access to the cloud must provide *application programming interfaces* (API) that allows for orchestration, automation, monitoring capabilities, and full integration with the billing infrastructure. See Chapter 4, "Network Services in the Cloud," to refresh your memory about cloud services management.

Securing the Cloud Edge

The edge of the cloud is a critical part of the architecture because it defines the interface characteristics and the service hand-off from a provider to the consumer of the cloud. Protecting the cloud edge requires the cloud services (Iaas, Paas, SaaS) to be protected from all sorts of attacks that might result in service interruption.

The cloud edge is also a trust boundary that establishes the "rules of engagement" between the provider and the consumer of the cloud. The provider needs to implement security mechanisms to guarantee the SLAs for the services offered. Service SLAs center on *reliability, availability, and serviceability* (RAS). When an enterprise subscribes to a cloud service, the cloud provider needs to ensure that the bandwidth pipe delivered to the enterprise is clean and secure. Some typical threats encountered include *bandwidth stealing and distributed denial of service (DDoS)* attacks that reduce the reliability and availability of the cloud services.

The following list highlights some of the malicious attacks that can be encountered in cloud deployments:

- Attackers use sheer weight of traffic to overwhelm the initial processing of the messages.

- Attackers bombard particular bottlenecks of the service, such as authentication, which requires a lot of processing.

- Packets can be spoofed to appear to have several source IP addresses (a spoof DDoS attack).

- Packets can be from a large number of real IP addresses, usually a collection of hijacked machines (a true DDoS attack or a zombie DDoS attack). This, in particular, is very dangerous because it provides a considerable bandwidth over which to originate the malicious messages.

- With port scan attacks, an attacker, in an attempt to break in, scans all the ports to find out which are all the "open ports" (ports with a listener).

Not protecting the cloud edge and not delivering the services with guaranteed SLAs will lead to a perception that the cloud provider cannot deliver. To avoid this negative perception, the cloud provider needs to deploy security mechanisms to assure SLAs. These security mechanisms should be able to localize the threat and prevent propagation of any attack that the service provider network encounters.

The goal is to provide the first line of defense at the edge of the provider to ensure that the cloud provider infrastructure and services are protected from the traffic that originates from the enterprise (the cloud consumer traffic is not trusted) and is either destined to the provider or to the Internet (outside traffic has never been trusted anyway).

Protecting the cloud edge in no way eliminates the need for the security devices (firewall, intrusion prevention system, and so on) that are deployed within the data center to deal with north-south traffic (traffic that leaves the data center) or east-west traffic (traffic that stays within the data center). Additional security devices, such as firewalls to protect VM-to-VM traffic and tenant-to-tenant traffic (each tenant could have many VMs), remain vitally important as well. Security within the data center is discussed in Chapter 6.

This section focuses on the evolution of NGN to support cloud security, *protecting the cloud edge* here refers to protecting the cloud provider's *point of presence* (POP) or data center.

Typical network security mechanisms such as access lists and NAT are a starting point to seal the data center entry points from certain well-known attack vectors. However, due to the static nature of access lists, they are not useful against most of the advanced attack vectors, which are dynamic and distributed in nature. So, access lists can reduce the impact of an attack for a while, but they ultimately fail during prolonged attacks.

In a cloud environment, a holistic and multitenant approach to security is required where a tenant under attack does not affect other tenants sharing the same cloud resources. A typical scenario is a DDoS generated in the Internet where a sophisticated attacker has found a way to launch an attack using a large botnet army.

Figure 9-5 shows a typical cloud provider network providing peering and data center services for its customers with a networkwide security solution deployed from a renowned vendor like Arbor. The pervasive security solution is called Peakflow SP that is managed by a Peakflow SP PI device acting as a leader (a central point for provisioning and management). A network detector deployed at the customer premise probes user traffic to identify specific signatures associated with an attack vector. A match of the signature triggers a policy activation controlled by the leader to treat the affected flow/stream. At policy invocation, all the suspect traffic (identified by the signature match) is redirected to the collectors deployed at each layer. The affected stream is then directed to an Arbor Guard/Threat Management System (TMS) that treats the affected flow/stream and either sinks it or cleans it (the legitimate traffic) and forwards it to the original destination.

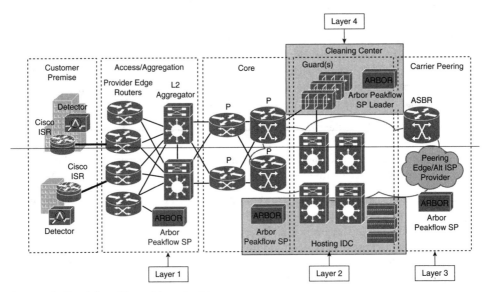

Figure 9-5   *Arbor Clean Pipes Architecture*

Internet-based DDoS attacks are not the only challenges that cloud providers face. Offering multimedia communications in the cloud comes with its unique attack vectors that need to be met with and call control requirements that need to be implemented to deliver these services with agreed-upon SLAs.

To be considered viable for the cloud, the multimedia security solution should at least offer the following capabilities:

- Call admission control polices per tenant to ensure individual SLAs.

- Call routing control policies per tenant to ensure traffic separation at Layer 7.

- Ability to configure and prevent DDoS attacks at the tenant level.

- Allow managing of the security services using cloud management tools.

Session Border Controller (SBC) is a unique breadth of solutions that target these requirements, allowing the cloud providers to offer cloud-based multimedia services with the required security.

Cisco is uniquely positioned to play a critical role here because it has the breadth of platforms and experience to push innovation required to complete the end-to-end security strategy for solutions including infrastructure, services, and transport.

Cisco Hosted Collaboration Solution (HCS) in the cloud is an example of offering a UC solution in the cloud. HCS offers the same feature richness and security as is available in the enterprise network and offers call admission, call control, number and header manipulation, call routing, load balancing, and attack prevention.

Similarly a hosted UC security solution ensures that the enterprise customers are offered a similar level of security and protection in the hosted cloud environment that existed in the enterprise premise.

Figure 9-6 provides an end-to-end view of hosted unified communications in the cloud. Each tenant is allocated its own instance of call managers, presence servers, and other unified communications services.

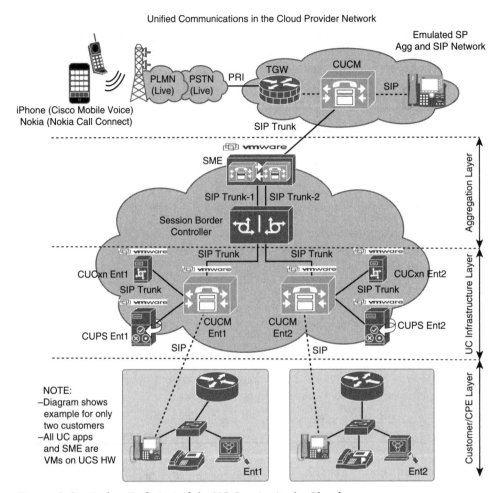

Figure 9-6   *End-to-End view of the UC Service in the Cloud*

Multitenant Traffic Separation

The cloud, by design, is multitenant, where infrastructure resources (compute, storage, network, and so on) and services (applications, databases, and so forth) are *shared across tenants* to realize cost advantages that the cloud promises to offer.

Cloud providers must offer the required security at every tenant level and prevent tenants from propagating malware, monitoring each other, and various other man-in-the-middle attacks.

Network segmentation is one of the most effective ways to realize multitenancy and isolate traffic and attacks. Cloud providers use these segmentation techniques to isolate customer traffic and attacks and localize them to a specific tenant while maintaining service to other tenants. For example, at the firewall level, segmentation enables a physical firewall to be partitioned logically into different firewalls each with a unique set of policies.

Various segmentation technologies exist; however, some of the key technologies are as follows:

- **Virtual local-area networks (VLAN):** The use of VLANs is one of the most commonly used methods because of its simplicity and ease of deployment. The cloud provider can deploy various services like web, database, and *Lightweight Directory Access Protocol* (LDAP) by simply configuring various VLANs and assigning them to various services. If a service is attacked under any circumstances, having a VLAN in place will restrict the attack to that VLAN only while keeping the continuity of service on other VLANs.

- **VRF:** The use of VRFs has been prevalent in the *service provider* (SP) space, where an SP can segment customer traffic across various tenants/customers using VRFs. Cloud providers can group tenants and offered services (web, databases, LDAP, and so on) in multiple VRFs to maintain isolation. Then, by using technologies such as Cisco *VRF-Aware Service Infrastructure* (VASI), VRF interworking is achieved.

Figure 9-7 provides an end-to-end view of HCS security and shows how different technologies discussed so far come together and work closely with each other. Virtual access in the data center is provided by a virtual firewall that supports inter- and intra-VLAN traffic. Firewalls can also be portioned using context awareness (for example, ASA Context-Aware Firewall). NAT can be used in the management VPN to use overlapping addresses and conserve scarce IPv4 address space. Cisco Unified Border Element (CUBE-SP) is used to protect the multimedia edge and enable inter-enterprise (enterprise 1 to enterprise 2 and vice versa) call flows. To realize effective multitenant separation, one or more VLANs can be mapped to a VRF so that overlapping IPv4 addresses can be assigned to multiple customers. This also enables the extension of the tenant separation from inside DC to the cloud provider IP NGN. This end-to-end tenant separation is a key differentiator and an effective use of existing network assets to offer cloud services.

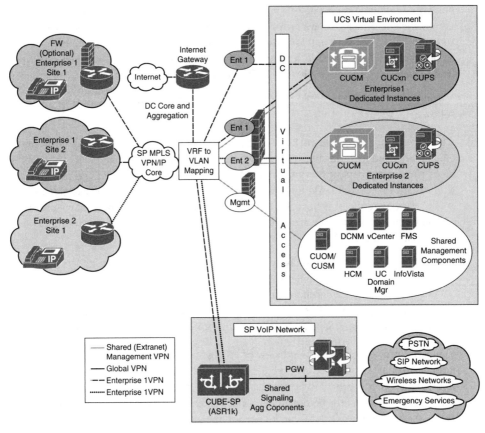

Figure 9-7   *End-to-End View of Security in HCS Deployment*

A firewall context is a logical group assigned per tenant that pools VLANs/VRFs in itself. Context helps achieve network segmentation per customer or tenant. Typical customer deployments have more than one VM associated with a tenant. Each tenant can be assigned to a set of VLANs to separate the actual data traffic from the management traffic. These VLANs are then mapped to VRFs at the edge of the data center and propagated across the cloud provider IP NGN. Both VLANs/VRFs are mapped in context to allow communication within the data center.

Traditional segmentation techniques exhibit scale challenges when applied to cloud architectures. Typically, these segmentation techniques either limit the scope of communication within the data center (VLAN scale while allowing any-vlan-anywhere) or limit the mobility of workloads within a data center (VRFs at the aggregation layer). Therefore, a breed of overlay solutions that work over an IP-based data center core are becoming popular. Some of these overlay solutions include VxLAN, NVGRE and STT. Although each of these technologies is based on a common principle to carry L2 segmentation (VLANs) over a tunnel, there are subtle differences. The VxLAN technology enables extending L2 segments (VLANs) flexibly across an IP (multicast-enabled) network. NVGRE uses a GRE tunnel transport L2 while using the 24-bit GRE key as the network discriminator. STT is a stateless tunnel transport technology that uses a TCP-like header instead of a GRE header to transport L2 frames. This enables seamless integration of services to the VMs.

Summary

To foster and accelerate adoption of the cloud, it is imperative to provide enterprises secure access to the cloud by securing the transport to the cloud. This chapter examined various IPsec and SSL VPN technologies that facilitate this secure access. Various IPsec-based VPN solutions exist that are known as DMVPN, FlexVPN, and GETVPN solutions. These solutions provide deployment options that differ in flexibility, complexity, and scale. Additional breadth of secure access solutions that are based on SSL VPN exist that are available in clientless and client-based modes.

The cloud provider not only needs to protect the cloud infrastructure from all sorts of attacks that exists today but also needs to have an optimal planning for future attack prevention. Threat mitigation within the NGN through signature matching (as provided by Arbor solutions) enables early detection, redirection, and cleanup of infected flow before threats affect service levels for legitimate cloud consumers. Additional threat prevention capabilities are available at the data center that protect VM-to-VM, tenant-to-tenant, and tenant-to-outside world. The cloud security offered by the evolved NGNs complements the security capabilities of the virtualized cloud data centers, which were explored earlier in Chapter 6.

You can leverage advanced solutions, such as application-aware firewalls, to further secure the cloud edge from clear-text traffic. Finally, securely offering multimedia services in the cloud calls for unique multitenant security capabilities that are provided by devices categorized as session border controllers, or SBCs.

Network segmentation is one of the most effective ways to realize multitenancy and isolate traffic and attacks. Cloud providers use these segmentation techniques to isolate customer traffic and attacks and localize them to a specific tenant while maintaining service to other tenants.

The wide range of security capabilities made available by cloud providers serves to bolster enterprise confidence as they embark on their migration of IT operations to the cloud.

Review Questions

You can find answers to these questions in Appendix A, "Answers to Review Questions."

1. Which VPN technology scales the most in the cloud?

   a. EZVPN
   b. DMVPN
   c. GETVPN
   d. All of the above

2. Which Cisco VPN solution is considered to be a "two-in-one" VPN solution?

   a. DMVPN
   b. GETVPN
   c. SSL VPN
   d. FlexVPN

3. Which is a true statement (choose as many possible)?

   a. Clientless requires software to be installed on the device that supports TLS-based access
   b. Clientless is lightweight because it uses a TLS-enabled Web browser to provide secure access to the cloud
   c. Full tunnel requires software (application- or device-specific) to be installed on the remote end point
   d. Full tunnel is considered a lightweight solution

4. Why is network segmentation important?

   a. It enables the separation of tenant traffic
   b. It restricts brute-force attacks to the tenant being attacked
   c. It allows the assignment of one or more VLANs to a tenant
   d. It allows tenants to be grouped in VRFs and communicated across cloud provider networks
   e. All of the above

References

1. Cisco Global cloud Network Survey, http://www.cisco.com/en/US/solutions/ns1015/global_cloud_survey.html

■ Santos, Omar. *End-to-End Network Security: Defense-in-Depth*. Cisco Press, 2007.

■ Earl, Carter. CCSP Self-Study: CCSP IPS Exam Certification Guide. Cisco Press, 2005.

■ DRAFT Cloud Computing Synopsis and Recommendations, http://csrc.nist.gov/publications/drafts/800-146/Draft-NIST-SP800-146.pdf

- Wainewright, Phil. What cloud computing can do for your enterprise; Lessons from the second generation of cloud adopters, http://thecloud.appirio.com/rs/appirio/images/Phil_Wainewright_cloud_Computing.pdf

- Cisco Hosted Collaboration Solution, http://www.cisco.com/en/US/partner/solutions/collateral/ns151/ns1086/solution_overview_c22-636326.html

Chapter 10

Optimizing and Accelerating Cloud Services

In this chapter, you will learn how to optimally:

- Place cloud services

- Offload services

- Consume cloud services

- Accelerate cloud services to achieve best performance

Enhancing Performance of Cloud Applications and Services

Adoption of cloud-based services and applications enables the enterprise to achieve business agility, cost savings, and efficiency of IT operations resulting from a usage-based model. For the cloud providers, the cloud opens up opportunities for new revenue streams.

The cloud applications and services, however, can offer a poor response time, resulting in a less-than-optimal user experience, which has slowed adoption of the cloud. Providing the same user experience to the enterprise consumers of the cloud as was available in the enterprise LAN remains a key challenge that needs to be addressed to accelerate the adoption of the cloud.

Role of IP NGN in Optimizing Cloud Applications and Services

Cloud providers with network assets are in a unique position to address this challenge. Leveraging the intelligence of their IP *Next Generation Networks* (NGN), these providers can differentiate their cloud offerings by delivering high performance and guarantee different service levels.

Supporting cloud-based services, such as accepting virtualized workloads into the cloud or streaming video content from any location to any location, can cause considerable drain on the cloud provider's network resources.

Adding to this is strong competitive and pricing pressure that requires the cloud provider's network infrastructure capacity to be utilized in an optimal manner. The goal is to reduce infrastructure costs by delivering cloud services in a manner that allows the network capacity to be effectively utilized.

Today's clouds are increasingly composed of multiple geographically dispersed data centers that are tightly integrated with the intelligent network infrastructure. The cloud service instance in one of these data centers will service a particular customer. The proximity of the data center to the enterprise location (where the service is consumed), along with the performance characteristics of the underlying network, can significantly impact the quality of the user experience.

Intelligently locating cloud-ready data centers on which to place cloud applications and services (infrastructure resources such as compute, storage, network, and network services like firewall, load balancers, and so on) is a critical aspect of service delivery because it allows the cloud providers to distribute the load and address scale and capacity demands appropriately.

If you do not understand the network topology, performance, and load, you might place cloud services in a data center that is already being overutilized or that is located on a less-optimized network path.

These demands require IP NGNs to become cloud services–aware and expose the network intelligence to cloud management tools to optimally place and deliver cloud services.

Figure 10-1 illustrates this two-way relationship, where cloud services are optimized by the intelligence shared by the network infrastructure and the network infrastructure is optimized through an increasing awareness of cloud services.

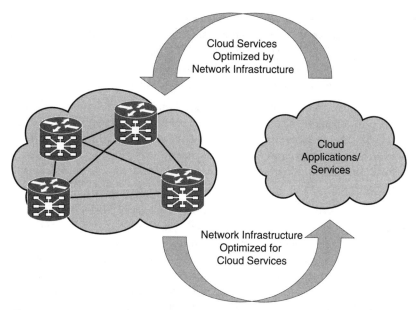

Figure 10-1 *NGNs Become Aware of Cloud Services*

How Cloud Services Are Placed Today

Today, a cloud service request by a consumer is usually fulfilled from a DNS-selected data center or from one that is geographically nearest to the consumer. Simple geographic proximity does not ensure that the network path between the consumer and the selected data center is optimal, nor does it guarantee low latency and jitter. The result could be a poor overall user experience due to numerous hops, high latency, jitter, and so on. Consequently, cloud providers struggle to offer any kind of performance guarantees in their *service level agreements* (SLA).

Selection of data centers, without considering available network capacity from the enterprise service consumption points to the data centers, leads to inefficient infrastructure utilization, which can result in capacity shortages in some parts of the network. To mitigate this, a provider may prematurely invest in upgrading network infrastructure capacity, leading to an overall increased cost of delivering cloud services.

Network Positioning System

Cisco *Network Provisioning System* (NPS) is the technology that enables IP NGNs to expose advanced network intelligence to the cloud to facilitate the optimized deployment and consumption of cloud services.

Enterprises want to ensure that the cloud services are placed in data centers that meet SLAs and that deliver high levels of user experience and application performance.

Cloud providers can meet the enterprise demands by sharing the intelligence of their NGNs to the cloud management tools to choose data centers that offer the best network performance metrics (accessibility, latency, jitter, packet loss, historical performance, and so on) but that also offer ideal network proximity (identifies resources based on hop or distances) to achieve reduced costs and excellent user experience.

Using real-time advertisements of network and cloud resource availability across multiple data centers, NPS maintains a global view of cloud capabilities. This allows NPS to align the provisioning of cloud services with the availability of resources, ensuring that the cloud services are placed at data centers with sufficient or excess capacity. This cloud awareness allows better utilization of the provider's cloud resources, while maintaining a superior user experience.

The fundamental role of NPS is to receive and respond to inquiries by cloud management tools that seek to provision services in the cloud-ready data centers. Again, these services could typically include infrastructure resources such as compute capacity, storage, and network services such as firewalls or load balancing. As illustrated in Figure 10-2, NPS responds to an inquiry with a list of the best data centers/resources ranked according to the ordering preferences of the cloud consumer. The ranking can be performed or based on criteria specified in the inquiry—such as proximity, latency, jitter, reachability, bandwidth.

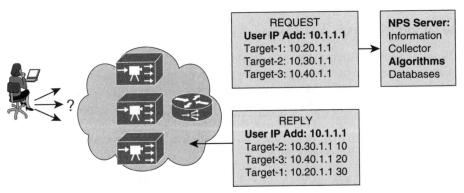

Figure 10-2 *NPS Provides a Ranked List of Data Centers on Optimal Paths*

Cloud Service Placement at an Optimal Location

NPS works the same way for the cloud consumer (that is, locate the optimal place of a cloud service) as the DNS of the Internet works for the web consumer (that is, locate the optimal place of a given web uniform resource identifier—Web URI).

Cloud fulfillment applications request the NPS to recommend an optimal data center for service placement.

NPS relies on the following subsystems to gather real-time network topology and capability information and traffic characteristics to make optimal service placement decisions:

■ **Network proximity:** Locates network resources in terms of hops and distances

■ **Network performance:** Identifies resources based on accessibility, latency, packet loss, and historical performance

■ **Data center network capabilities:** Maintains a global view of resource availability, with real-time updates across multiple data centers

■ **Network capacity optimization/demand engineering:** Leverages information about bandwidth availability between different parts of the network to recommend cloud service placement in a manner which leads to optimal utilization of available network capacity

Figure 10-3 illustrates a user request where an orchestration system requests the placement of a cloud service (for example, compute, storage, network, firewall, load balancer). Multiple data centers have available capacity to deliver the cloud service. NPS ranks them in order of network bandwidth, latency, or other specified criteria. Data centers that are suboptimal are ranked lower in the list and are therefore unlikely to be considered for service placement.

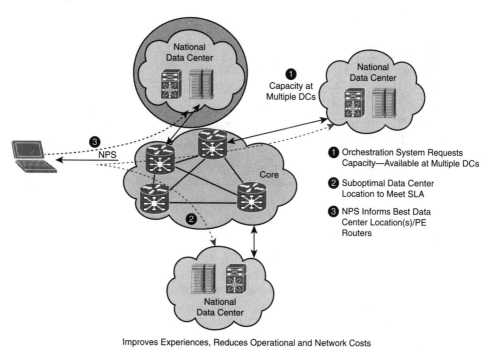

Figure 10-3 *NPS Enables the Placement of a Cloud Service at an Optimal Location*

We take a closer look at the operations of NPS while exploring the following two use cases:

■ **Service provisioning** at an optimal location

■ **Serving (cloud-based applications)** from an optimal location

Let's explore the steps that are usually involved in placing a cloud service using NPS.

Figure 10-4 shows the different steps involved in placing a cloud service at an optimal cloud location (that is, data center), beginning with the assumption (step 0 in the figure) that NPS builds a complete network topology view and collects comprehensive performance information from the NGN in real time. It also gathers resource capability information via advertisements from multiple data centers.

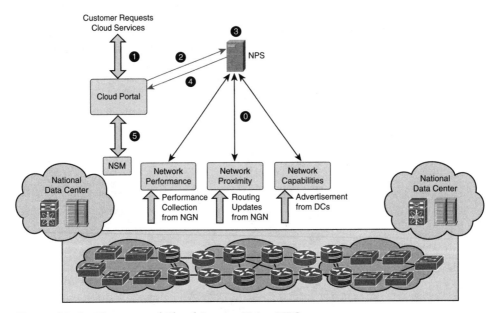

Figure 10-4   *Placement of Cloud Service Using NPS*

Step 1.   The customer requests the cloud services.

Using the service catalog/portal (IT Service Manager), the user selects the desired infrastructure resource capacity (compute, storage, network, and so on) and network service (firewall, load balancer, and so on). The cloud provider can offer different tiers of services using preconfigured templates like Bronze, Silver, and Gold that group different capabilities and SLAs in a single package.

Step 2.   The cloud portal requests the location of data centers that match the cloud service requestor's capability and SLA needs.

Step 3.   NPS determines the list of data centers with sufficient capabilities to meet the service request. It then sorts them based on the ranking criteria specified in the request, leveraging the real-time network information collected in step 0.

Step 4.   NPS replies back with a ranked list of data centers that meet the cloud service requester's needs.

Step 5.   The cloud service requester selects the top-ranked data center. The orchestration engine drives the service provisioning across various domain managers, including the *Network Service Manager* (NSM). The cloud service is provisioned at the optimal data center. You can find additional information about cloud service orchestration/management in Chapter 3, "Cloud Taxonomy and Service Management."

NPS Solution Components

NPS is composed of various solution components, as follows:

■ **XMPP Server:** *Extensible Message and Presence Protocol* (XMPP) is defined in IETF RFC 6120. XMPP is an *Extensible Markup Language* (XML)-based open standard that provides near real-time communication and information sharing across platforms. NPS uses Cisco Jabber, which is an implementation of XMPP and is enabled when NPS is configured on Cisco routers. XMPP Server, along with other NPS components (Capability Directory, Service Resolution Engine, and so on), is configured *on one of the data center facing provider edge (PE) routers.* In essence, XMPP clients (for example, data center resource managers that run within the data centers) publish information (for example, capability advertisement) to the XMPP server running on the PE router.

■ **Capability Directory (CD):** Capability Directory relies on XMPP client functionality to track capabilities (for example, compute, storage, network, firewall, load balancer) that are available in each data center. In this manner, it can maintain an up-to-date database of current capabilities at every data center.

Note that, in effect, an XMPP *application programming interface* (API) is exposed by NPS, which allows any cloud resource to advertise its capabilities. This information is then stored in the Capability Directory (CD). This provides a tremendous amount of flexibility, allowing NPS to be deployed in a vast number of scenarios, maintaining availability information for different types of resources beyond compute, storage, and network (for example, firewall services, load balancers, or video processors).

Figure 10-5 shows that, along with the network, compute and storage domain managers are sharing the capabilities with Cisco NPS.

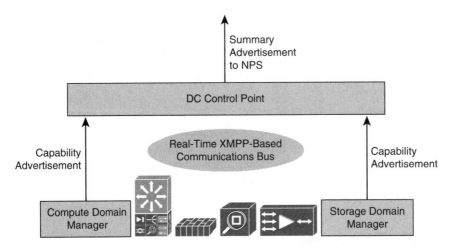

Figure 10-5   *Capability Advertisement to NPS*

Individual devices and services inside the data center could advertise their capabilities periodically or trigger upon a change to a central control point in the data center. Resource advertisement agents, including XMPP clients, would either function stand-alone (running inside a virtual machine [VM] or be embedded into devices), or as part of a device domain manager. The DC control point would then be responsible for summarizing the capabilities of the various resources at the DC level, and advertising to the NPS (where the advertised capabilities are then stored in the Capability Directory). One possibility is to modify and use existing *configuration management databases* (CMDB) to gather and advertise summarized DC-level capabilities.

- **Performance Manager:** Performance Manager is a key functional block of the NPS that relies on *performance routing* (PfR) / IP SLA probing to track network performance data such as delay, loss, and reachability between the *customer premises equipment* (CPE) router and data centers. Based on the requested ranking policy (for example, a user prefers to rank data centers from minimum to maximum delay), it then evaluates the available performance data and creates a list of data centers ranked according to the criteria specified in the policy.

- **Proximity Engine (PXE):** Proximity Engine "uses network routing proximity to select a data center based on its topological distance and path distance"[1] from the service consumption point. Proximity Engine relies on interior gateway protocols (Intermediate System-to-Intermediate System [IS-IS], Open Shortest Path First [OSPF]) and exterior gateway protocols (for example, *Border Gateway Protocol* [BGP]) to gather the path information. For a given service consumption point, the Proximity Engine analyzes the gathered topology information and returns a list of data centers ranked by network proximity

- **Service Resolution Engine (SRE):** The key decision-making component of NPS ultimately makes the placement recommendation. NPS fetches the relevant polices, tenant specified as well as cloud provider specified, which will eventually influence its ranking process. When the placement recommendation request comes in, NPS looks up the CD to create a list of candidate data centers that have sufficient capability (for example, compute, storage, network, and so on) to fulfill the service request. Now, based on the applicable policies, it consults the appropriate functional modules (for example, Proximity, Performance) and combines the results into a ranked list. Static and dynamic exclusion policies can also be applied to remove data centers that might be down for maintenance or that are facing an imminent natural disaster.

NPS Operation

NPS exposes a RESTful API that allows the cloud service management/portal to request an optimal data center. The request includes the specific cloud service/service tier specified by the cloud consumer on the cloud portal. It also includes the service consumption point (for example, branch CPE) and the ranking policies. The following is a sample request for the cloud service tier GOLD. This request gives network performance highest priority in the selection of a data center.

```
POST /sr HTTP/1.1
Host: sp.internal.net
Content-Type: application/xml;charset=UTF-8
<service_request>
<vdc_id>22222</vdc_id>
<user_handle>my_handle_1</user_handle>
<ce_list>
<ce address="10.10.10.1">
<pe address="10.10.10.2"/>
</ce>
</ce_list>
<policy_list>
<sr_ranking_policy>
<ranking_priorities performance="2" proximity="1"/>
<perf_ranking_priorities delay="2" loss="1"/>
</sr_ranking_policy>
<service_policy policy_type="model" name="GOLD"/>
</policy_list>
</service_request>
```

NPS receives the request and responds with a list of data centers ranked following the query criteria specified by the user (ranked using network performance in the preceding request).

A sample NPS response with the ranked list of data centers follows. Each data center could be reached by one or more PE routers:

```
HTTP/1.1 200 OK
Content-Type: application/xml;charset=UTF-8

<service_request_status>
<vdc_id>11111</vdc_id>
<user_handle>my_handle_1</user_handle>
<uri>https://sp.internal.net/sr/serv_req_00001234</uri>
<state>DONE</state>
<message>Service-request (id=00001234) successfully completed.</message>

<ranked_dc_list>
<dc id="dc1">
<pe address="30.30.30.2"/>
<pe address="20.20.20.2"/>
</dc>
<dc id="dc2">
<pe address="40.40.40.1"/>
</dc>
</ranked_dc_list>

</service_request_status>
```

Serving Cloud-Based Applications from an Optimal Location

With NPS, cloud providers can offload workloads in real-time from cloud-ready data centers that might get overloaded to data centers that have excess capacity.

A prime example of that is the Cisco *Virtualization Experience Infrastructure* (VXI) use case, where NPS can play a key role in offloading workloads to a data center that has excess capacity. VXI delivers next-generation virtual workspace by unifying virtual desktops, voice, and video. VXI is very resource intensive both in terms of WAN bandwidth and data center resources. When the resource demand exceeds capacity in a data center, NPS becomes aware of the resource crunch at that data center via resource advertisements. Subsequently, it would eliminate that data center from its ranked list of optimal data centers. This would enable the offloading of demand to other data centers that are underutilized and have excess capacity.

Another use case that could benefit from the NPS is cloud video gaming, as evidenced from the growth of companies such as Gaikai and OnLive, which offer cloud-based games.[2] As this market segment matures, and as more and more video games are offered through the cloud, it is essential to offer an optimized user experience. You can use NPS to identify the gaming server closest to the consumer of the game offering best network performance.

Caching and replication are essential to network traffic optimization, if they are coupled with the efficiency of a content distribution system, a more profound user experience will follow. NPS network proximity and performance are the key technologies that will enable the distribution efficiency by identifying the movie server cache that lies on the optimal network path for the user. By streaming content from the movie server closest to the user, cloud providers achieve efficient content distribution and utilization of their infrastructure while improving the user experience with the service.

Application Layer Traffic Optimization

Application layer traffic optimization (ALTO) proposes a standards-based API to be used to communicate the network-related information to the application so that the optimal delivery paths and content servers can be selected to achieve a higher-quality user experience. ALTO covers several use cases; among the notable ones are file sharing and live multimedia streaming. The end goal of NPS is very much aligned with ALTO: to locate the nearest copy of content, such as a movie, in the cloud or provision the compute/storage resources in the closest data center. Cisco NPS is considered an ALTO implementation, as depicted in the architecture diagram in Figure 10-6.

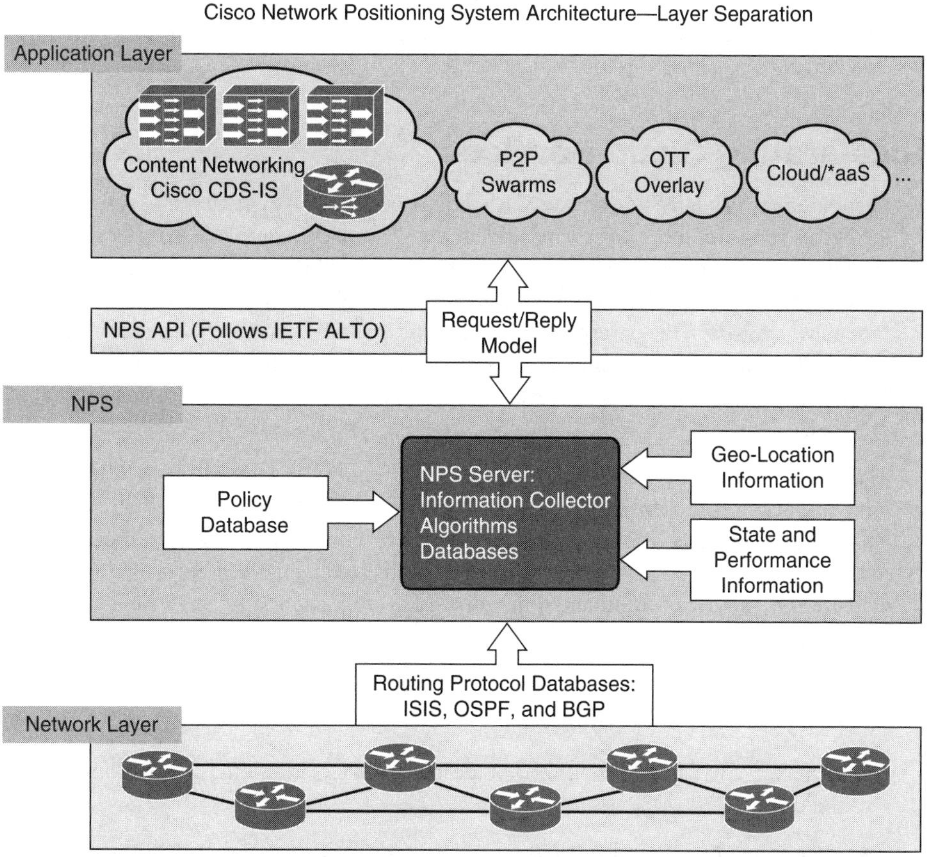

Cisco Network Positioning System Architecture—Layer Separation

Figure 10-6   *Cisco NPS Architecture in Line with the IETF ALTO Specification*

Next, let's look at how the network infrastructure is being optimized for the delivery of cloud services. A cloud *virtual private network* (VPN) is an example of such optimization.

Dynamic Extension of Customer VPNs

NPS enables the dynamic selection of the optimal data center for the placement of cloud services based on real-time topology, performance, and capability information. As discussed earlier in the chapter, the requested resources are eventually provisioned in the selected data center. These resources, including compute, network, and storage, should become a part of the customer's existing VPN in the *Multiprotocol Label Switching* (MPLS) network. This VPN needs to be dynamically extended to the PE router facing the selected data center.

Traditional VPN provisioning systems involve manual steps, which would slow down the overall service turn-up time. Customers would not be able to access their resources in the selected data center until the VPN provisioning is completed. In the future, as more APIs become available to do direct programming/provisioning of services on network infrastructure devices, this extension could be done in an automated fashion, either directly or through an intermediate provisioning system.

Accelerating Cloud Services

Reducing network latency over the WAN link is one of the key requirements for achieving better application response time and an excellent user experience from cloud-based services that will accelerate enterprise adoption of the cloud. One way to achieve this is to upgrade the WAN link to the cloud. Adding WAN bandwidth, however, is a costly proposition for both the enterprise and the cloud provider. Any upgrade cost would just weaken the primary driver for cloud adoption—cost savings from a usage-based model for the enterprise, and additional revenue streams from competitive offerings for the provider.

The value of the Cisco *Wide Area Application Services* (WAAS) solution becomes even more important for enterprises thinking of consuming applications from the public cloud, which is usually serviced over the Internet and that by design does not offer guaranteed *quality of service* (QoS). Moving applications to the public cloud will most likely increase the number of hops, and that will induce more latency and result in a poor user experience.

To overcome this challenge, a more innovative and comprehensive approach is desired that can

- Reduce WAN bandwidth utilization despite offering additional applications from the cloud

- Accelerate cloud-based *software-as-a-service* (SaaS) applications including virtual desktops, multimedia, and collaborative applications

- Be deployable in different cloud models: private, public and virtual private clouds

- Come in different form factors and support virtualization

- Support out-of-the-data-path or in-path scenarios

Offering cloud-optimized applications will generate new revenue opportunities for the cloud providers and encourage enterprises to migrate applications into the cloud.

Key Benefits of the Cisco WAAS Solution

Cisco WAAS is an innovative solution that optimizes WAN bandwidth utilization, accelerates cloud applications, and enables the delivery of applications from the cloud to any location to any device. Cisco WAAS seamlessly integrates with the enterprise WAN and the cloud provider IP NGNs.

The Cisco WAAS solution offers the following unique advantages that accelerate the performance of cloud-based applications:

- Mitigates latency and allows enterprises to migrate applications and services to the cloud. Reduced latency results in faster data transfer and improved application performance.

- Reduces WAN bandwidth utilization and results in more effective use of existing WAN bandwidth with less need to add more WAN bandwidth to improve user experience.

- Lowers *total cost of ownership* (TCO). The Cisco WAAS solution is available in various form factors, such as a Cisco WAAS Express (integrated into Cisco IOS) or Cisco WAAS (which can run on Cisco Service Ready Engine configured inside of Cisco Integrated Services Router Generation 2). This allows enterprises and cloud providers to repurpose their existing installed base while moving applications to the cloud.

- Allows enterprises to offer rich media and collaborative applications, desktop virtualization, and various other SaaS applications with high performance.

- Maintains regulatory compliance and business continuity by protecting the remote customer data.

The Cisco WAAS solution can be deployed by a self-managed enterprise where an enterprise can either co-locate the terminating device at the cloud provider data center or establish a network relationship with a cloud provider managed terminating WAAS device.

Cloud providers can also offer WAN optimization as a managed service to the enterprise, where the provider will either run Cisco WAAS as a dedicated device or run it as a virtualized service on Cisco Integrated Services Router Generation 2 configured with Cisco Service Ready Engine. At the data center, the cloud provider can run the

Cisco WAAS solution on a dedicated device like Cisco *Wide Area Application Engine* (WAE) or *virtualized Cisco WAAS* (vWAAS). See Chapter 7, "Application Performance Optimization," for additional information about vWAAS deployment.

Figure 10-7 shows a typical customer deployment using Cisco WAAS solutions.

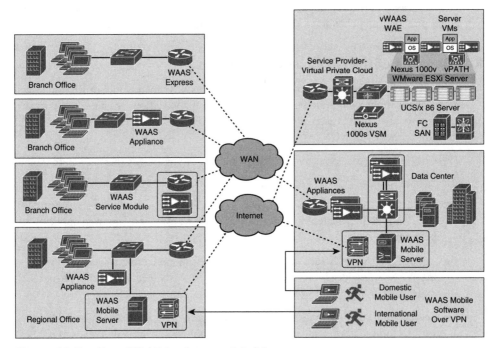

Figure 10-7 *Cisco WAAS Deployment Models*

The Cisco WAAS solution employs a range of techniques, such as TCP optimization and long-lived compression techniques, including standards-based compression, context-aware *data redundancy elimination* (DRE), and cross-protocol data suppression working in concert on clear-text or *Secure Sockets Layer* (SSL)-encrypted data to improve the performance of applications.

Cisco WAAS offers application-specific acceleration capabilities that would allow different vendors to validate their applications for encrypted and nonencrypted traffic. Cisco WAAS employs advanced techniques such as safe caching, multiplexing, read-ahead, and operation batching to improve the performance of a specific application. The result is full correctness with protocol specification, full coherency of data, and a dramatically improved user experience when compared with WAN access without WAAS deployed.

Figure 10-8 highlights the effects of Cisco WAAS WAN optimization techniques. The result is reduced WAN bandwidth utilization.

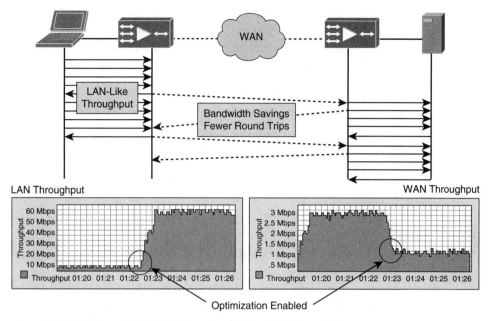

Figure 10-8 *Cisco WAAS Solution Providing WAN Optimization*

You can leverage Cisco WAAS for the following cloud use cases:

- **SaaS optimization:** SaaS existed long before the advent of the cloud. Enterprises resorted to SaaS to save capital and operational costs. Cisco WebEx and Salesforce. com are the two prime services that can be delivered from the public cloud. Cisco WebEx offers security via SSL and requires a separate connection for every user who participates in a meeting. A meeting in which a large number of users participate from a branch office could result in overutilization of the WAN bandwidth, resulting in increased latency and a poor user experience. With Cisco WAAS, you can optimize these WebEx flows, and you can reduce the bandwidth utilization significantly by 80 percent while maintaining the same security level.

- **Optimization of collaboration applications:** Collaboration applications (instant messenger, multimedia communication, file upload and download) that are intended to increase employee productivity are accelerated by the Cisco WAAS solution. Microsoft SharePoint is a prime example of this. A close look at Microsoft SharePoint reveals that this application can place intense demands on the WAN bandwidth, because it allows for the editing of documents using a PortalSever Workspace. Microsoft SharePoint allows editing and saving of the documents using an HTTP-based browser. With multiple people accessing the documents, and the chattiness of the protocol used, it can result in fully occupying the WAN bandwidth, which could result in increased latency and a poor user experience. Cisco WAAS has been shown to provide WAN data-link compression exceeding 80 percent and resulting in a significantly improved user experience.

- **Desktop virtualization optimization:** Enterprises armed with Cisco WAAS solution can deploy desktop virtualization solutions that are very bandwidth intensive and can suffer from serious performance issues. Cisco WAAS, can optimize, for instance, delivery of VMware View from private clouds, improving WAN link performance by 70 percent, and increasing the number of concurrent clients supported by 2 to 4 times. The same WAAS solution can be leveraged to increase the performance of IT applications like Microsoft Exchange, SAP Enterprise Portal, and so on.

- **VMware VMotion (vMotion) optimization:** The VMware VMotion use case to move the workload from an overutilized to an underutilized data center can also benefit from Cisco WAAS. With Cisco WAAS, you can reduce the workload (server memory content) from 512 MB to 30 MB and result in 94 percent compression. From the data center interconnect point of view, this is huge because it will result in reducing the bandwidth needed to support the WAN links connecting the data centers. The same bandwidth can be repurposed for other applications.

- **Data center data mirroring optimization:** Enterprises and cloud providers maintain high availability across data centers to achieve failover to avoid disaster and planned upgrades. All of this is driven by data mirroring technologies that replicate across data centers. Among the notable data replication technologies are SRDF/A – Asynchronous option for extended distances and NetApp SnapMirror applications. With Cisco WAAS, the WAN throughput performance usually improves by 10 times, significantly reducing the size of the backup window and the bandwidth occupancy on the links connecting data centers.

Summary

Application performance is a key challenge that needs to be addressed to accelerate cloud adoption by enterprises, especially for their business-critical applications and services.

This chapter explored how advanced NGN technologies such as Cisco NPS enable the network intelligence to be leveraged for selecting optimal data centers to place or consume cloud services. The selected data center would have sufficient resources to host the cloud service and would be optimal in terms of network proximity and performance characteristics from the point of service consumption. Such optimization leads to better utilization of provider capacity in addition to elevating the user experience.

Cisco WAAS is another method to enhance the performance of cloud services. Accelerating application and compressing bandwidth over the WAN link can help reduce the cost of delivering cloud services and enhance the application experience for branch and remote users.

Both solutions, optimization using NPS and acceleration using WAAS, improve the performance of cloud services, leading to a superior user experience that will ultimately lead to increased adoption of cloud-based services by business.

Review Questions

You can find answers to these questions in Appendix A, "Answers to Review Questions."

1. Network Positioning System enables which of the following?

   a. Optimal placement of compute and storage

   b. Provisioning of compute and storage

   c. Optimal distribution of routers

   d. Location of high-latency data centers

2. ALTO (application layer optimization) and NPS (Network Positioning System) are what?

   a. Competing technologies

   b. Complementary technologies

   c. NPS is an ALTO implementation.

   d. ALTO is an NPS implementation.

3. What are the benefits of Wide Area Application Services (WAAS)?

   a. Reduce WAN link bandwidth utilization

   b. Effective use of infrastructure

   c. Supports persistent LZ compression and context-aware DRE

   d. All of these answers are correct.

4. What techniques does the Cisco WAAS solution use to achieve reduced WAN bandwidth?

   a. TCP optimization

   b. Long-lived compression techniques, including standards-based compression

   c. Context-aware data redundancy elimination (DRE)

   d. Cross-protocol data suppression

   e. All of these answers are correct.

References

1 Cisco Network Positioning System Configuration Guide for the Cisco ASR1000 Router, Release 1.0, http://www.cisco.com/en/US/docs/routers/asr1000/nps/configuration/guide/b_nps_config_asr1k.pdf

2 How the Cloud Is Changing the Video Game Business, http://www.forbes.com/sites/johngaudiosi/2011/12/30/how-the-cloud-is-changing-the-video-game-business/

■ Cloud Computing Disrupts the Vendor Landscape, http://www.networkworld.com/supp/2011/enterprise6/120511-cloud-computing-253294.html?page=6

■ Extensible Messaging and Presence Protocol (XMPP): Core, http://xmpp.org/rfcs/rfc6120.html

■ Cisco Wide Area Application Services Software Version 4.4 Technical Overview, http://www.cisco.com/en/US/prod/collateral/contnetw/ps5680/ps6870/prod_white_paper0900aecd8051d5b2_ps6474_Products_White_Paper.html

Chapter 11

Connecting Enterprises to the Cloud

In this chapter, you learn about the following:

- Key enterprise motives for the cloud adoption

- Achieving optimized connectivity to the cloud

- Achieving optimal user experience with cloud services

- Achieving higher security, reliability, and availability for services in the cloud

- Streamlining operations and management of services in the cloud

- Defining what a Cisco Cloud Connector is, including its key benefits and how it helps enhance the cloud services

- Cloud Connector use cases: Enterprise Managed and Cloud Provide Managed

The cloud enabled by virtualization is a new computing paradigm that offers operational efficiencies to enterprises and helps them deal with shrinking IT budgets through various cost optimizations: reduced capital and operational costs (pay per use, self-serving portals, and so on).

Enterprises are motivated *to achieve per-server unit cost optimizations* by decoupling applications from the physical infrastructure and hosting them on virtualized environments.

"Without virtualization, Yankee Group estimates that as many as 40 percent of data center facilities would run out of power, space or cooling in 2011–2012."[1]

Services are also abstracted from physical locations and are available off-premise in the cloud. Moving to the cloud allows enterprises to reduce significant infrastructure and maintenance costs and achieve per user application cost optimizations.

By adopting cloud services, enterprises can reap the following key benefits:

- Applications are offered as a service over the network: pay per use without maintaining costly application infrastructure

- Compute and Network resources are offered and invoiced for use: pay as you go (scale-out when you need it, scale-in when you don't).

- Services (applications and resources) are rolled out very quickly—what used to be done in weeks can be done in minutes.

- Cloud services are available from any location to any type of device, meeting the needs of ubiquitous access and consumerization of IT (*bring your own device* [BYOD]).

Looking at various cloud deployment models discussed in Chapter 3, "Cloud Taxonomy and Service Management," not all the enterprises will be able to tap in to the full potential of the public cloud. For example, large enterprises that need to maintain very strict security and regulatory compliance cannot move resources to the public cloud. To realize cloud benefits, these enterprises will need to build *private clouds* by investing in a cloud-enabled infrastructure of their own to realize per-server and user cost optimizations and other benefits of the cloud.

Enterprises that do not need to maintain strict regulatory compliance and are faced with the push to move from a *capital expenditure* (CapEx) model to an *operational expenditure* (OpEx) model where the cost is optimized through pay per use will consider leveraging the public cloud in many cases, and will use hybrid cloud deployment options such as *virtual private cloud* (VPC).

Many small and medium-size enterprises and start-ups that do not have large budgets and trained IT staff are looking to the *public cloud* to meet most or all of their IT needs.

Despite the imminent benefits of adopting the cloud, enterprises have been slow to adopt the cloud due to security, control, availability, reliability, and ease of management concerns. Moreover, the enterprises would like to extend the same LAN-like application experience to their users when the services are moved to the cloud. Concerns for adopting the cloud have been discussed already throughout the book in different contexts.

Part II of this book looks at these concerns from the data center's vantage point and discusses how evolving data center networks can help address these concerns.

Part III of this book looks at these inhibitors and suggests solutions from the next generation network (NGN) point of view. Various chapters discuss the evolution of these networks, which help alleviate cloud adoption concerns.

This chapter looks at these concerns from the enterprise network's point of view, exploring existing and upcoming capabilities of these networks toward accelerating the enterprise adoption of the cloud.

In the Enterprise networks, the enterprise edge device (for example, Cisco Integrated Services Router Generation 2 or Cisco Aggregation Services Router 1000) is the critical control point, serving as the gateway to the cloud—all enterprise traffic to or from a cloud service must go through one of these WAN edge devices.

Enterprises are looking for these enterprise edge routers to become cloud-aware and provide capabilities that existing cloud deployment does not offer:

- **Brokering:** Requisite intelligence to broker connections between various cloud providers for IaaS and SaaS services

- **Streamlined policy:** Secure access and consistent business-focused enterprise security policy across multiple cloud services

- **Admission control:** Per-application and per-service bandwidth management

- **Consistent performance:** Control that delivers consistent user experience irrespective of location and type of the device

- **Availability and reliability:** Business-grade cloud services to ensure continued operation via fallback mechanisms if the cloud connection fails

- **Data management:** Data backup, encrypted archiving, and streamlined access from any devices and location

- **Flexible and optimized access to services:** File, print, and desktop services that are available to any device and location

- **Simplified Management:** Allow automated provisioning, managing, and monitoring of the cloud services

- **Regulatory compliance:** Compliance with Payment Card Industry Data Security Standard (PCI DSS), Health Insurance Portability and Accountability Act (HIPAA), Sarbanes-Oxley Act (SOX), Gramm Leach Bliley Act (GLBA), Federal Information Processing Standard (FIPS 140-2), and Common Criteria Evaluation Assurance Level 4 (CC EAL4)

Cloud Aware Enterprise Networks

Enterprise networking is an integral component of the cloud because it is the ideal point for enterprise policy enforcement, automation, monitoring, and management. As the workloads and applications move to the cloud, the value of the enterprise network becomes even more imminently important as this network provides the conduit to the cloud.

Enterprise network plays a critical role in providing the enterprise cloud consumers a consistent user experience and application performance because it sees all the data that stays within enterprise local-area networks (LAN), the wide-area network (WAN), and the data that ingress and egress the cloud.

Making enterprise networks cloud aware ensures that the same user experience and application performance is delivered no matter the location and the device used by the cloud consumer. Enterprise networks therefore must become more intelligent and intimately aware of cloud applications and services through the power of cloud connectors. The cloud connectors are available on Cisco Integrated Services Routers Generation 2 and Cisco Aggregation Services Routers 1000.

Cisco Cloud Connector is a piece of software that is either part of the *internetwork operating system* (IOS) or hosted on an enterprise routing platform. Cisco Cloud Connector helps "enable or enhance a cloud service."[2] These cloud connectors are offered on Cisco *Integrated Services Routers Generation 2* (ISR G2) or Cisco ASR 1000 Services Aggregation Routers.

Cisco Cloud Connectors capitalize on existing feature-rich capabilities of the network and further cement the linkage between the network and cloud applications to deliver a secure, consistent, and reliable user experience and highly available application performance (see Figure 11-1).

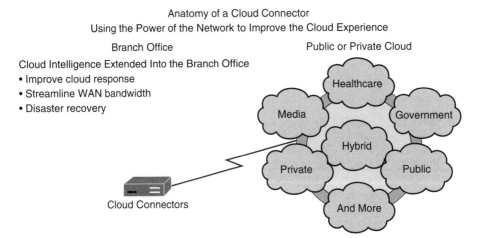

Anatomy of a Cloud Connector
Using the Power of the Network to Improve the Cloud Experience

Figure 11-1 *Cisco Cloud Connector Running on Cisco ISR G2 Router*

Connectors enable a deeper relationship between applications and networks on which they run, like never before. By interacting intelligently with the cloud applications, the cloud-aware enterprise network can deliver high levels of service expected of the cloud.

Cloud applications and services evolve and become more intelligent; they gain real-time knowledge of network conditions and adjust accordingly while delivering great application experience in a cost-optimized fashion.

How Enterprises Connect to the Cloud

The enterprise network provides the vehicle over which cloud applications and services and infrastructure resources are offered. The network defines the following:

- How enterprises connect to the cloud

- How cloud providers connect enterprises to the cloud

The following deployment models are available for the enterprises to connect to the cloud:

- **Enterprise managed:** Enterprises deploy and manage the device that hosts the cloud connector (for example, Cisco Integrated Services Router G2 or Cisco Aggregated Services Router 1000) to connect to the cloud.

- **Cloud provider managed:** Cloud providers deploy and manage the device that hosts the cloud connector (for example, Cisco ISR G2 and ASR1000 series of routers) at the enterprise edge and offer a managed cloud service. Managed cloud providers can offer a service from a partner as well.

Enterprise Managed Cloud Connector Deployment

An enterprise that has the IT staff to manage the network infrastructure could manage the cloud connector deployment. The enterprise has either built its own private cloud and would like to burst its additional workloads in a cost-optimized way to an IaaS provider or would like to consume a SaaS application from the cloud. Cloud connectors can provide ease of automation and monitoring and management of cloud services.

Cloud Provider–Managed Cloud Connector Deployment

A cloud connector solution is managed by the cloud provider, which could be one of the following:

- An incumbent service provider

- A cloud provider or over-the-top provider

Large-scale deployment of cloud connectors requires a centralized, multi-tenant deployment manager, which can allow for bulk installations, upgrades, and other operations on connectors over a large number of WAN edge/CPE devices.

Examples of Cloud Connectors

The cloud connector examples described in the following sections exemplify some key capabilities that a cloud connecting router (for example, Cisco Integrated Services Router Generation 2 and Cisco Aggregated Services Router 1000) can offer to an enterprise to enhance the capabilities of the cloud service being consumed.

Cloud Web Security Connector

A Cisco ScanSafe connector on Integrated Services Routers (ISR) G2 enables a cloud-based web security solution to protect the enterprise branch from malware attacks, reduce WAN backhaul traffic, and enable additional services such as video directly at the branch. With ScanSafe deployed in the branch, direct Internet access and malware protection is enabled directly at the branch. Traffic does not need to be backhauled over the expensive WAN links. Without ScanSafe enabled at the branch, the increased Internet access and video enablement would have caused the enterprise to add additional bandwidth to the WAN link and upgrade the infrastructure. With the ScanSafe connector deployed at the branch, required bandwidth upgrade costs are eliminated, existing WAN links are effectively used, and regulatory compliance is achieved with malware protection provided by the ScanSafe cloud.

ScanSafe connector on ISR G2 offers the following key benefits:

- Supports Active Directory integration for authentication and policy enforcement at the user level

- Provides creation and enforcement of security policies that are created based on categories, content, file types, schedule, and quotas

- Seamlessly integrates and runs security with IOS features such as QoS, multicast, and virtual routing and forwarding

- Provides a dual-stack security solution that support both IPv4/IPv6 and provides robust security required by cloud architectures

- Offers the Cisco industry-leading *virtual private network* (VPN) solutions *Dynamic Multipoint Virtual Private Network* (DMVPN), *Group Encrypted Transport Virtual Private Network* (GETVPN) to securely connect with the head-end and the cloud

Figure 11-2 shows how, by deploying Cloud Web Security connector at the branch, an enterprise can allow Internet access at the branch, reducing WAN bandwidth usage (traffic is not backhauled to the head end) while maintaining a consistent security policy.

Using Cloud Web Security to connect to the ScanSafe cloud service filters unwanted traffic and allows traffic to permitted websites, restricting traffic to unpermitted websites based on enterprise policy. Web traffic can also be filtered based on certain types of groups—of unwanted websites and of groups of users with access defined by the security policy. The Web Security component of ScanSafe ensures that enterprise branch is protected from malware and viruses. One of the key differentiators of Cisco ScanSafe is the support for secure mobility, which means the same filtering and protection is available to roaming users that is available to on-premise users. In a nutshell, Cisco ScanSafe cloud connector enables the enterprise to apply a uniformed security policy to any device at any location.

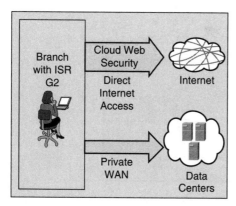

Figure 11-2 *Cloud Web Security on Cisco ISR G2 Series Routers Consumes Cloud-based Web Security*

Webex Cloud Connected Audio

Cisco WebEx Audio Connector is offered by the Cisco Unified Border Element (CUBE) feature that runs on the Cisco ISR G2 and Cisco ASR1000 family of routers. With Cisco CUBE deployed with Cisco WebEx applications, the audio portion of the meeting is routed over the enterprise VoIP network as opposed to expensive and legacy public switched telephone networks (PSTN) that would employ toll and international charges for the globally spread workforce.

Additionally, the Cisco CUBE Audio Connector shown in Figure 11-3 integrates seamlessly with cloud connector routing features and offers enhanced call routing and admission control features to ensure a great quality of service for the VoIP calls.

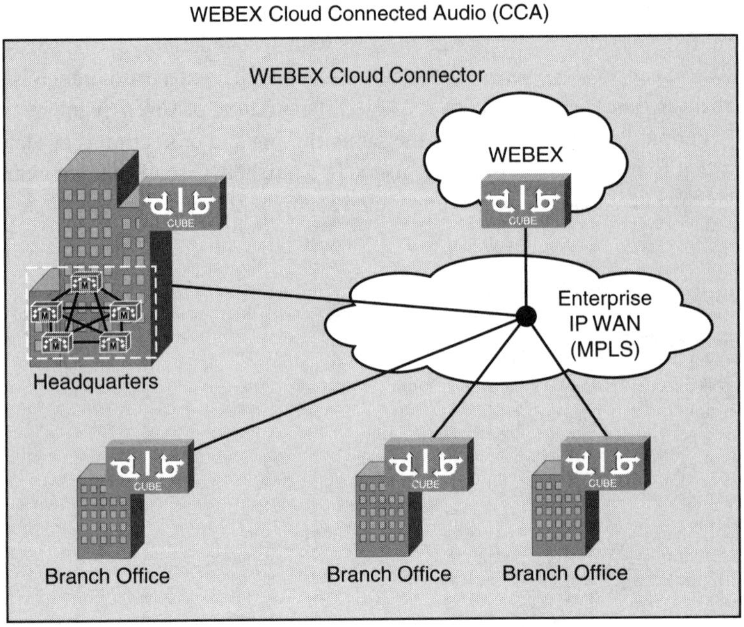

Figure 11-3   *Cisco WebEx Cloud Connector to WebEx Audio Conference on the Enterprise VoIP Network*

Ctera Cloud Storage Connector

With budgets either remaining flat or shrinking, it is difficult for enterprises' IT departments, especially at small and medium enterprises, to add additional storage capacity to existing data centers that have reached their maximum storage capacity. Building additional data centers to increase storage capacity is a difficult business preposition for any CTOs to justify. A cloud-based alternative becomes attractive for both data backup and archiving for the following reasons:

- Local storage and archiving for enterprises require dedicated equipment and staff that increases CapEx and OpEx expenses. To add more storage and archiving capacity, additional CapEx expenses are relatively difficult to justify; therefore, a cloud-based alternative that allows converting CapEx to OpEx is cost-effective and considered an operationally efficient approach.

- Time-sensitive projects that grow and unexpectedly require large data repository immediately cannot wait for the traditional IT approach of adding extra capacity to meet the increasing needs, because such a wait might affect the time to market. A cloud-based alternative is ideal for such a scenario; additional data can be pushed to the cloud in a timely manner without missing critical timelines.

Connecting with cloud-based storage and ensuring the appropriate security mandated by regulatory compliance and corporate policy can be achieved by deploying storage cloud connector software at the edge of an enterprise (main campus or a branch). Notable vendors that offer these cloud-based storage solutions include CTERA and Barracuda.

The CTERA storage connector on Cisco ISR G2 Series is an excellent example of how the small and medium-sized enterprises realize cost savings by storing and archiving data to the cloud. The CTERA cloud connector integrated with the Cisco ISR G2 running Service-Ready Engine offers on-premise and off-premise data-storage capabilities with most frequent data and client back data accessible right way with LAN-like high-speed access. The CTERA cloud connector running on the Cisco ISR G2 encrypts the data and mirrors it on the cloud storage in the background to optimize WAN bandwidth. The encrypted cloud data is managed by the cloud consumers using a single web portal. Figure 11-4 summarizes the benefits of CTERA cloud connector and how it contributes toward ease of managing on-premise and cloud stored data.

With a single web portal as shown in Figure 11-4, cloud users can create backup folders, archive data, and share data on demand, highlighting the flexibility of the solution. Enterprise admins using a single web portal can implement enterprise user accounts and policies to ensure streamlined provisioning and billing for the cloud service.

Cisco Cloud Storage Connector Solution
CTERA Cloud Connector Running on Cisco ISRG2

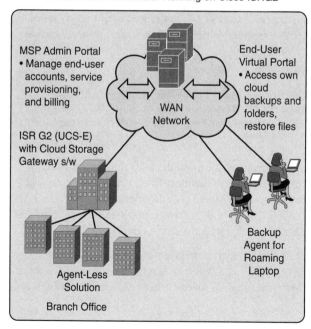

Figure 11-4   *Cisco Integrated Services Router G2 Running CTERA Cloud Connector*

Cisco Cloud Storage connector exemplifies a solution where a cloud storage provider, such as CTERA, is interested in enhancing the cloud services and has collaborated with Cisco to integrate its cloud connecting capabilities with the Cisco ISR G2 family of routers running Cisco Services Ready Engine (SRE).

Cisco Asigra Cloud Connector

Cisco Asigra cloud connector runs on Cisco ISR G2 configured with UCS-E Series blade. It enables a business-grade cloud backup and recovery system for an enterprise. The Asigra cloud backup solution offers comprehensive tools to ensure that the enterprise data is backed up in the most cost effective manner using "Global de-duplication and compression technology."[3]

Asigra cloud backup is an agentless solution that is

- FIPS 140-2 certified

- Deployable in hybrid, private, or public clouds

- Capable of delivering service-level agreements

- Capable of restoring data with validation capabilities

Asigra solution is composed of two main components:

- **Client side:** DS-Client that runs on Cisco ISR G2 configured with UCS-E Series blade. Asigra cloud backup also supports various types of smart devices, such as smartphones, tablets, and mobile clients, to deliver on the promise of delivering cloud service to any device and any location.

- **Cloud side:** DS-System is the cloud-based data aggregator system that receives the backup data from all types of clients, validates it, checks for the repository policy, and backs it up. The DS-System also restores data with full restore validation capabilities.

Cisco Asigra cloud backup connector runs on a central device, such as the Cisco ISR G2 configured with Cisco UCS-E Series blade. The agentless DS-Client software does not need to be installed on the machines (servers, desktops, and so on) that are on the LAN and must be backed up on the cloud. The DS-Client then compresses the data to utilize WAN bandwidth effectively and securely back up the data to the DS-System.

Cisco's pervasive footprint in the branch has attracted various cloud services and application providers to engage with it and jointly develop connectors that would differentiate their collaborated solutions. This has resulted in several other connectors that are listed as the following:[4]

- Cisco VMware VDI cloud connector

- Cisco XEROX cloud connector

- Cisco Infoblox cloud connector

Future Cloud Connector Concepts

Cloud connectors offer myriad possibilities in enhancing cloud services and applications. The cloud connector examples described in the following sections might not be available in a Cisco cloud connector device such as the Cisco ISR G2 and Cisco ASR1000 family of routers at press time.

Cloud Broker Connector

A cloud broker connector can communicate strong value when deployed at the edge of an enterprise (applicable to both self-managed enterprise and cloud provider–managed). For the self-managed enterprise, the enterprise can automatically burst workloads to an IaaS provider based on metrics such as cost, time of day, and latency. For example, an enterprise can burst workload into an IaaS provider that might be fewer hops away (and so offers less network delay), even though it might be more expensive. For the cloud provider–managed enterprise deployment, the provider can burst the workloads into its data centers based on metrics such as time of day, delay, and so on. The cloud broker connector relies heavily on the capabilities of Cisco Performance Routing (PfR) and Cisco Network Positioning System (NPS) to determine the least cost or delay path to one of its data centers.

Figure 11-5 shows the cloud broker connector deployed at the enterprise edge by the cloud provider, which selects one of its data centers based on predefined criteria that either optimizes cost or selects a low-latency network path to burst workloads.

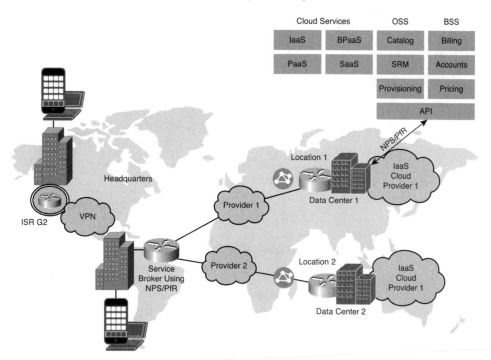

Figure 11-5   *Cloud Broker Connector That Selects a Lower-Cost Provider*

When bursting enterprise workloads to public clouds, it is important to ensure compatibility of workload formats between the enterprise and the provider. For example, an enterprise running VMware ESXi hypervisor requiring to burst workloads to an IaaS provider such as Amazon EC2, which is based on Citrix Xen hypervisor, needs dynamic conversion of its workload (VMDK/OVF) to match that of the cloud provider (AMI).

Hypervisor interoperability can be achieved at an enterprise edge or a cloud provider edge by converting the workload from one format to the other format by employing the capabilities of a cloud connector.

Figure 11-6 shows that the virtual machine (VM) translation is being done at the enterprise edge.

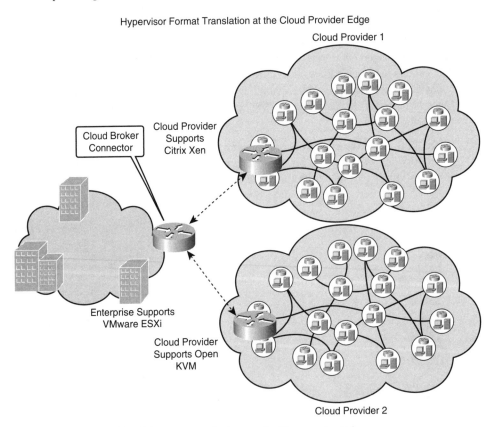

Figure 11-6 *Workload format translation at the Enterprise Edge*

A cloud brokering connector offered in a network device (for example, Cisco ASR1000 or Cisco ISR G2 router family) integrates well with the rest of the functions, such as routing, secure access, attack prevention, Performance Routing, Network Positioning System, and hierarchical QoS, to offer an optimal cloud service experience to the consumer of the cloud.

Brokering a more cost-effective and more reliable connection is not limited to IaaS. SaaS can also benefit from it, as well, as illustrated in Figure 11-7. For example, an enterprise that wants to offer an intuitive travel booking application can connect its legacy application to a SaaS provider while maintaining full control of the data on-premise.

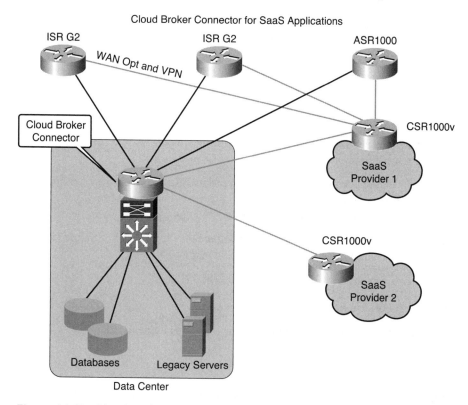

Figure 11-7 *Cloud Broker Connector to Provide Optimized Access to SaaS Applications*

Federated Identity Connector

Before the advent of the cloud, enterprises used to host business-critical applications on-premise in their physical data centers. The cloud changes that on-premise model and allows for a means to offer the same business-critical applications using off-premise model of the cloud using the SaaS paradigm. Associated with this is the challenge of ubiquitous access with *single sign-on* (SSO).

Enterprise users who want to access cloud services are and should be subjected to the same stringent requirements that are in effect for on-premise services. Users identify themselves to the enterprise with some sort of user ID and are required to maintain a unique complex password as dictated by security login policy of the enterprise.

Managing accounts becomes more complex as passwords expire after a set duration and as users are forced to change them with a unique new password.

Users access different enterprise services without logging in again by relying on mechanisms such as SSO and expect the same mechanisms will work when they access the same services or new services from the cloud.

Not providing SSO can wreak havoc in the user community of an enterprise. Imagine a large enterprise of tens of thousands of users who are subscribed to multiple cloud services and are required to change passwords and maintain unique passwords every time one expires. The resulting effect is that the enterprise cloud consumers are over burdened. As IT attempts to mitigate this and enforce strict password polices requiring special characters and so on, the enterprise users will record them somewhere else.

What is really needed here is to eliminate multiple passwords while at the same time enforcing a strict password policy.

SSO with federated identity meets such requirements. With SSO, enterprise users are authenticated and authorized just once in the enterprise domain and can access multiple services offered in the cloud without ever having to log in again.

Federated identity allows enterprises and cloud providers to establish trust and exchange user credentials without requiring the user to log in multiple times.

There are two approaches to achieve federated identity:

- *Security Assertion Markup Language* (SAML)
- OAuth, an open standard for authorization (including authentication)

SAML

SAML is an XML-based standard resulting from the work of several companies formed into the *Security Services Technical Committee of the Organization for the Advancement of Structured Information Standards* (OASIS). SAML provides a mechanism to communicate authentication information and establish user authorization to various services that are offered in the cloud. SAML enables SSO at the enterprise edge and relies on its assertions to communicate user identities and entitlements to cloud-based services without users ever having to log in multiple times.

Figure 11-8 shows SAML in action and illustrates various steps of an enterprise user attempting to access Salesforce.com, a cloud-based SaaS.

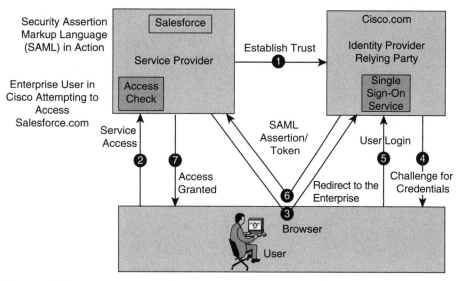

Figure 11-8   *SAML in Action*

OAuth

OAuth Version 1.0 has been discussed in the informational RFC 5849. OAuth provides mechanisms for a client (for example, a web application) to access resources (artifacts placed on a webserver, photos, videos, contact lists) on behalf of a resource owner (the one who has placed artifacts on a web server). OAuth also defines a process "for end-users to authorize third party access to their server resources without sharing their credentials (typically, a username and password pair)."[5] OAuth employs temporary tokens that are given to a web client to access specific resource; for example, one token is issued to access photos, while the other is issued to access videos. These tokens have a finite lifetime and can be revoked independently. OAuth is designed to work with HTTP and HTTPS.

OAuth has the following key roles, the understanding of which will help you learn how OAuth works (see Figure 11-9):

- **Resource owner:** An entity that owns a resource; for example, an individual who posted pictures, videos, and contacts on the cloud web server.

- **Resource server:** This is the web server that hosts the resources. This server can accept and respond to requests for the protected resources.

- **Client:** This is the third-party web application that requests protected resources on behalf of the resource owner, with its authorization using the access tokens.

- **Authorization server:** This is the web server that issues access tokens to clients to access the resources made available by the resource owner.

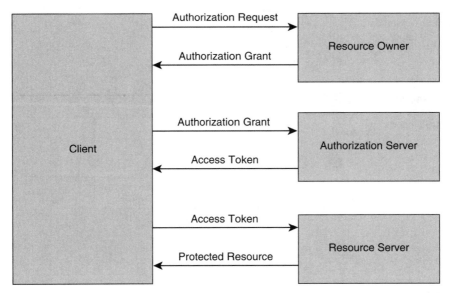

Figure 11-9   *OAuth in Action (Source: http://tools.ietf.org/html/draft-ietf-oauth-v2-23)*

Cisco Ping Identity Connector

Cisco has partnered with Ping Identity to develop a cloud connector that interacts with the enterprise-grade Identity Bridge product from Ping Identity to enable features such as single sign-on (SSO) and Federated Identity Management. Running an identity cloud connector solution on a centralized device such as Cisco ISR G2 adds real value to the operations of a large enterprise that runs local applications requiring access from a large number of partners. Consider the example of a large automobile manufacturing company that allows its partners access to various parts inventory applications. The automobile manufacturing company would not want to maintain access grant permission for different users coming from its partners. Instead, it would want to federate the identity of the user in the partner's on-premise authorization system. The partner maintains its database of users (for example, Active Directory) and runs Identity Service, which integrates with the Active Directory and automobile manufacturer's Identity Server. When deployed on a cloud connector device at an enterprise premise, the Cisco Ping Identity connector works seamlessly to federate the identity of a partner user back to its origins and provides hassle-free SSO to various applications.

For example, traffic can be intercepted and redirected to a local identity provider (in the branch) to obtain full network/device/user context that reduces latency greatly because all the traffic can be processed inside the router—all the way to SAML assertion.

Cisco Extensible Cloud Connector Solutions

Cloud connectors can offer immense opportunities for companies such as independent software vendors (ISV), enterprises, and cloud providers that are willing to improve the performance of the cloud services and applications.

With the growth of cloud-based applications on the rise, providers and enterprises are looking for ways to tightly interact and integrate with network devices (that is, routers and so on) and leverage the network intelligence to enhance application performance.

The Cisco onePK (One Platform Kit) toolkit addresses this strong need, offering an easy-to-use API that connectors can use to interact with the network at various levels. Cisco onePK is a framework "that provides rich network interaction to applications through a common *software development kit* (SDK)."[6] Providing this programmatic kit will allow enterprises, ISVs, and cloud providers to develop their own connectors to leverage the network intelligence and enhance the cloud services.

Additionally, Cisco Integrated Services Routers Generation 2 equipped with Cisco Unified Compute System (UCS) Express capabilities provides an environment to host industry-recognized virtual machines. Again, the enterprises, ISVs, and cloud providers can develop the cloud connectors, as shown in Figure 11-10, and host them in the virtualized environment.

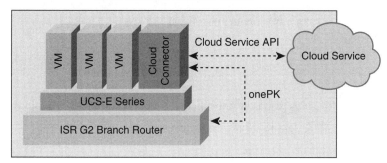

Figure 11-10 *Cisco Cloud Connector Toolkit*

Summary

Despite the obvious benefits of adopting the cloud, enterprises have been slow to adopt it due to security, control, availability, reliability, and ease of management concerns. Moreover, the enterprises want to extend the same LAN-like application experience to their users when the services are moved to the cloud.

The enterprise network is an integral component of the cloud because it is the ideal point for enterprise policy enforcement, automation, monitoring, and management. As the workloads and applications move to the cloud, the value of the enterprise network becomes even more important as this network provides the conduit to the cloud.

The enterprise network plays a critical role in providing enterprise cloud consumers a consistent user experience and application performance because it sees all the data that stays within enterprise LANs, WANs, and the data that ingress and egress the cloud.

Making an enterprise network cloud-aware ensures that the same user experience and application performance is delivered, regardless of the location and device used by the cloud consumer.

The enterprise network therefore needs to become more intelligent and intimately aware of cloud applications and services through the power of cloud connectors. The cloud connectors are available on Cisco Integrated Services Routers Generation 2 and Cisco Aggregation Services Routers 1000.

With the growth of cloud-based applications on the rise, providers and enterprises are looking for ways to tightly interact and integrate with the network devices (routers and so on) and leverage the network intelligence to enhance cloud performance. To meet this strong need, Cisco developed a network-aware programming interface called Cisco onePK (Cisco One Platform Kit).

Cisco cloud connectors increase the service awareness of the network and network awareness of the cloud service and further cement the link between the network and cloud services to deliver a secure, consistent, and reliable user experience and highly available application performance.

Review Questions

You can find answers to these questions in Appendix A, "Answers to Review Questions."

1. The evolved NGN offers what benefits in the cloud?

   a. Intelligence to optimally place the cloud services
   b. Secure access, compliance, and threat prevention
   c. Optimal connectors to connect with multiple cloud providers
   d. All of the above

2. What are the key benefits of adopting the cloud?

   a. Cost optimizations through virtualization
   b. Instant turning on/off of services
   c. Ability to scale up and down on demand
   d. Reduced operational costs

3. What are the benefits of single sign-on?

   a. Identity management and federation
   b. No logging in at multiple places and times
   c. Enhanced security because user credentials are not available at multiple places
   d. All of the above

4. Which of the following describes a cloud connector?

   a. Software that enhances a cloud service by sharing the network intelligence
   b. Runs on a dedicated device
   c. Runs on a virtualized device
   d. All of the above

5. Who developed SAML (Security Assertion Markup Language)?

   a. OASIS
   b. IETF
   c. OASIS and IETF
   d. IEEE

References

1 Any Device, Anywhere: The Next Phase for the Enterprise: http://www.cisco.com/web/solutions/trends/intelligent_network/docs/Any_Device_Any_Where.pdf

2 Cisco Cloud Connectors: Bringing Network Intelligence to the Cloud: http://www.cisco.com/en/US/prod/collateral/routers/ps10536/white_paper_c11-706801.html

3 Asigra Cloud Backup: https://marketplace.cisco.com/catalog/products/3116

4 The Network is the Path to Accelerate Adoption of Cloud Services: http://blogs.cisco.com/borderless/the-network-is-the-path-to-accelerate-adoption-of-cloud-services/#more-89188

5 The OAuth 1.0 Protocol: http://tools.ietf.org/html/rfc5849

6 Cisco ISR Web Security with Cisco ScanSafe Data Sheet: http://www.cisco.com/en/US/prod/collateral/vpndevc/ps6525/ps6538/ps6540/data_sheet_c78-655324.html

Chapter 12

End-to-End Cloud SLAs

In this chapter, you learn about the following:

- Cloud SLA elements
- Service-level metrics
- Provisioning, managing, and measuring end-to-end SLAs

The previous chapters have discussed the various elements that are integrated to deliver a cloud service. These elements usually include compute, network, storage, and application services, and are flexibly bound together by the fabric that spans multiple data centers as well as transport (*Next Generation Networks* [NGN]) and enterprise networks (*customer premise equipment* [CPE]). To deliver a reliable service, you must be able to provision, manage, and measure the *service level agreement* (SLA).

SLAs are a measure of the quality metrics that a service provider guarantees when delivering a service. It is a legal contract the service provider abides by and hence is a major part of any service offering. Traditionally, services such as compute and storage (web/application hosting services), transport network, and application services were delivered by different providers, and therefore the SLAs were delivered by the respective service providers. The cloud disrupts this model because all of these elements are virtualized to host a service, and the SLA now refers to the quality metrics of the hosted cloud service.

With a plethora of vendors in the market specializing in one or more of the cloud elements, the price points for building cloud services with these elements vary. Effectively, a cloud service provider aims to build the infrastructure with the best combination of price and functionality that can deliver the intended cloud service that meets the SLAs it wants to be able to offer to its customers. Another perspective is that of an IT manager transitioning business applications to the cloud. In doing so, it is evident that the aggregate of all the SLAs is what matters to the cloud service rather than SLAs of individual components.

To maintain certain SLAs such as application latency, network bandwidth, vCPU/memory/IOPS for database, *quality of service* (QoS) on CPE, or service availability, the workload needs to be mobile. The capability of the cloud infrastructure to enable a seamless environment for the workload to move based on resource availability and optimization is key to designing an elastic and agile cloud service. This capability enables the cloud service to be power and space efficient. Finally, the quality of a cloud service depends on each of the elements and the overall design of the underlying infrastructure. The challenge here lies in guaranteeing a consistent and predictable QoS and experience for the tenant.

These are some of the considerations regarding the SLA of the cloud service. This chapter explores each of the SLA components and defines the requirements to make the cloud SLA easy to provision, manage, and measure across multiple elements and domains that comprise the cloud service.

Defining and Monitoring SLAs

Service providers such as network, server, and application service providers focus on delivering infrastructure services to connect or host software applications. Therefore, the SLAs seek to guarantee the reliability and availability of the specific infrastructure. Service providers offer measurable SLAs that can be easily tracked and audited. Following are a few examples:

- **Installation or provisioning time:** Refers to the process of physically and logically enabling service as per customer SLAs. The duration is measured as the amount of time taken from the subscription request from the customer to the ability of the customer to reliably use the service. Thus, for an *Internet service provider* (ISP) this means installation of the optical or copper cable to the customer premises and enabling the Internet service; for a data collocation provider this means installation of a rack of servers, network, storage, and other service appliances as the case may be and providing reliable and redundant power to the racks.

  Figure 12-1 illustrates a simplified process followed by service provider to provision a service for their customers. Depending on the complexity of the service, the service enablement time usually varies between a few days to months.

- **Service reliability and availability:** Refers to the capability of the service to be resilient to failures in infrastructure used for service delivery. It is a measure of the maximum downtime the infrastructure might experience due to any failure or maintenance operations. Metrics such as *recovery point objective* (RPO), *recovery time objective* (RTO), service uptime, and service convergence time are used to quantify this SLA. Typical strategies to deliver availability include using a redundant design or using multipathing such that the risk of service failure is spread over multiple devices. Similarly, disaster recovery and backup strategies increase the reliability of the service.

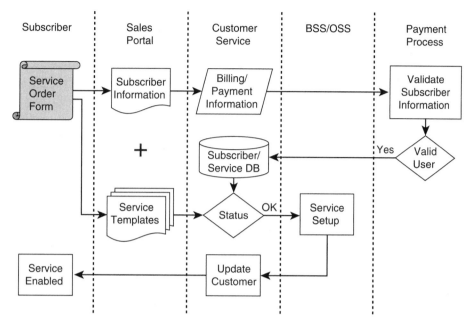

Figure 12-1 *Service Provisioning Process*

- **Security:** Refers to the capability of the infrastructure to thwart attacks on the service. Security affects many aspects of the service, including reliability, availability, and quality of experience. Because it is a complex service applicable at multiple layers of hardware and software, it is offered as a layered service, which can be enabled at any time. Infrastructure is periodically audited for security readiness, and the report is made available to subscribers.

- **Performance guarantee:** Performance refers to the characteristics of the service such as application performance (*mean opinion scores* [MOS], jitter, latency) and network performance (packet delivery, network bandwidth, and *time-to-repair* [TTR]). These metrics allow the infrastructure to support multiple service levels, which in turn enable the service provider to offer multiple SLAs on their infrastructure.

Some examples of services offered by service providers discussed in the sections that follow should help you understand the complexity of SLAs defined and the methods used to measure the SLA for each type of service.

Network Service Provider

A network service provider, as illustrated in Figure 12-2, delivers network services, including Internet, VPN, mobile, Ethernet and peering, to name a few.

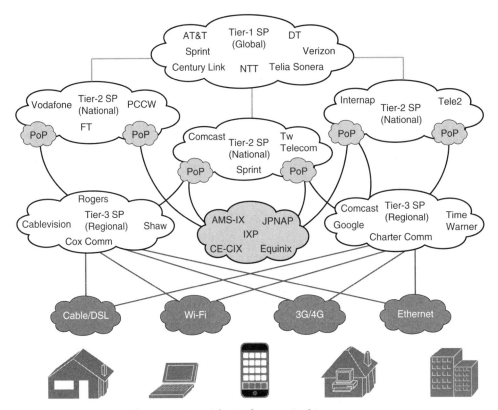

Figure 12-2 *Network Service Provider Reference Architecture*

These services could be dedicated or shared. Some key deliverables of network service providers to their customers include the following:

- Physical circuit installation

- Network availability

- Latency

- Packet delivery

- Security against denial of service (DoS) and other attacks

- Incident reporting

- Network jitter

- MOS scores

- TTR

Colocation Service

A colocation service, as illustrated in Figure 12-3, refers to the hosting of an enterprise customer's physical data center infrastructure (such as routing, servers, storage, and so on) in the network service provider facilities and providing network connectivity/peering for that infrastructure.

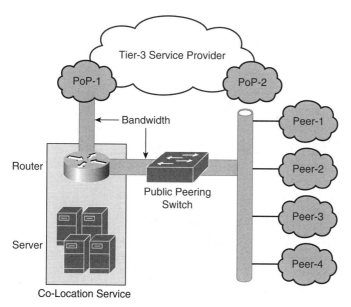

Figure 12-3   *Colocation Service*

Colocation enables a subscriber to create a carrier-grade environment for the services hosted. The management of the collocated services infrastructure is entirely a subscriber responsibility. Key deliverables of data center collocation *service providers* (SP) include the following:

- Power availability

- Internet bandwidth availability

- Network latency, jitter, packet delivery

- Security

- Outage reporting

- Storage backup and restore

- Site and physical security

- Business continuity and disaster recovery services

- Standards compliance: SAS, HIPAA, PCI-DSS, and so on

Application Hosting Service Provider

An application hosting service, as illustrated in Figure 12-4, is an extension of the collocation service, where the SP provides the platform and support to host the enterprise application. An enterprise usually benefits from the cost-effective solution with carrier-grade reliability, availability, security, and technical support.

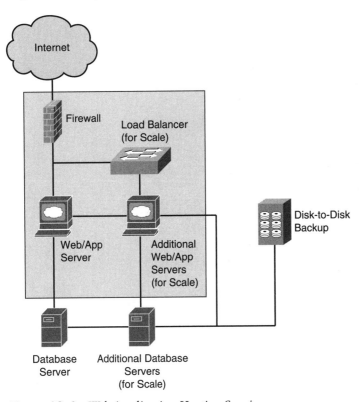

Figure 12-4   *Web Application Hosting Service*

Key deliverables of application hosting SPs include the following:

- Server uptime

- Persistent storage

- Network services: load balancers, firewall

- Network characteristics: latency, jitter, packet delivery for internal and external connectivity

- Domain name services
- Support response time
- Security

SLA Targets and Penalties

It is evident from the preceding examples that as the service offering becomes more complex the SLAs must also become more complex. An important part of the service provider's deliverables are SLAs around the areas of support and troubleshooting (TTR) assistance. This factor, among others, is key to determining the success of a particular service. Service providers usually offer very strict SLAs to attract business and offer financial credits back to the enterprise in the event they do not meet those SLAs. Table 12-1 lists typical SLAs offered by an ISP that guarantees network availability, performance, and service restoration in case of failure. Such SLA guarantees depend on the infrastructure architecture, hardware capabilities, and the manageability of the equipment. Notice that the SLA targets are less strict than the typical actual metrics, giving the service provider a "cushion" between how they maintain their network and events that might cause them to miss meeting SLAs.

Table 12-1   *Typical ISP SLA*

Metric	Target	Actual
Installation interval	5 calendar days	3 calendar days
Network availability %	99.99	99.999
Latency (roundtrip) ms	40.0	28.0
MOS score	4.0	4.2
TTR	4–8 hrs (depending on service)	2–6 hrs
Packet loss	0.1	0.011

Service disruption can be caused by a number of factors, including hardware failures, software upgrade procedure, power failures, capacity shortage, or other factors. Typical service architecture includes fault tolerance and failure recovery measures to maintain business continuity and minimize the service disruption. When such a disruption violates the SLA negotiated with the subscriber, penalties are incurred by the SP because of the subscriber business impact. Table 12-2 is a typical credit offered for the data center collocation service failure by an SP.

Table 12-2   *Typical Business Colocation SLA*

Service Level	Credit
99.99% managed data center network availability	If more than 4 minutes managed data center network unavailability in any month, then in addition to any credits to which customer is entitled under Section 2 herein, 5% of the charges for all affected devices
99.9% availability for each redundant device	If between and including 44 and 220 minutes service unavailability in any month, 10% of the charges for the affected redundant device; or if between and including 221 and 440 minutes service unavailability in any month, 20% of the charges for the affected redundant device; or if more than 441 minutes service unavailability in any month, 30% of the charges for the affected redundant device
99.5% availability for each device which is not a part of a redundant device	If between and including 220 and 440 minutes service unavailability in any month, 10% of the charges for the affected nonredundant device; or if between and including 441 and 880 minutes service unavailability in any month, 20% of the charges for the affected nonredundant device; or if more than 881 minutes service unavailability in any month, 30% of the charges for the affected nonredundant device
1–2 servers: 10 business days 3–10 servers: 15 business days 11+ servers: negotiated	10% of the initial fee per affected device for each day beyond the delivery commitment, not to exceed the total initial fee for such device

SLA Assurance and Methodology

Service assurance is a major component of the SLA assurance model that defines processes to meet predefined service quality levels (see Figure 12-5). Service assurance involves integrating fault, performance, incident/problem management, and remediation, which are typically referred to as *day-2 operations*, into the *operations support system* (OSS). These functions enable the service provider to deliver SLAs to its customers. As such, the equipment hosting the services needs to support a range of tools that provide feedback to the OSS to track the health of the components delivering the service.

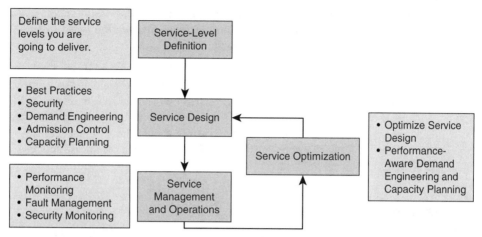

Figure 12-5   *SLA Assurance Model*

The SLA assurance model depicted in Figure 12-5 describes the broad categories of functions required to assure service performance, reliability, and availability. These include the following:

- **Service level definition:** Refers to the classes of service that can be supported by the infrastructure. Alternatively, predefining the SLAs could help in deploying infrastructure that can accommodate the classes of SLAs required to drive business. These are the SLAs that are guaranteed to customers by the service provider. SLAs can be categorized as network-, compute-, and storage-level SLAs. Examples in the earlier section "Defining and Monitoring SLAs" form the elements of these categories.

- **Service design:** Includes implementing best practices for deploying and delivering each SLA defined in the aspects of security, demand engineering, admission control, and capacity planning. Based on the service level definitions, a best practice template is implemented to provide a consistent and predictable SLA. This allows the service provider to automate the process of SLA delivery to its customers. Securing the infrastructure and the service is critical to protecting the SLA metrics. Demand engineering, admission control, and capacity planning are part of the operations to sustain and grow the business. These functions determine the size of the infrastructure required to provide service with the guarantees defined in the SLAs.

- **Service management and operations:** Refers to the tools and framework that collects data from the infrastructure to project the health of a service and its SLA in real time. This is a critical component of the service assurance model that binds the business requirements to the infrastructure. Functions such as *fault management* (FM), *performance monitoring* (PM), and security monitoring are the critical components of service management. A more exhaustive set of functions is defined in the FCAPS

(Table 12-3). These functions depend on tools such as *operations administration and management* (OAM), IP SLA, NetFlow, *Message Information Bases* (MIB), and a security framework in the infrastructure.

■ **Service optimizations:** Refers to the feedback mechanism that enables the OSS to react to a condition. This usually results in resource management and capacity planning of the infrastructure. The data generated by the service management and operations component is used as feedback to the service design components to manage demand engineering and capacity planning. Ultimately, the best practices are fortified dynamically to resolve business challenges for which the infrastructure is deployed.

SLA Management Framework

Besides service assurance, accounting and billing for a service require accurate measurement and validation of the service usage. Figure 12-6 briefly illustrates the components of Business/Operations Support System (B/OSS) and service assurance.

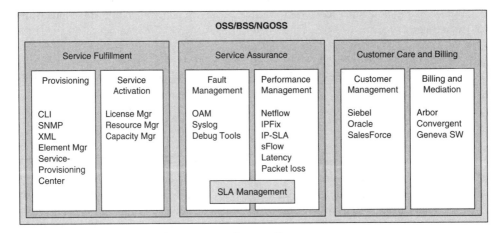

Figure 12-6 *Business and Operations System Support*

The B/OSS and New Generation Operations support system (NGOSS) defines a framework for service management, including service fulfillment, service assurance, customer care, and billing. All these modules are key business processes that sustain a service with manageable quality. Figure 12-6 includes the necessary tools required to deliver each function. SPs traditionally used FCAPS (see Table 12-3) to manage SLAs in the network infrastructure. The major components of the FCAPS model are fault, configuration, accounting, performance and security management.

Table 12-3 *FCAPS Functions*

Fault Management	Configuration Management	Accounting Management	Performance Management	Security Management
Fault detection	Resource initialization	Track service/ resource usage	Utilization rates	Selective resource access
Fault isolation	Autodiscovery	Cost management for services	Error rates	Network element functions
Fault correction	Network provisioning	Accounting limits/policies	Performance data collection	Security event reporting
Network recovery	Backup/restore	Quotas for usage	Performance reporting	Data privacy
Alarm generation	Resource shutdown	Audits	Performance data analysis	Role-based access rights
Alarm handling	Change management	Fraud detection and reporting	Capacity planning	Detect security breaches
Alarm filtering	Pre-provisioning	Support for accounting models	Maintaining and examining historical logs	Security audit trail logs
Alarm co-relation and clearing	Inventory/asset management		Problem reporting	Security information distribution
Diagnostic tests	Configuration management			
Error logging	Remote configuration			
Error handling	Batch job scheduling			
Error statistics	Automated software distribution			

As the services offered by the service providers extended beyond the network infrastructure, the SLA management model evolved to a service based approach. *Information Technology Infrastructure Library* (ITIL) defined a framework that provided the necessary processes to extend the FCAPS model to services. The ITIL framework includes business processes, service delivery, service support, infrastructure management, and security management.

Figure 12-7 illustrates the various components of the ITIL framework that are based on *service-oriented architectures* (SOA). This architecture breaks a service into multiple functions, as shown in the figure, and each function is associated with one or more processes. These processes use tools that are implemented in the infrastructure and push information to the processes to fulfill the function. A number of tools, such as *operations administration and maintenance* (OAM), IP SLA, NetFlow, *Internet Protocol Flow Information Export* (IPFIX), sFlow, and so on are implemented on the infrastructure. Service assurance applications such as service manager, service delivery, and service support use these tools to provide the end-to-end measurement of an SLA. The SLAs are defined at trust boundaries where service delivery is realized. Hence the tools used to measure SLA need to be standards based.

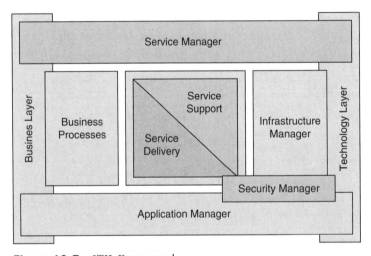

Figure 12-7   *ITIL Framework*

SLA in a Cloud Environment

A major difference between the traditional services and the cloud services is that of virtualization. Virtualization introduces the concept of a workload that can be moveable, restart-able, extendable, and cloneable. This introduces a set of new metrics to be considered to guarantee a cloud service (that is, cloud SLAs). These metrics are characteristic of the service or application in addition to those defined for the infrastructure.

Complexity of Cloud SLA

Compared to traditional services, the cloud provider faces additional challenges in offering, measuring, and managing SLAs. The shared and dynamic nature of virtualization and the cloud introduces complexities for service assurance.

The dynamic mapping of virtual services to physical resources, a key characteristic of the cloud, means that additional tracking capabilities are needed to enable the provider to identify the virtual/tenant services impacted by failure of a physical device or to identify the physical device responsible for performance degradation of a virtual/tenant service.

Multitenancy in the cloud implies that multiple tenants share the same physical resource and have different SLA requirements. Service assurance needs to be tenant-aware.

To match the speed and zero-touch operations of the cloud, SLA measurement elements need to be dynamically enabled/allocated when a service is provisioned and then revoked/de-allocated along with the service.

Service assurance needs to be able to scale with the elastic cloud infrastructure.

Whereas the traditional SLAs are bound to a particular part of the service (for example, application hosting, Internet service, data center, and so on), a cloud SLA usually encompasses two or more of these scopes. Therefore, a subscriber has a single SLA addressing all their service requirements instead of peering with a group of service providers for specialized services.

The following sections discuss these metrics required to be able to deliver a cloud SLA in greater detail. We also explore the deployment aspects (automation and abstraction) of these SLAs.

Service Level Metrics

This section explores the metrics that define cloud SLAs. More specifically, this section explores the cloud level, network container level, network service level metrics, and location and scope of these metrics.

Cloud Service Level Metrics

This section explores the cloud service level metrics that define cloud SLAs. More specifically, the list that follows describes the agility, elasticity, quality assurance, and management simplicity metrics tied with scalability and multitenancy capabilities:

- **Agility:** This metric is a measure of the capability of the cloud service to be provisioned, modified, and revoked within a short amount of time. This is important because the cloud infrastructure is shared; reuse of the resources fast enough optimizes the utilization of available hardware. This is enabled by workflow automation and enhanced by the abstraction of the platform *command-line interface* (CLI) via an *application programming interface* (API). The time taken to reserve and revoke platform resources, including ports, bandwidth, contexts, and so on; configuration to enable or disable platform services such as segmentation (*virtual LANs* [VLAN], *virtual private networks* [VPN]); IP addressing and policies (*quality of service* [QoS], *access control lists* [ACL], *policy-based routing* [PBR]); and *virtual machine*

(VM) **characteristics such as** cloning, mobility, and restartability—all these determine the agility of service. There is a huge dependency on the platform CLI/API constituting the cloud service to achieve agility. Together, these capabilities enable **on-boarding and** faster replication of workloads with minimal to no impact on the cloud service. For example, a complex service SLA deployment, including multiple network segments, application tiers, certification (PCI, HIPAA, GLBA, and so on), and secure storage could be guaranteed by the cloud provider to deploy or revoke in 60 minutes depending on the number of infrastructure elements it touches; however, a simple compute-based SLA with basic network connectivity could be guaranteed to deploy/revoke in less than 5 minutes.

- **Elasticity:** As the cloud service scales, it might not always be possible to reserve resources within a single location or domain. To scale the workload cluster across multiple locations or domains seamlessly, the cloud needs to be elastic and extensible. This is enabled by the network fabric via L2 extensions or L3 subnet extensions across the fabric and the clustering technology used by the workload. Elasticity metrics could include guarantees on the capacity that could be added or removed to a tenants' service in a fixed time period (for example, one hour), either as absolute capacity or as a percentage of current capacity. Example for compute could include the number of VMs of a particular type that could be provisioned in an hour.

- **Quality assurance:** Quality of a cloud service depends on the infrastructure that hosts the service and the applications or services hosted on the infrastructure. A major benefit of a cloud service is that the service provider certifies the infrastructure that hosts the service. This implies that the service provider assures the quality of infrastructure, including the servers, storage, network fabric, and network services. The service provider would usually provide benchmark metrics for the application and WAN performance, workload high availability, and on-demand scale. If the subscriber has a custom application that uses the service provider infrastructure, a quality benchmark can be established using sandboxing capabilities on the infrastructure. A predictive quality is key to quality assurance consistency.

- **Management simplicity:** The complexity of managing a cloud service depends on the underlying infrastructure, provisioning, troubleshooting, event logging, and other operational tools. Simplifying the management process includes developing logic that interfaces with applications (APIs) and a capability to automate operational tasks so that human intervention is reduced to a minimum.

Network Container Level Metrics

A network container is a depiction of a virtual tenant topology on a physical network fabric that is associated with a predefined SLA. Containers such as Bronze, Silver, and Gold are some examples that have been traditionally offered, as shown in Figure 12-8. In a cloud model, however, a network container includes the entire infrastructure to deliver services and resources such as compute and storage. Because the network fabric binds the service elements together, network container SLA is a depiction of the cloud SLA itself. Depending on the services such as load balancers, firewall, application accelerators that are used to optimize network bandwidth (more specifically WAN bandwidth), the guarantees would vary from best effort to very strict SLAs. Metrics including latency, jitter, packet drops, and throughput are usually provided as benchmark performance for the network. Besides this, operational metrics such as resource availability and proximity determine the most optimal use of network resources.

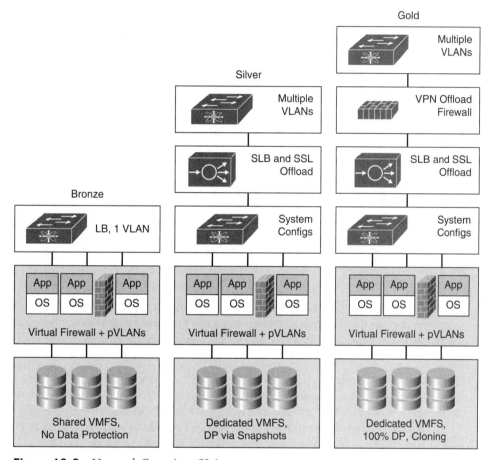

Figure 12-8   *Network Container SLAs*

A network container allows predefined budgets for the network metrics previously mentioned to predict the application/service performance.

Besides these, the network container SLAs also include disaster recovery and business continuity metrics such as infrastructure uptime, RPO/RTO, and storage backup capabilities to guarantee service reliability.

Component Level Metrics

As shown in Figure 12-8, services such as WAN accelerators and hardware engines for security (IPsec) in the network container yield better SLAs compared to a best-effort (Bronze) service. Introducing a service, however, implies packet processing, and this can be achieved only at the cost of latency in the packet path. Other component-level metrics include the throughput limitations and jitter introduced by these service appliances in the packet path. Besides the network services, storage and compute SLAs are critical to cloud SLAs. For example, storage SLAs define metrics such as storage uptime, IOP transactions per second guarantees, and encryption capability. Similarly, compute or VM SLAs such as high availability, restart priority, and heartbeat time interval are a few metrics that are usually included.

Location/Scope for the End-to-End Measurements

To deliver on the cloud SLA metrics, the cloud provider needs to be able to make appropriate measurements. The scope of the metric determines the location for the measurement. Component-level metrics, such as latency, can be measured as the packet path latency introduced across the component. But network container level metrics for a tenant, such as latency, jitter, packet loss, and bandwidth would need to be broken down into more specific metrics based on the scope—inside the container and outside the container.

Inside the container, there could be metrics based on the latency measured between two components of the container, such as the application server VM and the storage component. There could also be metrics around ingress and egress bandwidth available to the container.

For metrics with scopes extending beyond the container, one of the endpoints for the measurement would be located outside the container. This could include measurement of latency between a specific component inside the container and the *customer premise equipment* (CPE) across the WAN.

Such extra-container performance metrics depend on the performance of the enterprise network and the service provider *Next Generation Network* (NGN) that facilitate access to the services hosted within the data center. To preserve the cloud service experience across network boundaries, appliances that accelerate or offload the protocol processing such as *Wide Area Application Services* (WAAS) and IPsec appliances could be deployed to guarantee quality at scale.

Figure 12-9 illustrates a use case based on the Cisco Network Positioning System discussed earlier in Chapter 10, "Optimizing and Accelerating Cloud Services," where the scope of the metric measurement extends beyond the network container, all the way to the CPE at the point-of-service consumption. An enterprise client accessing services instantiated in one data center would not appreciate a change in performance when the service moves to a different data center. This can be streamlined and automated by using a placement algorithm to determine the best location that can meet the quality of experience goals of the service. This algorithm makes use of end-to-end network metrics and availability of resources such as CPU, storage, bandwidth, services, and also any business requirements to determine a location that would best serve the quality goals.

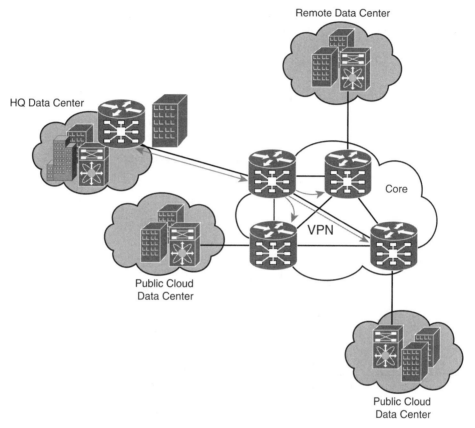

Figure 12-9 *Scope of Measurement for Cloud SLA Metrics*

Guaranteed SLA

Earlier in this chapter, you learned about the complexities of offering and managing SLAs in a cloud environment. This section explores how a cloud provider can address some of those challenges and successfully offer performance and availability SLAs to its customers.

Traditional service assurance systems simply break down in the cloud environment, unable to cope with the dynamic nature of the cloud and its rapid rate of change. When a cloud service request from a portal is automatically fulfilled and placed into production, there is no time to manually update tools and components. Updating configuration databases in batch mode is not fast enough. In addition, they lack multitenancy and the ability to scale as needed to manage vast numbers of resources in the cloud.

Figure 12-10 illustrates the Zenoss Cloud Service Assurance system, which is a key component of Cisco *Cloud Service Assurance for Virtualized Multi-Service Data Centers* (CLSA-VMDC). The various layers work together to enable resource management and impact analysis functionalities. Leveraging a variety of methods—secure access, management APIs, and synthetic transactions—the resource manager gathers inventory, utilization, fault, and performance data. Device models (for example, Nexus 7K and UCS) help transform this data into relevant state events that are fed into the *service impact* and *root cause analysis* (SIA/RCA) engine.

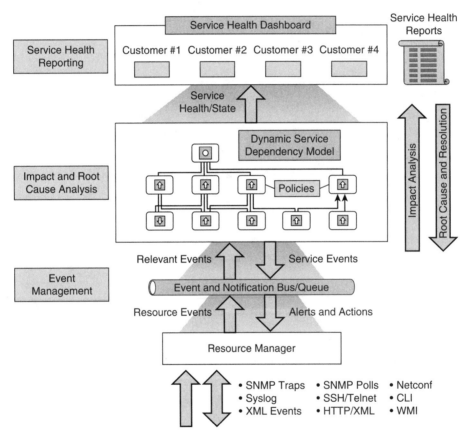

Figure 12-10   *Zenoss Cloud Service Assurance System*

Per-tenant and per-service service assurance information can be made available to the service reporting layer as perceivable and actionable metrics. This information could drive rapid triage or closed-loop automation and service remediation. Analytics can be used to trend the data over time or detect patterns that could trigger remediation to prevent potential problems, thus proactively protecting the SLA. Presenting such information/ dashboards on the tenant's portal can help address some of their concerns around loss of visibility and control in the cloud. Figure 12-11 illustrates the key integration interfaces for cloud assurance system. By integrating with service orchestration systems such as *Cisco Intelligent Automation for Cloud* (CIAC), BMC, and so on, service assurance can obtain additional information beyond that available from autodiscovery. For example, it can learn about the tenant ID tied to the provisioned service. Such tenant awareness is a key capability for service assurance in the multitenant cloud environment.

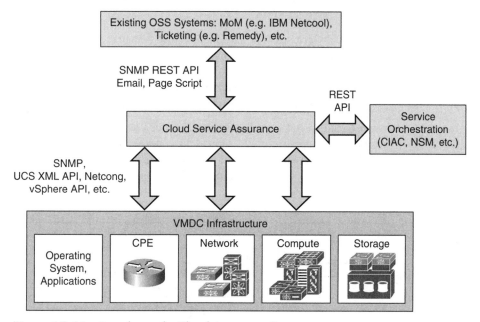

Figure 12-11   *Interfaces of a Cloud Assurance System*

Intelligent autodiscovery and integration with service orchestration enables service assurance to be dynamically enabled/revoked with the provisioning/deprovisioning of the tenant service. Such zero-touch operations are mandatory in simplifying and maintaining the operational efficiency and cost benefits of the cloud. Finally, horizontal scaling allows the service assurance system to scale as needed for handling hundreds of thousands of nodes in the elastic infrastructure.

SLA measurement is a bottom-to-top process. The network, compute, storage, and services implement tools such as IP SLA, IPFIX, OAM, or some agents that periodically transmit the health and statistics of the resource. The cloud resource manager uses this information to determine whether infrastructure has the capacity to host a service and meet the quality metrics. The *configuration management database* (CMDB) stores this performance information and matches it with conditions or thresholds set by the orchestration layer to trigger actions to modify the resource allocation. Finally, the orchestration layer presents this information to the customer portal as perceivable and actionable metrics.

End-to-End SLAs

The end-to-end path and SLA for a cloud service extends beyond the data center to include the SP IP NGN/WAN in addition to the enterprise network where the cloud service is consumed. Earlier chapters in this book have explored how data center, IP NGN, and enterprise networks can enhance the performance, security, reliability, and availability—and contribute to the SLA of cloud services.

This end-to-end path usually crosses multiple administrative domains, such as data center operations, NGN/MPLS VPN operations and application operations. While each operations team maintains detailed information related to monitoring and assurance within their own domain, they do not have much details about the other domains. So, how can providers offer, measure, and manage end-to-end SLAs to their customers?

Figure 12-12 illustrates end-to-end delivery of a cloud service, such as a collaboration or business productivity application. As shown, the end-to-end cloud service sits on top of several other services—managed enterprise network service, WAN service, *infrastructure-as-a-service* (IaaS) and applications—which work together to deliver the end-to-end service.

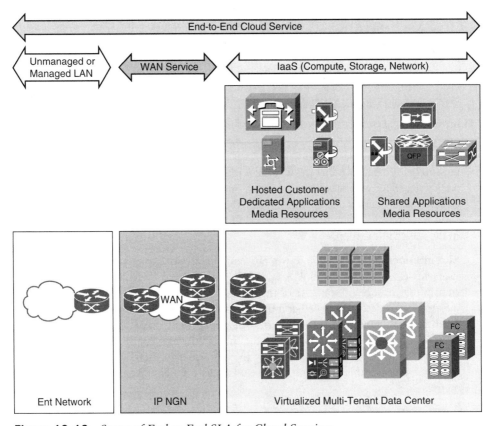

Figure 12-12 *Scope of End-to-End SLA for Cloud Services*

It is evident that the end-user experience and the end-to-end SLA depend on the entire traffic path, which traverses multiple operational domains and service legs that need to be stitched together to deliver the end-to-end service. A service overlay approach, illustrated in Figure 12-13, can help enable assurance for the end-to-end service.

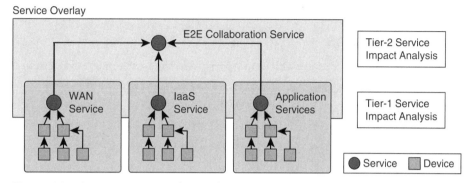

Figure 12-13   *Components of an End-to-End Service SLA*

Each of the underlying services would deal themselves with the thousands of events coming from the devices in their domain. Only the abstracted data is fed to the upper-level service—the end-to-end collaboration service shown in the diagram. Instead of having to deal with all the devices in multiple domains, the complexity for the assurance system can be greatly reduced by feeding abstracted events from a few underlying services. In addition, attempting to deal with information from all the devices is unnecessary, given the existence of segregated operational domains we discussed earlier.

In the example in Figure 12-13, the collaboration service shouldn't be notified about the failure of an individual device in the infrastructure, such as a Nexus7k, if it will not impact the collaboration service itself. If service impacting events exist in the *data center* (DC) infrastructure, however, the IaaS service would send an abstracted notification to the collaboration service.

This multitiered service impact analysis helps stitch multiple services together and monitor for end-to-end SLAs. With each service leg having an associated SLA, the corresponding service events and *key performance/quality indicators* (KPIs/KQI) would be monitored and correlated at the service edges, ultimately enabling end-to-end SLA for the higher-level service.

Summary

A cloud SLA represents a single subscriber SLA that spans the data center, WAN, and client premises. Besides delivering the traditional SLA metrics for a service, the cloud service provider needs to consider additional metrics such as workload agility and elasticity. The complexity of the cloud SLA is simplified using a multitenant service assurance layer that can dynamically track the infrastructure dependencies of a service, with near real-time service dependency graphs. This layer is the crux of service SLA management in a cloud environment.

Service overlays allow stitching of multiple underlying services to deliver end-to-end cloud service SLA spanning the application hosted on DC infrastructure and the IP NGN to the enterprise network at the point-of-service consumption. Such seamless end-to-end SLAs enable true business-grade cloud services, allowing the consumer to migrate confidently to the cloud.

Review Questions

You can find answers to these questions in Appendix A, "Answers to Review Questions."

1. Which of the following SLAs are relevant to colocation service?

    a. Power availability
    b. Server uptime
    c. Network latency
    d. Compliance certification

2. Which of the following are the correct cloud service level metrics?

    a. Server uptime
    b. Agility
    c. Quality assurance
    d. Network latency

3. Which of the following services are required to deliver end-to-end SLAs?

    a. Server load balancers
    b. Application accelerators/ protocol offloaders
    c. WAAS
    d. All of the above

References

- Enterprise Data Center Management, http://www.cisco.com/en/US/docs/solutions/Enterprise/Data_Center/Management/Zenoss.html

- Capacity and Performance Management Best Practices, http://www.cisco.com/en/US/tech/tk869/tk769/technologies_white_paper09186a008011fde2.shtml

- Network Configuration Management, http://www.cisco.com/en/US/technologies/tk869/tk769/technologies_white_paper0900aecd806c0d88.html

- Performance Management Best Practices, http://www.cisco.com/en/US/tech/tk869/tk769/technologies_white_paper09186a008014fbf3.shtml

- Service Level Management Best Practices, http://www.cisco.com/en/US/tech/tk869/tk769/technologies_white_paper09186a008011e783.shtml

- Problem Management, http://www.cisco.com/en/US/technologies/tk869/tk769/technologies_white_paper0900aecd806c3eee.html

Chapter 13

Peeking into the Future

In this chapter, you learn about the following:

- The next big things in the cloud world: the Intercloud and the Internet of Things

- How networks and network services are enabling the success of these futuristic clouds

- Emerging network innovations and trends involving application-network interactions and Software-Defined Networking (SDN)

Clouds today have crossed well beyond the initial hype, bringing about transformational changes in how IT resources are offered and consumed. A plethora of infrastructure, platform capabilities, and applications are offered as on-demand services (*anything-as-a-service* [XaaS]), presenting significant cost savings and agility for the customer. These services are making a significant positive impact in how businesses are able to innovate, extend their reach into more markets, and boost their productivity. Governments can empower their citizens with greater access to education, health care, and community information; and they have also started adopting the cloud to operate with improved efficiencies and transparency.

And by all accounts, these cloud services are rapidly mushrooming, not only in volume but also in their impact. In fact, the cloud transition is shaping up to be as powerful and transformative as the previous one—the Internet—if not more so! But where are we in terms of the life cycle of this transition? We might very well be at just the beginning of this cloud era, with a long journey ahead of us. So, how is the future cloud shaping up?

This final chapter looks further out on the cloud journey and examines a couple of phenomena that are poised to be the next big things: the Intercloud and the Internet of Things. These two future clouds bring huge opportunities and have the potential to significantly alter the landscape of the cloud market. Significant challenges remain to be overcome to successfully reach these envisioned destinations. The network has a huge role to play in facilitating the realization of this futuristic vision. Today's "cloud-ready" networks and network services need to evolve further to successfully address these upcoming challenges. In this chapter, you peek into the exciting trends shaping these future networks.

Future Clouds

Let's delve into these clouds of the future—the Intercloud and the Internet of Things—and understand the drivers and use cases fueling these phenomena. Each has its own set of challenges, though, and we discuss the role of networks and network services in addressing them.

The Intercloud

With the growing competition in the cloud market, providers are innovating and offering specialized clouds to address a niche where they can differentiate themselves. Some of them seek to address a particular segment of the customer base (for example, financial, government, or healthcare verticals). This is leading to a diverse, vibrant marketplace teeming with an ever-growing number of cloud providers—a world of many clouds.

Inspired by the web services philosophy, these clouds often make their services available via rich *application programming interfaces* (API) for other cloud providers to consume. This service-oriented architecture finds new cloud applications leveraging existing cloud services to provide increasingly higher value to the business. We are already seeing this phenomenon taking hold with various applications tapping into the Google Maps API or authenticating unregistered users with their Facebook credentials.

In addition, clouds could lean on each other to handle overflow capacity. Similar to offloading of excess data traffic from one network service provider to another, an *infrastructure-as-a-service* (IaaS) provider could divert incoming workload to another provider's infrastructure if its own facilities are running at near capacity and unable to adhere to the contracted *service level agreement* (SLA). There could be several reasons for utilizing the resources and services of another provider's cloud. Maybe it just makes economic sense to do so at that particular time based on cooling costs (follow the moon). Or maybe the workload needs to stay close to the active user base (follow the sun) to ensure a stellar user experience.

Note Follow the moon: The concept of reducing data center (DC) energy costs by processing workloads at night, when power is cheaper and outside temperature is lower. With DCs distributed around the globe, power savings can be achieved if workloads can be dynamically diverted to those geographies where it is nighttime.

Follow the sun: Another cloud computing concept, this idea focuses on enhancing the user experience by processing workloads at DCs that are close to the consumer. The phrase derives from the notion that consumers tend to consume services, especially business services, mostly during the daytime. This would mean that user-experience-sensitive workloads would be processed at "local" DCs during the daytime.

Over time, these interprovider relationships could evolve into an ecosystem, rich with multiple clouds, each offering its services to other clouds based on open and interoperable standards. A single application could integrate services from five, ten, or more clouds, based on the end goal of securely providing the desired functionality with the best experience and cost for its end users. Workloads could be dynamically migrated between clouds based on cost and performance considerations. This future cloud marketplace, with federation based on open standards, is being called the *Intercloud* (see Figure 13-1).

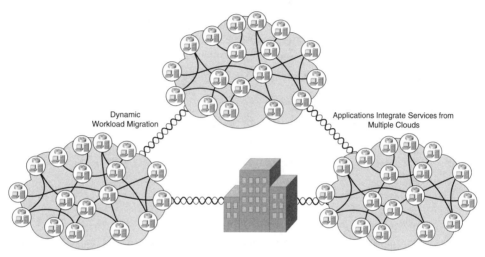

Figure 13-1   *Intercloud: Flexible Infrastructure and a New Applications Platform*

Internet Analogy

The evolution of the Internet provides an interesting analogy to draw on as we discuss the cloud's evolution from the mostly closed approach of today's cloud marketplace toward the open standards-based interoperability of the Intercloud. Before the Internet era (yes, there actually was such a time), service providers provided a "walled garden" experience for their customers, each operating their networks in proprietary fashion, without interoperating with each other.

With the emergence of "killer apps" such as email, customers, no longer satisfied with the proprietary solutions from their providers, demanded the ability to exchange email with other organizations. Routers and TCP/IP emerged to connect disparate networks, and application-specific open protocols such as POP, SMTP, and MIME emerged to allow email servers from different providers to interoperate with each other. A huge paradigm shift ensued, and walled-garden experiences eventually morphed into today's open Internet, based on application interoperability and open specifications.

Parallels can be drawn from this scenario with how the cloud market could evolve, as illustrated in Figure 13-2. Today, we have a bunch of walled clouds, with a focus on initial customer capture. Over time, with killer apps such as workload mobility, the precedent of the Internet tells us that customer demands will speed up the move toward interoperability between clouds, leading to the open standards-based Intercloud.

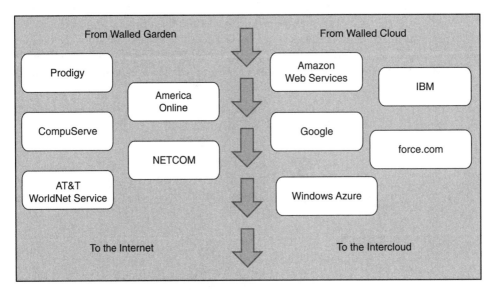

Figure 13-2   *Internet-Intercloud Evolution Analogy*

Just as this open Internet decoupled consumers from providers of web content and communications, resource consumers in the Intercloud would be able to find resources without any preexisting agreement with the resource provider. But, to enable such a vision, resource naming and discovery techniques similar to the *Domain Name System* (DNS) used on the Internet are needed in the Intercloud to facilitate the dynamic identification of providers that are willing and able to meet a particular resource demand. In addition, to enable such transactions, trust mechanisms similar to certificates used on the Internet could be leveraged to establish trust among the numerous entities in the Intercloud.

Intercloud Use Case

This section examines the provider-to-provider workload migration use case in some detail so that you can better understand how such an Intercloud could operate and the new requirements and challenges it presents. The basic premise is that a cloud provider has decided to move its workload to another provider, for reasons that could be technical, economic, or regulatory; we touched on some of those drivers earlier.

Enabling such a migration to happen in an automated, policy-driven manner requires the completion of several steps, as illustrated in Figure 13-3. To start with, the *consuming cloud* must discover the *serving cloud* that can satisfy its workload-migration requirement. Once discovered, the two clouds must establish a trust relationship (for example, using certificates), and then negotiate high-level policies, including billing, security, and SLA.

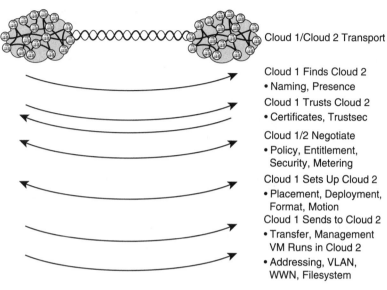

Figure 13-3 *Workload Migration in the Intercloud*

After completing the negotiations, the two clouds can finally get down to working on the migration of the workload. Metadata for the migration, such as format and placement, is first passed to the serving cloud, after which the actual workload transfer can take place. As the workload begins to execute in the serving cloud, it could share management, monitoring, and metering data with the consuming cloud, enabling SLA, compliance, and billing awareness.

As you can tell, negotiations and information exchanges need to happen at several levels to facilitate such dynamic workload migrations across clouds. Consequently, interoperability through open standards is a key enabler.

Deeper Dive into the Intercloud Vision

A potential reference topology for realizing the vision of the Intercloud described in IEEE P2302 Draft Standard for Intercloud Interoperability and Federation is illustrated in Figure 13-4. Based on the public Internet infrastructure, here public clouds (analogous to *Internet service providers* [ISP]) can interoperate with and offer services to other public clouds and private clouds. Intercloud exchanges, similar to Internet peering points, facilitate this interoperability between clouds, assisted by services provided by the Intercloud root element.

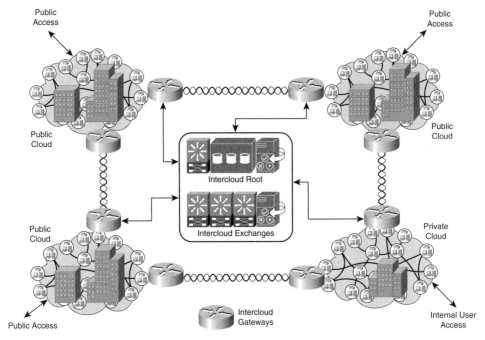

Figure 13-4   *Intercloud Topology (Source: IEEE P2302 draft)*

The Intercloud root element could host services such as trust authority, naming authority, and directory services to facilitate the secure federation and seamless discovery of resources between clouds. The Intercloud exchanges, together with the Intercloud root, are able to mediate the initial Intercloud negotiations between heterogeneous consuming and serving clouds. Another major element is the Intercloud gateway, much akin to the Internet router itself, which implements the Intercloud protocols. Such gateway functionality needs to be enabled at each element in the Intercloud topology that wants to participate in Intercloud transactions.

Intercloud Challenges and the Role of Networks

You can think of the Intercloud as an overlay built on a reliable and secure network infrastructure, connecting individual clouds into an open standards-based marketplace. This network is poised to play a critical role in enabling the vision of the Intercloud and is best placed to address the major Intercloud challenges:

- **Intercloud security:** Two aspects of interprovider security stand out. Providers need to secure their cloud infrastructure from attacks directed through other potentially compromised clouds by leveraging identity-based peer authentication and resource authorization. In addition, they need to ensure that their customer's security policies are carried over and enforced in the serving cloud.

Cloud networks are positioned to evolve toward solving the dilemma of securing the cloud infrastructure from threats originating in external clouds, while still facilitating the seamless consumption/sharing of resources and services between clouds. The challenges are none too easy. With the massive distributed pools of resources that such an Intercloud would bring together, how could compromised sections be rapidly contained? How can trust and authorization be tied to the sharing of resources/services between clouds?

- **Intercloud SLA management:** The cloud user negotiates an SLA with the provider, which usually includes availability and performance metrics. If the provider determines that its own cloud might not be able to guarantee the negotiated SLA, it starts identifying an appropriate serving cloud that can conform to the required SLA. When multiple serving clouds are involved, this chaining of SLAs can quickly get complex to manage, monitor, and report. To ensure that multiple parties are on the same page (that is, have the same view of the service performance and availability), it is imperative to be able to share monitoring information across providers, allowing them to discuss SLA conformance and violations based on data/facts.

  The network is a tried-and-tested place where service delivery metrics can be monitored, measured, and objectively discussed between multiple independent parties. Such network-based data collection can allow providers to offer, measure, and enforce SLAs between each other, ultimately enabling them to offer meaningful SLA guarantees to their customers.

- **Interoperability across cloud providers:** Interoperability is critical to achieving the vibrant marketplace of the Intercloud. Several areas of interoperability challenges need to be resolved, including the following:

  - API mapping

  - Workload interoperability with standardized virtual machine (VM) formats such as OVF

  - Live workload migration considerations such as different network address schemes in different clouds

  Interoperability based on server-side translation of APIs and workload formats can be enabled through an intelligent cloud-aware network.

Apart from the technical considerations discussed in the preceding list, myriad barriers (business, legal, and even political) remain, and we might be several years away from realizing this vision of the Intercloud. But keeping an eye on this future can help guide strategic planning and decisions for cloud providers, consumers, vendors, brokers, developers, and carriers—anyone seeking to play a role in this future ecosystem. It can also provide direction for the future evolution of networks.

Internet of Things

The Intercloud phenomenon would bring together a planetary-scale cloud with an unprecedented scale of resources at its command. The other cloud rising on the horizon is one made up of network-connected machines—sensors, actuators, smart and not-so-smart devices—and is often referred to as the *Internet of Things* (IoT). Sometime during the year 2008, the number of machines connected to the Internet exceeded the world's human population, and the era of the Internet of Things is said to have commenced. Since then, new devices continue to be added faster than ever before, connected by means of various network access technologies, including cellular (2G/3G/4G and beyond), local wireless technologies (WiFi/ZigBee/DSRC), as well as wired. The total is estimated to reach 50 billion connected devices by 2020, spread across diverse application domains such as utilities, health care, transportation, manufacturing, home automation, and environmental monitoring.

Today, a massive number of connected devices are deployed in huge sensor networks. For example, Cisco's Planetary Skin and HP's CeNSE (*Central Nervous System for the Earth*) involve global dispersed networks with billions of sensors. Information collected through these massive networks cuts across silos, enabling public- and private-sector entities to make decisions based on a complete picture of the planet's environment and resources.

In addition, as illustrated in Figure 13-5, advances in *microelectromechanical systems* (MEMS) sensors, ultra-low-power processors and memory, thin-film battery, and onboard wireless radio with antenna are bringing down the power needs and size of sensors, while Moore's law keeps pushing down the costs, thus opening up a multitude of new application areas. For instance, edible microchips from companies such as Proteus/Novartis can be added to patient medication. When stomach acids activate the chip, it can collect and wirelessly transmit internal body information such as heart rate and temperature to a patch worn on the patient's skin. Doctors can then monitor this information over the network.

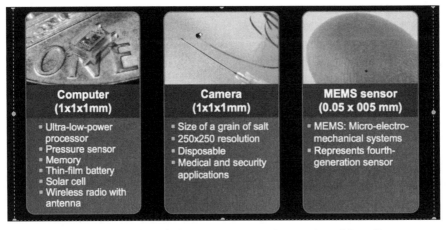

Figure 13-5 *Honey, I Shrunk the Sensors! Next Generation of Low-Power Miniaturized Sensors (Source: Dave Evans, Cisco Chief Futurist, and Cisco Internet Business Solutions, U of Michigan, Fraunhofer 2011)*

A Bigger Cloud

Although we tend to think so, clouds are not limited to the servers and other infrastructure inside DCs. This pervasive cloud, illustrated in Figure 13-6, extends out from the DC, encompassing the multitudes of smart meters, health monitors, and consumer electronic devices linked to the network.

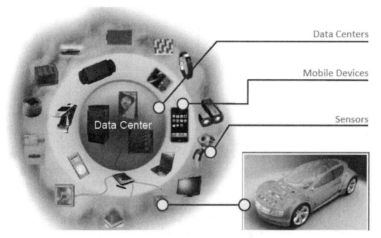

Figure 13-6   *Cloud of Sensor Devices and Mobile Consumer Devices (Source: J. Rabaey, "A Brand New Wireless Day," Keynote Presentation, ASPDAC)*

These connected "things" become a part of the cloud. They often carry enhanced capabilities for processing and data storage, which allows parts of the business logic to be decentralized outside the DCs and executed at the edge of the network—a phenomenon also known as fog computing, named to indicate that this cloud is closer to the ground (that is, more local). This distributed processing can help significantly improve scalability, lower latency, and enable local decision-making, as discussed in the use cases that follow. In addition, these devices on the periphery can communicate with each other to form a local network, which can bridge different communication networks, thus extending the reach and pervasiveness of the overall cloud.

IoT Use Cases

Let's explore two use cases, each covering an IoT application that has already started showing results today and where the future holds a lot of promise.

Smart Cities: Parking Automation

Urban areas provide one of the most interesting and powerful use cases for the Internet of Things. With multiple sensors mounted on street lamps, parking meters, and other places in the city, a huge amount of data can be continuously collected about various aspects of the city, such as the environment, traffic, and noise levels (enabling a huge number of opportunities). Here, we focus on the specific use case of helping citizens find an available parking spot.

In several big cities, parking spaces are in high demand. Finding a parking spot usually involves driving around and hoping to find an available spot. Without up-to-date data to guide the driver, this approach results in wasted time and fuel, in addition to worsening the traffic problem. The parking automation solution illustrated in Figure 13-7 aims to solve these problems by providing real-time availability of parking spots, along with directions, to drivers on their smartphones.

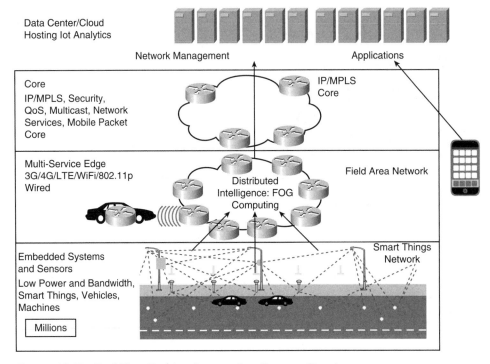

Figure 13-7   *Real-Time Parking Automation (Source: Cisco)*

Low-power, low-bandwidth sensors in parking spots or parking meters would convey the availability of each parking spot. The data from this vast collection of sensors needs to reach the DC, where powerful applications running on a scalable cloud infrastructure can process the incoming data streams to compute citywide parking availability. This near-real-time parking information is then made available to the public through the web or smartphone apps, as illustrated in Figure 13-7.

Enabling the transfer of data from the huge number of sensors to the cloud DCs presents a couple of challenges. First, each sensor must have its own 3G/4G wireless module to communicate its parking availability data, which would increase the cost of each sensor device, significantly pushing up the overall cost of the deployment. Second, having each sensor device communicate over its own cellular data connection could significantly impact the network operations cost.

Smart gateway devices, such as the Cisco ISR 819 M2M Gateway, allow for increased scale through aggregation of sensor devices. The parking sensor radios need to communicate only over short ranges with the gateway, bringing down device costs associated with long-range radios. The gateway then aggregates the data streams from multiple sensor devices over long-range WiFi/3G/4G wireless networks. In addition, because the gateway sends data over the expensive long-range wireless links only when there is sufficient data collected or when urgent data is handed to it, ongoing network costs for the deployment can be lowered.

In addition, such gateways could help scale the cloud-based management of these sensor devices. For example, when upgrading the sensor devices, the cloud would perform a one-time push of the upgrade patch to the gateway, which would then upgrade each of the sensor devices individually over the local network. This is much more cost-effective than having to push out the upgrade patch from the cloud to each sensor device over expensive long-range wireless links.

These smart gateways could potentially run pieces of the distributed parking application locally, which allows them to parse and partially process the sensor data. The field-area network in Figure 13-7 illustrates an instance of the fog computing concept. Such local processing could filter out nonrelevant sensor data, leading to a reduction in the volume of data that needs to be crunched by the application running in the cloud DC. This allows a larger scale of sensors to be supported without requiring vast pools of DC compute, storage, and networking resources.

Connected Vehicles

The automobile industry is undergoing a major technological upgrade and is poised to break in to the era of highly intelligent, automated, and connected vehicles. Modern cars today are already equipped with hundreds of sensors. They monitor and collect data from various systems within the car in the form of engine and brake performance, tire pressure, fluid levels, and so much more. Using various mobile wireless technologies, these cars could connect and share the collected data with the car manufacturer's cloud DC.

With powerful analytics software hosted in their DCs, vehicle manufacturers could analyze the data streams from multiple components and then indicate to the driver when it's time for maintenance or repairs, greatly enhancing vehicle safety. In addition, the manufacturer could dynamically improve the vehicle efficiency by controlling certain actuators. At the same time, security becomes very important in these network-based interactions, as unauthorized parties need to be denied access to vehicle systems (such as brakes, for instance).

Beyond the manufacturer's cloud, automobiles are moving toward consuming services from multiple clouds. Subscription services from public clouds could provide entertainment in the form of music, television and movies, or information services in the form of local weather, news, and restaurant reviews. These modern cars seek to connect to enterprise clouds over secure tunnels and access business and collaboration applications. Such productivity enhancers are particularly beneficial in developing countries such as India and China, where a significant number of professionals are chauffeured to work and want to attend meetings or prepare for meetings during their commute.

Automobiles could also want to connect and communicate with other vehicles in their vicinity, and learn locally relevant information such as road conditions or accident-induced traffic jams coming up ahead of them. The ability of these vehicles to securely and dynamically form ad hoc networks with others around them can enable several such interesting use cases. Wireless access protocols such as 802.11p/Dedicated Short Range Communications enable such geographically localized low-latency communications in a highly mobile environment, not just with other vehicles (V2V) but also with the roadside infrastructure (V2I), as illustrated in Figure 13-8.

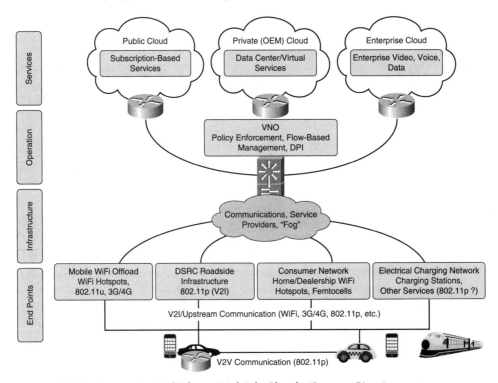

Figure 13-8   *Connecting Vehicles to Multiple Clouds (Source: Cisco)*

Apart from 802.11p, Figure 13-8 illustrates other wireless access technologies such as 3G/4G and WiFi, which enable these smart and connected vehicles to communicate with applications hosted in several clouds. Similar to the parking automation use case, parts of the application logic could be hosted closer to the vehicles, in the communication service provider's fog, allowing for local processing.

One challenge with this cloud connectivity is the need to maintain a superior level of user experience despite the high mobility of these vehicles and the bandwidth constraints of some of the widely deployed wireless access technologies. The network needs to facilitate seamless mobility across these access technologies, without any disruption to ongoing user sessions. In addition, WAN optimization and application acceleration technologies such as Cisco *Wide Area Application Services* (WAAS) become increasingly crucial with the growing adoption of data-intensive cloud applications. WAAS, discussed earlier in Chapter 10, "Optimizing and Accelerating Cloud Services," could significantly enhance the delivery of cloud applications to these connected vehicles, improving the user experience with business productivity and collaboration applications from multiple clouds.

Sensor Networks and IP

A large number of specialized sensor networks have been built for a variety of applications, including planet-scale environmental monitor networks, automated smart energy meter networks, and urban parking sensor networks (described in the preceding IoT use cases). Several of these smart devices or sensors took the path of proprietary network technologies, assuming incorrectly that IP would be too heavy for the extremely low footprint and power requirements that these devices operate under. But this choice brought in complexity associated with designing, managing, and deploying protocol translation gateways and limited the reach of these sensor networks.

Today, several optimized IP stacks are available—both commercially and under open source—which can meet the low memory footprint and processing power and severe energy constraints of these smart devices. The RAM and ROM footprints of these lightweight IP stacks, such as uIP, NanoStack and lwIP, are limited to less than 20Kb, which is perfect for the low-cost, low-power processing environments of these devices.

Several of these smart devices implement IEEE 802.15.4, which specifies a wireless link for *low-power personal-area networks* (LoWPANs). To get IP to work over these low-power links, 6LoWPAN was introduced as an adaptation layer between the IP stack's link and network layer, enabling the efficient transmission of IPv6 datagrams over 802.15.4 links. LoWPAN networks can now communicate natively over IP, which means that they can connect to the Internet and other IP networks by using IP routers. The ubiquitous availability of global IP networks enables these IP-based sensors to efficiently and reliably connect to the cloud, leveraging the proven strengths of an end-to-end IP architecture.

Note Why IPv6? IPv4 addresses are already on the verge of exhaustion. IPv6 expands the addressing space from 32 bits to 128 bits, a huge expansion, allowing for the assignment of 100 addresses for every atom on the Earth's surface! Or 4.8 trillion addresses for every star in the known universe! With billions of devices being rapidly added to the Internet of Things, IPv4 is not an option. IPv6 is needed.

Complementing the efficiencies provided by 6LoWPAN at the network layer, we are also seeing the emergence of more efficient protocols at higher layers of the stack. For instance, *Constrained Application Protocol* (CoAP) performs functions analogous to HTTP transport in constrained environments, while *Efficient XML Interchange* (EXI) optimizes XML encoding, as shown in Figure 13-9. Compared to today's web services, the Internet of Things demands a specialized protocol stack that limits the message overhead to the order of 10s of bytes. With some of these sensor networks scaling into the millions of sensor endpoints, such efficiencies ultimately help reduce the data transportation, storage, and processing load in the cloud DCs.

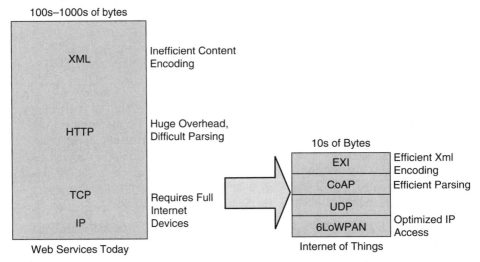

Figure 13-9   *Optimizing the Messaging Overhead in the IoT*

IoT Challenges: Networks to the Rescue

Even as the Internet of Things goes mainstream, it faces several challenges in reaching its envisioned potential. Let's examine some of the significant barriers for IoT and how networks are well positioned to play the rescue role:

- **Scale:** With the IoT scaling to billions of sensors distributed across the globe, we are looking at an unprecedented number of data streams being sent to the cloud, mostly over wireless access technologies. Huge numbers of wireless connections and data transactions initiated from these sensors will need to be supported by various parts of the network, including the mobile packet core. In addition, the clouds of the future will need to handle the massive volume of incoming data, while crunching that data to make sense of it—sometimes for near-real-time decision making.

  The gateway aggregation model previously described in detail for the parking automation use case can help bring down the number of connections and significantly lower the data transactions being sent over the network. These smart networks can efficiently handle the growth of the IoT. Also, distributed application processing and data filtering in the fog at the edge of the network can significantly lower the amount of data that needs to be sent to the cloud. This prevents compute, network, and storage requirements in the cloud from becoming bottlenecks that hinder the IoT from scaling to billions of endpoints.

- **Cost:** To remain profitable, operators need to support the huge scale of sensor networks while controlling costs—the cost of sensor devices, their network access, and the cloud resources needed for that IoT application. Again, the gateway aggregation model described in the parking automation use case can help lower both capital and operational expenses. The inclusion of intelligent data aggregation on the gateways means that sensor devices with basic processing capabilities and without expensive long-range wireless radios would suffice, thereby bringing down the per-unit cost of these smart devices. In addition, because the gateways can reduce the number of connections and transactions needed on expensive wireless networks such as 3G/4G, the operating costs associated with the network can be significantly reduced.

  The introduction of IP in sensor networks allows the move toward end-to-end IP network architectures, as discussed in the preceding section. The reach of global IP networks and cost-effective IP connectivity can be leveraged to bring down the cost associated with connecting vast numbers of IoT endpoints to other networks, including cloud networks.

- **Reliability:** With its reach into the physical domain, IoT breakdowns have the potential to become life impacting/threatening—for example, failures of traffic lights, truck fleet management, or building air conditioning. With the limited processing power (and corresponding exception-handling capabilities) of sensors and other smart devices today, machine-to-machine transactions tend to be inherently less failure tolerant than machine-to-human transactions. An ultra-reliable self-healing network becomes a critical asset in avoiding the catastrophic consequences associated with system meltdowns. Such networks can intelligently mitigate the effects of device and subsystem failures and ensure that data can reach its intended destination (to other devices/systems or to the cloud).

- **Security:** The devices in the IoT have the means to affect the physical environment. This greatly raises the stakes for security. The increasing significance of the IoT makes it a target for a variety of attacks, including virus/worms, *man-in-the-middle* (MITM), *denial-of-service* (DoS), and insider attacks. These attacks could span multiple IoT components, ranging from malicious/compromised smart devices to infected applications running in the fog or all the way in the cloud.

  The security challenge is compounded by the large number of diverse devices (different levels of processing and security capabilities) distributed over vast distances, some of which may be mobile. A network-centered security approach can help enable policy enforcement and governance of these smart and not-so-smart devices attaching to the network fabric. Multidimensional contextual information (for example, who, what, when, where, and how) can help ensure that only the required levels of privileges are granted when accessing virtualized applications in the cloud.

The Internet of Things fuses the digital and physical world, bringing together vastly different elements—in terms of functionality, technology, and application domain—on the same communication network. These "things" communicate with each other and can even form local networks that bridge together existing communication networks and extend the reach of this future cloud. Such aspects bring novel challenges that influence the evolution of networks.

Network Evolution Continues

Chapter after chapter in this book explained how cloud providers can leverage modern networks and network services to successfully deliver differentiated cloud services. We explored the remarkable changes that are underway in networks—inside DCs and in the NGNs/WANs outside, and extending all the way to the WAN edge at the enterprise campus/branch—that are enabling cloud providers to achieve their goals. In particular, these changes have driven network and network services toward becoming more flexible, virtualization aware, API-driven, and capable of achieving incredible scale while managing cost through optimization of resource usage.

And this network evolution continues. The following sections examine two major trends affecting the future of networks, and their influence on cloud networks: *software-defined networking* (SDN) and application-network interactions.

Software-Defined Networking

SDN has been generating quite a buzz of late, promising to open up new opportunities for innovation in the science of networking. OpenFlow, discussed in Chapter 1, "Virtualization," has been gaining in popularity as an instance of SDN. OpenFlow allows the network control plane to be moved out of network boxes to a centralized controller located on a server. This controller maintains a view of the entire network and communicates (using the OpenFlow protocol) with different types of network boxes—switches, routers, or firewalls that are OpenFlow enabled—over a secure channel, as illustrated in Figure 13-10.

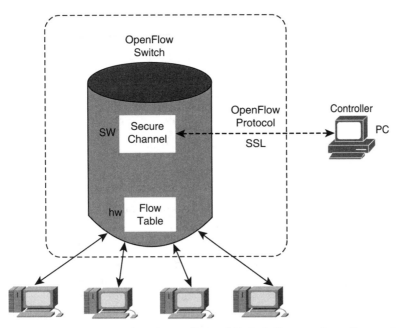

Figure 13-10   *OpenFlow Controller and Switch (Source: Openflow.org)*

The ability for a centralized controller to maintain a view of the entire network topology, including the capabilities of each network box, could potentially allow for efficient utilization of network resources in cloud DCs. In addition, in the case of cloud networks, SDN could provide the flexibility to dynamically create tenant networks on top of heterogeneous physical network boxes. Such flexibility is key in enabling the on-demand multitenant nature of the cloud operating model.

Applications could then be developed on top of this controller, which can perform functions such as load balancing and firewall security; the possibilities are endless. However, mature and battle-hardened software for such capabilities already exists on network platforms today. And so, the benefits obtained would need to justify the resource-intensive investments in re-creating on the OpenFlow controller the huge suite of existing networking software. And that brings up the all-important question: When does the use of SDN/OpenFlow make sense?

Hybrid Approach

Existing distributed control plane software (for example, routing protocols) is highly optimized and mature and functions well in a large number of network deployment scenarios. Using SDN/OpenFlow in these scenarios might not bring any significant benefit and could instead expose the deployment to the risk associated with much lower maturity software. However, certain network deployments demand an increased level of customized optimization. These optimizations could be based on multiple network properties, and the inputs to these optimizations can keep changing with high frequency. Solving these problems with the current distributed control plane protocols would involve a lot of data-heavy interactions between the distributed nodes and bring in significant complexity. An SDN/OpenFlow approach could make sense in such cases.

To achieve the best of both worlds, a hybrid option has been considered, where the same network box is controlled by existing on-box control plane as well as off-box control planes such as OpenFlow. How do the on-box and off-box control planes coexist as "ships in the night?" Work continues in the Hybrid Working Group of the *Open Networking Foundation* (ONF) to investigate the conflict-free sharing of forwarding plane resources across multiple control planes.

Challenges

Apart from the ecosystem maturity issue touched on earlier, scalability is another significant challenge facing OpenFlow today, particularly in cloud deployments. The controller, being the central coordinating entity, could easily become the bottleneck when scaling the deployment. One option is to distribute the controller functionality over a cluster of controllers, and the challenge then is to scale the cluster without growing significantly in complexity. Another option involves reducing the controller's interactions with the network devices by pushing more intelligence into those network devices. The challenge in this case is to add those capabilities without significantly increasing the cost of those network platforms.

Application-Network Interactions

OpenFlow/SDN provides a programmable forwarding plane and enables the development of new control planes. While OpenFlow allows a level of programmability for the selection and management of specific traffic flows, this is only a single example of network programmability. Broad network programmatic automation involves much more, requiring APIs for configuring, managing, monitoring, and data-mining networks.

The Cisco *Open Network Environment Programming Kit* (onePK) offers a comprehensive API for developers to access a rich services set, spanning low-level constructs for data path punt and inject, up through higher-level configuration, element, and topology information. Figure 13-11 contrasts the feature richness of the onePK API with OpenFlow and the OpenStack quantum API. While OpenStack enables provisioning capabilities as discussed in Chapter 4, "Network Services in the Cloud," it is currently limited in the richness of its networking API. OpenFlow, as discussed in the previous section, remains focused on controlling the forwarding plane of network devices but not on application development capabilities. onePK is unique in its ability to span multiple layers, enabling access to a rich set of network intelligence through its program model and application development environment.

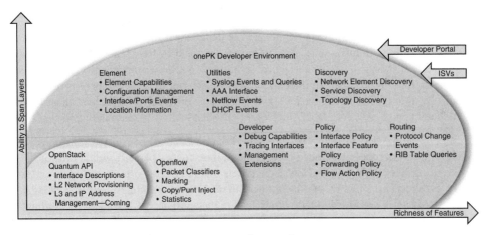

Figure 13-11   *OpenStack Quantum, OpenFlow, and onePK*

These APIs are key to enabling the application-network interaction cycle illustrated in Figure 13-12. The interactions can be summarized with these two questions: How can applications be optimized based on information queried from the network? And then how can networks be optimized based on information received from applications?

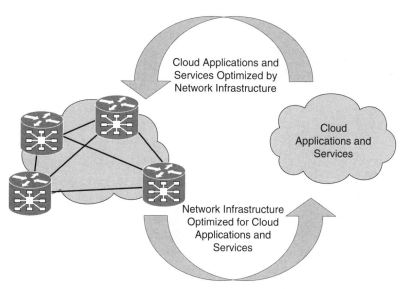

Figure 13-12 *Application <-> Network Interaction Cycle*

Accordingly, these network APIs can be divided into two categories:

■ **APIs that allow the networks to expose intelligence that can be consumed by applications to optimize their behavior:** The network intrinsically carries a trove of valuable data, but applications can leverage this information only if it is made available programmatically via well-defined APIs. Chapter 10 discussed Cisco's cloud *Network Positioning System* (NPS), which allows optimal cloud service placement based on the network location of the point-of-service consumption. Such network intelligence capabilities allow cloud services to be placed in appropriate DCs that can meet the desired service levels (for example, latency, jitter, packet loss, or network proximity). Figure 13-13 shows a use case, with the ITSM (*IT Service Management*) application querying the NPS API to achieve optimal service placement.

Apart from the example in Figure 13-13, applications can consume information from the network to better understand the capabilities of the end-user device and their access characteristics and adjust their own behavior accordingly. In addition, applications could derive granular billing information via an appropriate network-usage API. The possibilities are endless, and cloud applications today have the opportunity to deliver a truly differentiated user experience by being aware of the network.

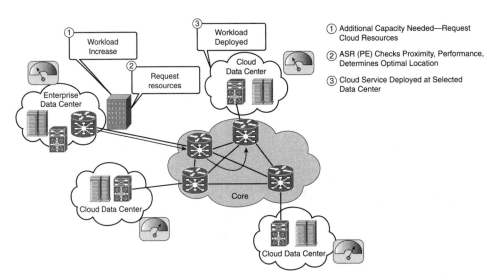

Figure 13-13 *Cisco NPS Exposing Information About Network Proximity and Performance*

■ **Applications specifying what they need from the network:** Today, networks essentially spy on the application traffic and use sophisticated and computationally expensive traffic-analysis techniques to take a best guess about which application is running and what it needs from the network.

But if the network were to provide APIs that let applications indicate their service profile, service topologies, and bandwidth requirements, networks would be able to fine-tune their behavior to meet the specific requirements of the application at that point in time. This enables the consistent delivery of superior experience with the application while optimizing the network's resource usage and lowering the operating cost.

The combination of network-aware applications and application-aware networks opens up powerful possibilities, enabling the flexible and cost-effective delivery of next generation business-grade cloud services.

Apart from these two trends, lots of research is being conducted on cloud networks, both academically and in the business realm. Case in point is research in use of 60-GHz wireless links on top of DC racks to offload peak traffic from wired DC networks. This exciting technology has the potential to deal with busy-hour congestion issues without expensive re-wiring in the DCs and may prove to be a huge success when reliability and tenant-isolation concerns are addressed in the coming years. Another example is increasing the scale of tenants supported by the network infrastructure inside huge DCs. VLANs are used for tenant isolation, and are limited to a scale of 4K using conventional methods, but with newer technologies such as *virtual extensible local-area network* (VXLAN), discussed in earlier chapters in this book, DC networks can extend isolation to millions of tenants.

These exciting network architectures and technologies promise to address the future growth of clouds and to enable the successful delivery of tomorrow's cloud services. Their cost benefits, flexibility, scale, and API richness can also help in realizing the vision of the Intercloud and the Internet of Things.

Summary

The outlook on the future of clouds is bright and sunny, with cloud services continuing to make an ever-increasing impact across the planet. Several high-value IT services are now within reach of user segments that could not afford such access in the past. Big data in the cloud is helping solve complex challenges that will unlock new fields of research. Entrepreneurship and innovation opportunities have been unleashed, riding on new business models.

This chapter explored further out into the clouds of the future and discovered how two phenomena—the Intercloud and the Internet of Things—are poised to become game changers, creating far-reaching changes in the world of clouds. We then zoomed in on some of the deployment scenarios before delving into the barriers faced by these future clouds and the role of the network in helping overcome those challenges.

Networks today are evolving rapidly, with the cloud being a strong driver for the changes. We looked at how software-defined networking can increase the speed of innovation in networks. We explored how the overall trend toward programmability in all aspects of the network and the ability to learn from and influence applications through APIs are leading to immensely flexible networks. These cloud-centric networks enable CIOs to confidently move more and more of their core workloads to the cloud. Today, not only businesses are counting on these networks to deliver the next generation of cloud services. Governments, communities, and consumers are counting on them, too!

Review Questions

You can find answers to these questions in Appendix A, "Answers to Review Questions."

1. Which of the following upcoming phenomena are poised to shape the future of clouds?

   a. Virtualization
   b. Intercloud
   c. Internet of Things
   d. Internet

2. Which of the following could be Intercloud use cases?

   a. Workload migration across cloud providers
   b. Cloud application leveraging cloud services from multiple clouds
   c. Three-tier application hosted inside a data center
   d. Interconnect a cloud provider's data centers through Layer 2 extension

3. Which of the following is an instance of software-defined networking?

  a. OpenFlow

  b. OpenFoundry

  c. OpenCompute

  d. OpenOffice

4. Which of the following are key areas of evolution for networks in the cloud?

  a. Automation/API

  b. Flexibility

  c. Scale

  d. All of the above

References

- Intercloud Topology: IEEE P2302 draft

- Blueprint for the Intercloud - Protocols and Formats for Cloud Computing Interoperability: http://ieeexplore.ieee.org/xpls/abs_all.jsp?arnumber=5072540

- Global Inter-cloud Technology Forum: http://www.gictf.jp/index_e.html

- A. Dunkels and J.P. Vasseur, IP for Smart Objects (IPSO) Alliance White Paper, September 2008

- IPv6 over Low Power WPAN (6lowpan) Working Group. Internet Engineering Task Force (IETF): http://www.ietf.org/html.charters/6lowpan-charter.html

- Next-gen IoT sensors: Material sourced from Dave Evans, Cisco Chief Futurist, and Internet Business Solution

- OpenFlow, https://www.opennetworking.org/index.php

- Internet of Things Web Services Stack: http://www.sensinode.com/EN/technology.html

- Wireless to Supplement Wired Networks in DC: http://www.nytimes.com/2012/01/15/business/a-wireless-way-around-data-center-traffic-jams.html

Answers to Review Questions

Chapter 1
1. b
2. b
3. b
4. d

Chapter 2
1. d
2. c
3. b

Chapter 3
1. c
2. a
3. b
4. b

Chapter 4
1. d
2. a
3. c
4. d

Chapter 5
1. c
2. b
3. a and b
4. c and d
5. c

Chapter 6
1. a, b, and d
2. a
3. a and d
4. a and c

Chapter 7
1. b
2. b and d
3. a, b, and c
4. a, b, c, and d
5. d

Chapter 8

1. a and d
2. a
3. d
4. a
5. a

Chapter 9

1. c
2. d
3. b and c
4. e

Chapter 10

1. a
2. c
3. d
4. e

Chapter 11

1. d
2. a and c
3. d
4. d
5. a

Chapter 12

1. a, c, and d
2. b and c
3. b and c

Chapter 13

1. b and c
2. a and b
3. a
4. d

Index

N

FREE
Online Edition

Your purchase of *Designing Networks and Services for the Cloud* includes access to a free online edition for 45 days through the **Safari Books Online** subscription service. Nearly every Cisco book is available online through **Safari Books Online**, along with thousands of books and videos from publishers such as Addison-Wesley Professional, Press, Exam Cram, IBM Press, O'Reilly Media, Prentice Hall, Que, Sams, and VMware Press.

Safari Books Online is a digital library providing searchable, on-demand access to thousands of technology, digital media, and professional development books and videos from leading publishers. With one monthly or yearly subscription price, you get unlimited access to learning tools and information on topics including mobile app and software development, tips and tricks on using your favorite gadgets, networking, project management, graphic design, and much more.

Activate your FREE Online Edition at
informit.com/safarifree

STEP 1:   Enter the coupon code: ROMJQZG.

STEP 2:   New Safari users, complete the brief registration form.
Safari subscribers, just log in.

If you have difficulty registering on Safari or accessing the online edition,
please e-mail customer-service@safaribooksonline.com